1983

THE
UNITED STATES
AND IRAN

STUDIES OF INFLUENCE IN INTERNATIONAL RELATIONS

Alvin Z. Rubinstein, General Editor

THE
UNITED STATES
AND IRAN

The Patterns of Influence

R. K. Ramazani

PRAEGER

PRAEGER SPECIAL STUDIES • PRAEGER SCIENTIFIC

Library of Congress Cataloging in Publication Data

Ramazani, Rouhollah K., 1928-
    The United States and Iran.

    (Studies of influence in international relations)
    Includes bibliographical references and index.
    1. United States--Foreign relations--Iran.   2. Iran
--Foreign relations--United States.   I. Title.
II. Series.
E183.8.I55R28   327.73055   82-3811
ISBN 0-03-049001-4   AACR2
ISBN 0-03-048996-2 (pbk.)

Published in 1982 by Praeger Publishers
CBS Educational and Professional Publishing
a Division of CBS Inc.
521 Fifth Avenue, New York, New York 10175 U.S.A.

23456789   145   987654321

Printed in the United States of America

To Edwin E. Floyd and Vincent Shea
who made the writing of this
book possible

EDITOR'S PREFACE

These are troubled times for the United States and Iran. Once allies, they are now enemies. The partnership they formed in the early 1970s to safeguard their mutual interests in the Persian Gulf and Arabian Peninsula region has dissolved in bitterness. Iran, once considered a pillar of U.S. power in the Middle East, has become a dangerous dilemma. The United States, once the ultimate guarantor of Iran's independence against a covetous and expansionist Soviet Union, has been denounced and cast as a satanic and imperialist threat to the Islamic revolution wrought by Ayatollah Khomeini. The extensive economic relationship on which the Shah determined to transform Iran into a modern and industrial nation is in shambles, rent by Khomeini's factious followers who look backward for a societal model that never existed rather than ahead to the harsh alternatives that confront them. After toppling the Shah, Khomeini imposed a policy that is profoundly hostile to the United States. His millenarian vision of an integrist Islamic Iran is hard, particularistic, and revolutionary. He is committed to the export of the Iranian Revolution to the other regimes in the region.

Although all of this has metamorphosed the United States-Iranian relationship, Iran is of intrinsic strategic and economic importance. In Washington or in Tehran, the present discontinuity in United States-Iranian relations should not be considered as signifying a permanent lack of interest in returning to a semblance of diplomatic normalization.

The collapse of the United States' special relationship with Muhammad Reza Shah, the Pahlavi ruler who reigned from 1941 to 1979, and the traumatic 444-day hostage crisis that erupted in Tehran only nine months later serve as vivid reminders to all students of international politics of the sudden turnabouts to which internal systems and international relationships are heir in this anarchical age. They also demonstrate that in our complex and fragmented international system, even governments possessing enormous power find that the exercise of influence over a putative client can be frustrated by the surprising ability of the weaker party to resist domination and, indeed, to exploit the asymmetries in the relationship to its own advantage. This irony, which is so dramatically typified by an examination of relations between the United States and Iran, goes a long way toward explaining the important role played by medium-level powers in regional and even global politics.

In the outpouring of memoirs and commentaries on various aspects of the origins, evolution, and determinants of the United States-Iranian relationship, this study by Professor R. K. Ramazani of the University of Virginia sets a standard against which other works will inevitably be judged. A prolific scholar and internationally recognized authority on the Middle East in general and especially on Iran, Professor Ramazani has written a superb work of synthesis and interpretation. His study assesses the Shah's era and the domestic and external considerations that shaped Iranian policies and interactions with the United States. It places events in historical perspective, provides insights into the multifaceted motives that impelled the behavior of the key figures of the period, and places developments in their regional and global context. This book spans the roles of U.S. oil companies, arms transfers, trade, strategic cooperation, power projection in the Persian Gulf, and Soviet-United States rivalry in the often difficult, always complicated, relationship between the Shah and eight successive U.S. presidents.

Professor Ramazani brings to the subject a lifelong intimacy with Iranian society and culture. He has lived in Iran for many years, visited the region frequently, and known most of the leaders whose policies and actions he so perceptively relates. On a number of occasions, such as during the hostage crisis, he was a consultant to the White House and State Department, and his scholarly works are essential reading for students and specialists alike. This learned and lucidly written book is a valuable addition to the Praeger series, *Studies of Influence in International Relations.*

Alvin Z. Rubinstein
University of Pennsylvania

PREFACE

The primary objective of this study is to examine the United States-Iran influence relationship during the Shah's regime from his accession to the throne in 1941 to his downfall in 1979. As such, it is neither intended as a study of the Iranian Revolution, nor of the U.S. policy during that revolution. Yet by its very nature and scope this study cannot escape either subject matter to the extent that each bears on its primary objective. As a matter of fact, I hope that this study will shed some light on both topics for two reasons. First, since it will emphasize the intimate linkage between Iran's domestic politics and foreign policy toward the United States, I hope it will reveal the contribution of that relationship to the Iranian Revolution. Second, since it will involve examination of the development of U.S. policy toward Iran, I hope it will also help bring about a deeper understanding of the nature of U.S. influence in Iran. That understanding, I hope, will divulge the oversimplifications that characterize most of the existing debate on "who lost Iran."

This study began before the fall of the Shah's regime as a case study of influence relationship between superpowers and Third World states. When I began this volume it was particularly designed to cover the United States-Iran relationship after 1973, since I had already treated the earlier United States-Iran relationship in great detail in *Iran's Foreign Policy, 1941–1973* in 1975. But the fall of the Shah's regime made it seem more useful to cover the entire period of the Shah's rule. I had emphasized in the 1975 study that contrary to the conventional view, the Shah had exercised considerable influence in Iran's foreign policy in general and toward the United States in particular from his accession to the throne in 1941 rather than simply after his return to power in 1953. The enlargement of the scope of this study involved not only new research on the pre-1973 period because of the publication of new source materials published since 1975, but also incorporated research in the classified files of the U.S. Department of State for the revolutionary period before the Shah's downfall in 1979. I am grateful for the permission to examine the files for background information without attribution.

I would like to thank Professor Alvin Z. Rubinstein for understanding my reluctance to rush into print simply because the Iranian Revolution and the hostage crisis had captured worldwide attention.

I should also like to thank Professor James A. Bill, Professor Richard Cottam, Captain Gary Sick and Professor Marvin Zonis for consenting to read the manuscript despite their busy schedules. No one mentioned, however, is in any way responsible for the facts and interpretation in this study. The responsibility for these is solely mine. The research assistance of Thomas Vandever, Bahman Bakhtiari, and Joseph Kechichian is also appreciated. I am also indebted to my colleagues in the Woodrow Wilson Department of Government and Foreign Affairs at the University of Virginia for their understanding of my need for leave of absence from the chairmanship in order to complete this volume. Most of all, I feel an abiding gratitude to Professors Edwin E. Floyd and Vincent Shea for making my leave from the chairmanship possible.

CONTENTS

INTRODUCTION

One of the most important intellectual lessons of the collapse of U.S. influence in Iran is the need for a deeper understanding of influence relationships between superpowers and Third World states in world politics. The continuing debate on "who lost Iran" graphically reflects the persistence of that need. Whether one places the blame on the Nixon or the Carter Administration for one reason or another, one cannot escape the underlying assumption that the United States enjoyed dominant control over the Shah's regime. Yet that basic assumption is found to be wanting when the entire fabric of the United States-Iran relationship is subjected to an objective analysis from the perspective of influence relationship between the superpowers and Third World states.

The primary objective of this book is to examine the United States-Iran relationship during the Shah's regime as a case study of influence relationship between the superpowers and Third World states in this series. On the basis of this case study, I shall set forth a number of theoretical propositions below. But before doing so, it will be helpful to indicate first that although in most respects Iran qualifies as a Third World state, there are differences that distinguish it from most others. Let us examine some of these differences.

First, Iran is the neighbor of a superpower, sharing about 1,200 miles of boundaries with the Soviet Union. The fact that so much of the East-West global and regional competition for power and influence has centered on the Middle East and Southwestern Asia after World War II partly distinguishes Iran—which straddles both regions—from most other Third World states.

Second, unlike most Third World states, Iran is an oil-rich state, and it is also the only such state that physically dominates the world's most vital oil chokepoint: the Strait of Hormuz through which over 55 percent of the world oil trade flows. Although Oman also straddles the strait, neither physically nor in terms of resources is it comparable to Iran in its overall strategic importance in world politics.

Third, unlike most Third World states, Iran's foreign policy during the Shah's regime represented an alignment relationship with a superpower.

Fourth, unlike most Third World states, Iran represents an old-new state; it was "the sole superpower of the ancient world," according to Arnold Toynbee, and yet it is a "new" state in the sense of sharing many of the socioeconomic and sociopolitical problems of most other developing nations.

And fifth, unlike most Third World states, Iran is not a former colony of Western imperial powers, although its independence was nominal during most of the nineteenth century and part of the twentieth.

The list of differences between Iran and most other Third World states can be extended. Nevertheless, there are many similarities that justify a number of theoretical propositions based on the Iranian experience that may be relevant to the study of influence relationships between the United States and other Third World states. I offer the propositions below in the hope that they will reveal the complex nature of the phenomenon itself and the difficulties involved in its assessment in contemporary international politics.

First, the differentials in power do not always translate into differences in influence. In other words, the state possessing a greater amount of material and other forms of power does not necessarily exercise a greater degree of influence over the lesser power at all times. According to Alvin Rubinstein, "Influence is manifested when A affects the behavior of B so that it redounds to the policy advantage of A."[1] Taking A as a superpower and B as a Third World state, there is no automatic influence of A over B simply because of the inferiority of B's power relative to A's. The key word in this definition of influence is "when," indicating that there are times when the greater power of A translates into greater influence over B, but there are also other times when it does not. The truth of this proposition, I submit, is borne out by the example of the United States-Iran relationship over nearly four decades.

Second, influence is not only time-bound, but it is also issue specific. Simply stated, this means that even at a given point in time A's influence over B or vice versa is not uniform with respect to every issue. For example, the Shah's overpricing of Iranian oil in the 1970s—assuming total U.S. opposition, which is an assumption that some dispute—reflected the greater influence of the Shah's regime over the United States on that specific issue, but no comparable influence was exerted during the same period on the United States by that regime, for example, on the issue of nonoil trade.

Third, governments are not the only influence players. Private individuals, corporations, and other nonstate actors exercise considerable influence in the overall relationship between the United States and a Third World state. By virtue of its greater capacity, U.S. non-state players, corporations, and individuals are far more numerous than those of a client state. For example, at one time hundreds of U.S. private corporations and about 45,000 U.S. nationals exercised considerable influence in various sectors of the Iranian economy and society, but no comparable influence was exercised by Iranians in the United States; Iran simply lacked comparable private actors. Empirically, there is no necessary "symbiotic relationship" between U.S. private interests and the interests of the U.S. government just because the United States is characterized as a "capitalist state." Conversely, the interests of the U.S. government in Iran, for example, were marked primarily by strategic, rather than economic, considerations.

Fourth, domestic political instability and external vulnerability place the most serious limits on the exercise of influence by Third World states in their relationship with superpowers. Third World regimes in power and sociopolitical forces vying for power are at times inclined to invite, court, and cultivate the power and influence of foreign powers in their own societies as a means of consolidating domestic power and resisting the pressures of perceived foreign enemies. Nevertheless, client or surrogate states exercise considerable influence over their patrons—depending on time, circumstances, and the issue at hand—as long as the ruling elites can successfully manage the challenge of political opposition. The failure to do so may destroy their domestic power and the influence of their superpower patron all in one stroke.

Fifth, and finally, the most serious limits on the effective exercise of influence by a superpower in its relationship with a Third World client state may stem from three principal flaws in its basic approach: (1) obsession with East-West strategic considerations; (2) inordinate emphasis on economic development—defined primarily as the rate of economic growth—at the expense of adequately appraising the challenges of domestic political change and continuity in the client state; and (3) a superpower's inability to take into account in its decision-making process the intangible factors underlying political and diplomatic behavior in Third World states.

The importance of the third point cannot be overemphasized. If the concept of influence is said to concern only who gets what, where, when, and why, then it would be inadequate for an analysis of the foreign policy and political behavior of many Third World states. The Western concept of influence is basically secular; it is a byproduct of the post-Westphalia Western state system. But the secular and the sacred are largely inseparable in the political culture of most Third World states. Hence, in applying the concept of influence to these societies, we should modify it to allow for strong religiously based moralistic considerations as well. So modified, the concept of influence should then mean not only who gets what, where, when, and why, but also who *should* get what, where, when, and why.

Neither in pre-Islamic nor in Islamic Iran, for example, have the concepts of power and piety been separable, whether they are viewed in the contexts of Zoroastrian or Shi'i Islamic tradition. This is partly why power politics within the Iranian society and between the society and the outside world should be perceived not so much in terms of the struggle for, or accommodation of, power and influence, but the ultimate triumph of good over evil power and influence. The more prevalent this kind of concept of power politics in a Third World society is, the less the value of give-and-take and compromise is in its domestic and foreign policy behavior. All this, however, does not mean that a monolithic concept of power and influence exists within a given Third World society. It only means that even when there is no consensus on what constitutes good or bad influence in a society, the concept of the inseparability of power and piety persists and significantly affects political and foreign policy behavior in Third World states.

NOTE

1. Alvin Z. Rubinstein, ed. *Soviet and Chinese Influence in the Third World* (New York: Praeger, 1975), pp. 1-18.

THE
UNITED STATES
AND IRAN

1

THE SHAH COURTS
U.S. INFLUENCE IN IRAN

The main feature of the United States-Iran relationship during the Shah's regime was the exercise of initiative by the Shah in involving U.S. power and influence in Iran. That was a classic example of the exercise of influence by a lesser power over a greater power. That important initiative preceded by more than a decade the U.S. intervention in favor of the Shah in 1953 at the peak of his domestic power struggle with the Iranian nationalist leader, Dr. Muhammad Musaddeq. It is often simplistically assumed that the Shah could not have exerted any significant influence on the direction of Iran's foreign policy before 1953 because: (1) the Shah was young and inexperienced during that period; (2) he began to consolidate domestic control largely after 1953; (3) the United States-Iran relationship developed largely during the subsequent decades; and (4) during part of that period the country was occupied by Britain and the Soviet Union. I hope this chapter will dispel the myth that the Shah was not influential in guiding Iran's foreign policy during this period.

This erroneous myth is a remarkable example of how influence is equated with power. Since the Shah did not seem to have significant domestic control before 1953 how could he have exercised any major influence on Iran's foreign relations? The assumption that he could not have is empirically indefensible. The Shah had both the intention and the requisite capability to influence the direction of Iranian foreign policy in general and the development of United States-Iran relations in particular.[1]

The Shah's intention was rooted paradoxically in the interplay

1

between his own sense of personal insecurity and the country's external and internal insecurity. The fall of Reza Shah, his father, as a result of the Anglo-Soviet invasion of Iran in 1941 had a traumatic impact on the son's sense of security. The domineering character of Reza Shah, his son's confined childhood experiences, and the over-bearing influence of the young Shah's twin sister, Ashraf Pahlavi, who left Iran with her father after his abdication but returned to Iran subsequently, were powerful influences on his desire to protect himself against a chaotic scramble for power by numerous political factions, parties, and individuals mushrooming on the Iranian political scene after the fall of his father. Nationalists, Muslim fundamentalists, and communists either poured out of his father's jails or returned from exile. Few, if any, seemed friendly to the son of a hated dictator.

The intention of Muhammad Reza Shah to influence events in his own favor was inseparable from the interests of his country as he saw them. He was no different from other Iranian monarchs, who had always considered the country as the extension of themselves. His country was occupied, although it was technically made an ally of the invaders in 1942. The Soviets had been his father's bête noire; they were his, too. The British were not necessarily admired, but to him they represented the lesser of the two old evils. They could be relied on to checkmate Soviet encroachment.

The Shah's want of effective domestic control was not totally hopeless, either. He inherited his father's supporters, especially the members of the aristocracy and military leaders. Such experienced and fatherly prime ministers as the distinguished scholar-philosopher Muhammad Ali Foroughi, his first prime minister, helped him greatly. Even such ambitious prime ministers as Ahmad Qavam could be counted on to carry out his wishes most of the time. Qavam, in particular, enjoyed the longest tenure of all the prime ministers during the war; he served the Shah well in spite of differences over various issues. In addition, members of the aristocracy in the Majlis (Parliament) and in the civilian and military bureaucracy could often be counted on to support the Shah's wishes. Most of all, the military was the proud creature of his father. He himself had been trained in the Iranian Military College, and he firmly believed that strengthening the military was the key to the survival of his nascent regime, and to the internal and external security of the country. The collapse of the military before the invading Soviet and British forces was disturbing, but its revival was not regarded impossible.

The British government recognized Muhammad Reza Shah's accession to the throne of Iran after the abdication of his father in September 1941. But it did so on condition that he would return the lands forcibly taken by his father to their rightful owners, that he would observe the Iranian Constitution, and would carry out "all the reforms considered necessary by the British government."[2] These might have seemed intolerable conditions, but the Shah had no real choice.

The observance of the constitution, however, was potentially a source of trouble. The potential opponents of the Shah's regime, especially among the urban middle classes, the merchants of the Bazaar, and the Muslim fundamentalists, were already referring to the fall of his father as the "revival of constitutionalism" (*ehya-e mashroutiyat*). Each group foresaw a different scenario of future political developments.

The clerical leaders wanted the revival of the constitutional provision that had never been implemented by his father, namely, the supervision of the acts of the Majlis by a committee of five leading clergymen. For example, Ruhollah Musavi Khomeini, who was not the prominent religious leader during World War II that he became subsequently, argued vociferously that Iran's government must become a "government of God" (*hokoumat-e haq*). He did not advocate either the destruction of the monarchy or the overthrow of the Shah. Nor did he believe that the Shah must be a *faqih* (religious leader). But he advocated that the kind of government that he envisaged could materialize by "implementing that one provision of the Constitution" regarding the religious supervision of laws passed by the Majlis. Such an implementation, he argued, would turn the country around, and would raise it to a unique position in the world. "The Shah must obey the law," must not abuse the monarchy for personal "lust and robbery" (*shahvat-raniha va qarat-qari-ha*), and must not become a party to the destruction of life, property, and integrity in the country. Only the religious supervision of the secular laws could accomplish these and similar objectives.[3]

The nationalist elements also foresaw new developments in the revival of the constitution. Their prescriptions, as those of the religious elements, could pose a potential threat to the emergence of a strong monarchical regime. Domestically, they aspired to the true implementation of the provisions of the constitution, the reform of the electoral laws, and many other political and legal reforms that would result in a limited monarchical rule under the constitution. The Shah should reign rather than rule; that was the nationalist article of faith. Reza Shah's dictatorship should not be repeated. Freedom of the press and assembly must become meaningful, parliamentary elections must become truly free, and, above all, the military must be placed under civilian control. The leading advocate of these internal political changes, Musaddeq, also demanded a foreign policy of "negative equilibrium" (*syasat-e movazeneh-ye manfi*) or nonalignment between the superpowers.

All told, the demand of the British government for the observance of the constitution, the Allied occupation of Iran, and potentially unfriendly religious and political forces seemed to provide no real opportunity for strengthening the Shah's rule and for resisting the pressures of the occupying powers on him. There was a clear need for reliance on a third foreign power. That could only be the United States. The example of his father's action immediately before the Anglo-Soviet invasion of Iran provided a model. When Winston Churchill decided to establish "the fullest communication with Russia" as a means of aiding Moscow with the help of Iran in the fight against Germany, Reza Shah reversed his position of trying to prevent the invasion of Germany. He had for decades cultivated the friendship of Germany before the war partly as a means of strengthening his domestic control and resisting the Anglo-Soviet pressures. As soon as the threat of the Anglo-Soviet invasion became imminent, however, he turned to President Franklin D. Roosevelt for U.S. intercession. The attempt failed, but the lesson was learned. Why should not his son also turn to the United States for help?

The Shah, therefore, took a historic initiative on October 8, 1941. He approached the U.S. minister in Tehran. He told the minister that his father had been surrounded by "bad advisers"—which meant that this had been the reason for his disregard of the Iranian Constitution—but "he would govern constitutionally and look after the welfare of his people." More to the point that he really had in mind, the Shah told the minister that he "would be very happy to be an ally of America."[4]

This was a bold vision. It was the first time in the history of Iran's foreign policy that a leader had envisaged an *alliance* with the United States. Traditionally, the Iranian leaders had tried to develop relationships with the United States as a "third power" that would be a counterweight against external pressures from Britain and Russia, and, of course, as a means of strengthening domestic control of the ruler through modernization and centralization. That had always been based on the fundamental assumption that the United States was a "distant and disinterested" power, and hence could not dominate the country in the way that the British and the Russians had done. To appreciate this important point more fully, a brief look at the inception of the United States-Iran relationship will be helpful.

TRADITIONAL INITIATIVE

The Anglo-Russian rivalry in Iran began in earnest early in the nineteenth century, but it reached a new peak by the time the Iranian leaders took initiative to establish diplomatic relations with the United States in 1881. As Iran continued to weaken, particularly after two disastrous wars with Russia that ended in 1813 and 1828, the crown prince, Abbas Mirza, launched a campaign of modernizing the motley and primitive Iranian armed forces along European lines, and others tried subsequently to follow suit. Yet by the late nineteenth century, the Iranian armed forces were as "contemptible" as ever by any standards of regular European armies in terms of pay, equipment, transportation, command, and other considerations.[5]

Nevertheless, modernization spread from the military field into other spheres, and the Anglo-Russian rivalry took the form of fierce competition, especially for concessions in economic, commercial, transportation, communication, education, and other fields. The grant of concessions to Britain and Russia became a source of easy income for the ruling elite. The monarch could grant all sorts of concessions almost at whim. The public began to see an increasing identity of interest between the royal court and the rival foreign powers, and a growing encroachment of foreign interest on its own. Foreign enterprises and commerce threatened the interests of the merchant classes of the Bazaar and those of their traditionally close allies in the mosque, the *ulama*, or the religious leaders.

The first historical example of this clash of interest between the ruling elite tied to foreign interests and the public occurred in 1872. The government granted a far-reaching concession for railways, mines, and a bank to Baron Julius Reuter, a British subject. The public protest forced the Shah to cancel the concession, and his minister was accused by the *ulama* of having tried to "Christianize Iran."[6]

That minister was Haji Mirza Hussein Khan Sepahsalar, one of

Iran's earliest modernizers. He was also the Iranian official who took the initiative to establish diplomatic relations with the United States. On May 21, 1881 he persuaded the U.S. representative, John W. Foster, in St. Petersburg to recommend to Washington the establishment of diplomatic relations with Iran.[7] The United States Committee on Foreign Affairs moved that the House approve Bill H.R. No. 6743, on August 3, 1882, which it did, as did the Senate. And the first U.S. representative presented his credentials to the court of Nasser ed-Din Shah on June 11, 1883. The Shah was happy to learn from Minister Benjamin that the U.S. legation would be a permanent one, and hoped that the two countries would benefit from each other.[8]

What were the U.S. interests in Iran at the time? Gleaning the information from the congressional record, the following will suffice: To persuade the House to approve the bill mentioned before, the Committee on Foreign Affairs used three major arguments. First, the U.S. missionaries in Iran needed protection. They had begun their work in Azerbaijan in 1834, and had traditionally enjoyed the protection of the British Embassy, which was no longer certain because the relations between Iran and Britain had become "seriously disturbed." Second, the establishment of diplomatic relations with Iran would help increase U.S. trade, for which a treaty had been signed as early as 1856. Iran was already importing not only U.S. cotton, but— interestingly—U.S. petroleum. And third, the United States should establish diplomatic relations with "the oldest government in the world" that was of such "strategic importance."[9]

Although the fierce Anglo-Russian competition for economic concessions in Iran did not leave much room for U.S. activities at the time, the Shah asked the U.S. minister in 1886 to help the course of Iranian "progress" (*taraqi*). He knew little about the United States, which he called *Yangee Dunya* (Yankee World), but he told the U.S. minister that Iran's interest in the United States was not only diplomatic, but also economic and technical. In the same year, the U.S. minister recommended to the Shah the employment of U.S. engineers for the study of Iranian economic capabilities and problems. He also added, significantly, that the United States' help to Iran was more "appropriate" than that of other foreign powers (meaning Britain and Russia) because "undoubtedly it is not interested in interfering politically in the internal affairs of other countries."[10]

This must have been gratifying to the Shah, but the Anglo-Russian rivalry and its entanglement with the domestic political struggle within Iran had already shown that the involvement of a great power with the ruling elite could hardly be separated from Iranian domestic politics. That point was dramatically demonstrated on two subsequent occasions. Once again Nasser ed-Din Shah granted a lavish concession to British interests and the public rose in protest. The opposition was led again by the religious leaders. The Shah was forced to cancel the concession. This is known as the Tobacco Protest of 1891–92 because it involved the grant of a tobacco concession.[11]

This protest preceded the Iranian Constitutional Revolution (1905–11) in which the U.S. financial adviser, Morgan Shuster, became deeply involved and was later forced to leave the country. The revolution was a popular movement, which involved the leadership of religious, secular modern-educated, and Bazaari elements. It was directed primarily against the political and economic dominance of Britain and particularly Russia, and the tyranny of the monarch. The lower classes as well as traditional middle classes also supported the movement. The Russo-Japanese war had ended the export of kerosene and sugar to Iran, which hurt the lower classes more than any other group.[12]

The leaders of the new Parliament in Iran hired the U.S. advisor to set the country's financial house in order, but this brought him into a head-on collision with Russian interests. Great Britain, which was then Russia's ally (since 1907) against the perceived threat of Germany, went along, in effect, with the Russian pressure to force Shuster out of Iran. But the departure of Shuster was also a result of the Iranian domestic politics. The aristocratic members of the Cabinet opposed Shuster because the reforms he had tried to institute with the blessing of the nationalist Parliamentarians had threatened their vested interests.[13]

The last instance of a U.S. involvement in Iran before World War II was again the object of domestic opposition. In the early 1920s the U.S. mission under Dr. Millspaugh, as the Shuster mission before it, was a private undertaking with the aid of the U.S. government. Millspaugh, as Shuster, was hired by the Iranian Parliament, but Reza Shah forced him to leave because he denied the Shah funds for strengthening his nascent army. The vain Shah told the U.S. minister that Millspaugh had "one serious fault, lack of consideration for the dignity of the government and the state. . . ." He added, "The government would rather put up with difficulties and preserve its independence than have everything running smoothly and enjoy no freedom of action."[14]

THE SHAH'S COURTSHIP OF THE UNITED STATES

The young Shah, however, had every intention of involving U.S. power and influence in Iran. The war, he knew, had breached the traditional U.S. isolationism. The opportunity to follow through on his ideas dramatically improved in 1942 when about 40,000 U.S. troops arrived in Iran to assist the British and the Soviets in the prosecution of war against Germany through the use of an Iranian access route to the Soviet Union. Between then and the rise of Musaddeq to power in 1951, the Shah singlemindedly used every possible method to deepen the U.S. stakes in Iran. Let us look at his main methods and tactics.

The Shah made the strengthening of the Iranian security forces the primary objective of his policy. Toward that end, the government hired a U.S. mission, headed by Colonel H. Norman Schwarzkopf, for the reorganization of the Shah's Imperial Gendarmerie. He was put in charge of "the entire administration and control of the Gendarmerie." Parenthetically, Schwarzkopf played a major part in the covert U.S. intervention in favor of the Shah 11 years later in 1953. To strengthen the Iranian army, the government also obtained a U.S. military mission in 1942, headed by General Clarence S. Ridely, who was deeply trusted by the Shah.

In the same year, the Shah's government hired a U.S. financial mission, headed by Dr. Millspaugh who had been forced out of a similar job by the Shah's father, as discussed. Again, however, Dr. Millspaugh's mission was caught in the web of Iranian politics and foreign policy. The Shah trusted him at first, but when the going got rough he withdrew his support. The main opposition to Millspaugh, however, stemmed from two sources: first, from the Soviets, and second, from the Iranians. The latter proved to be decisive as a strange mixture of traditional and new middle classes combined efforts with those members of the upper classes who felt their vested interests threatened by the reforms instituted by the U.S. advisor. The representatives of these forces within the Majlis finally repealed the powers of Millspaugh in 1945.

Another method used by the Shah's government to involve U.S. interests in Iran was the attempt to grant oil concessions to Standard and Sinclair oil companies. But that attempt also failed. The main opposition was posed by the Soviets. While the U.S. companies were involved in negotiations with the Iranian government, a Soviet delegation suddenly appeared on the scene in Iran; it was headed by Sergey I. Kavtaradze. He asked the Shah on October 1, 1944, in the presence of the Soviet ambassador in Tehran, for exclusive rights over a five-year period for petroleum exploration by the Soviet government in an area of 200,000 square kilometers in northern Iran, stretching from Azerbaijan to Khorasan.

Although the Shah's government believed that the Soviet move was part of the traditional Russian imperialist designs in Iran, the United States believed differently. George F. Kennan, the U.S. chargé d'affaires in Moscow at the time, for example, told the State Department that the oil of northern Iran "is important not as something Russia needs, but as something it might be dangerous to permit anyone else to exploit. The territory lies near the vital Caucasian oil centers which so closely escaped complete conquest in the present war. The Kremlin deems it essential to Russian security that no other great power should have even the chance of gaining a footing there. . . ."[15] In any event, since the Shah's government was reluctant to comply with the Soviet demand, it decided to postpone granting oil concessions to any foreign interests until after the war, and the Majlis prohibited oil concession negotiations completely. The leader of this total opposition to the grant of oil concessions to foreign interests, even after the war, was Musaddeq.

Nevertheless, the Shah did not consider his failure to involve U.S. interests in Iranian oil at the time as a total defeat. The crisis prompted the U.S. government to come out publicly against the Soviet pressures for the first time, in spite of the wartime alliance between Washington and Moscow. On November 1, 1944, the U.S. ambassador in Tehran told the Soviets that the U.S. "policy in this case is based on the American Government's recognition of the sovereign right of an independent nation such as Iran, acting in non-discriminatory manner, to grant or withhold commercial concessions within its territory."[16]

This unequivocal U.S. stand against the Soviet Union was the prelude to the full U.S. support of the Shah's government during the crisis of 1945–46. The crisis was over two main issues in dispute with the Soviet Union: the Soviet interference in Azerbaijan and Kurdistan; and the Soviet reluctance to withdraw its forces from Iran six months after the cessation of hostilities, as required by the 1942 Tripartite Treaty of Alliance between Iran, Britain, and the Soviet Union. The Shah considered the solution of both issues in favor of Iran impossible without the enlistment of full U.S. diplomatic support. Long before the expected legal date of evacuation of all foreign troops from Iran, therefore, the Shah's government repeatedly appealed to the United States to pressure the Soviets to prepare for withdrawal of the Red Army troops. Before V Day, and afterwards, at every Allied conference, the United States and Britain considered it in their own interests as well to comply with the Iranian pleadings. They discussed the issue with the Soviets at the Malta, Yalta, Potsdam, London, and Moscow conferences, trying to extract the promise of an exact date for the withdrawal of Soviet forces. That magic date was March 2, 1946.

But when that date came, instead of preparing for the withdrawal of its forces, the Soviet Union dispatched fresh troops to northern Iran the following day. All that did, however, was to strengthen the U.S. resolve to support the position of the Shah's government even more firmly against Moscow. Secretary Byrnes believed that it was clear then that the Soviet Union was shifting from political subversion to military invasion, and told his colleagues in the State Department, "Now we'll give it to them with both barrels."[17] On March 6 and 8 the United States formally objected to the arrival of new troops in Iran, and called on the Soviet Union to withdraw "immediately all its forces from the territory of Iran." Years later Harry S. Truman claimed, in 1952 and again in 1957, "I personally saw to it that Stalin was informed that I had given orders to our military chiefs to prepare for the movement of our ground, sea and air forces. Stalin then did what I knew he would do. He moved his troops out."[18] Although I have not been able to verify this claim, there is no doubt that the full U.S. support of the Shah's regime, within and outside the nascent United Nations, helped decisively in the eventual withdrawal of the Soviet forces from Iran on May 6, 1946.

The Shah's successful enlistment of U.S. diplomatic support, in this case, however, was paralleled by the successful efforts of his shrewd prime minister, Ahmad Qavam, who finally outpoliticked both Molotov and Stalin. The Shah worked closely with his confidants, Hassan Taqizadeh and Hussain Ala, within and outside the United Nations and in close cooperation with Washington. Qavam, on the other hand, pursued a parallel twofold policy toward the rebel regimes in Azerbaijan and Kurdistan, and toward Moscow. His inclusion of a few Tudeh communist party members in his Cabinet had irked both the Shah and the United States for fear that Iran might lose its freedom of action. But, actually, the differences between the two leaders were more tactical than substantive in nature. Qavam, no less than the Shah and the United States, was determined to bring down the rebel regimes, and to get the Soviet troops out of Iran.

Toward these ends, Qavam negotiated with the rebel regimes and, at the same time, with the Soviet leaders. In his visit to Moscow in February 1946, he encountered a demand by Molotov and Stalin for oil concessions. He linked the promise of meeting that demand to the withdrawal of Soviet forces from northern Iran. He argued successfully that he would agree to meet their demand, but any such agreement would have to be approved by the Majlis. First, however, a new Majlis had to be elected because the term of the old one had expired. Knowing well that the forthcoming Majlis would reject his agreement with Moscow—because the law forbade any government to negotiate such agreements with foreign interests—as early as 1944, he demanded the withdrawal of Soviet forces as a prerequisite of free elections. He and the Shah then coordinated efforts to bring about the anticipated result. The Shah personally supervised the movement of Iranian troops into Tabriz on December 13, 1946 and into Mahabad on December 17, when both the communist and Soviet-supported regimes collapsed amidst Soviet protests. The new Majlis then did what it was all along expected to do; it roundly rejected the so-called Qavam-Sadchikov agreement on October 22, 1947.

By this important date, the Shah's vision of an alliance with the United States seemed closer to realization than at any time since October 8, 1941 when he launched, and assiduously pursued, his courtship of Washington. Just over a month before the Majlis rejected the oil agreement with the Soviet Union, the U.S. ambassador in Tehran had made it even more firmly clear than during the 1944 oil crisis that Iran's "resources belong to Iran" and it could do with them what it pleased. "Patriotic Iranians," said Ambassador George Allen, on September 11, 1947, "when considering matters affecting their national interest, may therefore rest assured that the American people will support fully their freedom to make their own choice."[19] This was, in a nutshell, some kind of a Truman Doctrine for Iran. It was enthusiastically embraced by the Shah and his supporters, but the nationalist elements, who had enjoyed Iran's overall success in opposing the Soviet Union and its puppet regimes in northern Iran no less than the Shah had a different vision of the next phase of their national struggle for independence.

The Shah was determined to make Iran an ally of the West in the emerging Cold War, but the nationalist elements believed that with the Soviet troops finally out of Iran, the next task must be the elimination of British influence. That influence, they believed, was exercised through the Anglo-Iranian Oil Company (AIOC). As early as 1944, Musaddeq had advocated publicly in the Majlis the control of the Iranian oil industry by "Iranian hands." To him and his supporters, Iran's foreign policy in the emerging Cold War had to follow his theory of "negative equilibrium."

But the nationalists also believed that not only should Reza Shah's dictatorship not be repeated by his son, but that the new Shah must reign rather than rule under the Iranian Constitution. The Muslim fundamentalists, on the other hand, demanded the restoration of an Islamic government by means of the full implementation of the provision of the constitution regarding the supervision of all acts of the Majlis by a committee of five religious leaders. As seen, this was the view of Ruhollah Musavi Khomeini during World War II. After the war, however, the leading religious leader was Ayatollah Abolqasem Kashani. In the emerging postwar power struggle between the Shah and his opponents he first joined the National Front led by Musaddeq. But basically, his stated position on the future shape of the Iranian government resembled that of Khomeini. Kashani also believed that Islam and politics in Iran must be considered inseparable, and that those Iranians, such as Ahmad Qavam, who believed in the separation of religion and politics were the instruments of the British, who had always opposed the unity of the two as detrimental to their imperialist interests in Iran.

U.S. INTERVENTION

After the departure of Soviet troops, the Shah's government tried to pursue the courtship of the United States, and at the same time negotiate a new oil agreement with the AIOC to provide greater revenues than had been possible under the old 1933 oil agreement. Both courses of action aimed at the twofold objective of continued strengthening of his regime and resisting Soviet pressures. Both courses of action, however, proved unsuccessful.

The Shah tried to court the United States at this time by three main methods. First, his government pressed for acquisition of U.S. military equipment, which it had requested on September 30, 1946, but the negotiations for which had dragged on during the crisis with the Soviet Union. In 1948 the United States finally agreed to sell Iran $26 million worth of noncombatant equipment with some light combat material. This was the first time in the history of the U.S.-Iran relationship that the sale of U.S. weapons to Iran took place. Washington extended the necessary credit to the Shah's regime.

Second, the Shah tried to institute a seven-year development plan with the aid of U.S. consultants. The U.S. ambassador believed that the Iranian goal was to effect "far-reaching economic reforms which Iran needed urgently."[20] Max Thornburg, the president of the American Overseas Consultants Incorporated (OCI), however, analyzed the Iranian motive more accurately. He believed that the development plan was destined to fail because the ruling elite preferred industrial over agricultural development and over educational and health improvement projects. He also believed the plan would be doomed to failure because of the government's "political interference" in economic development planning. Actually, the oil nationalization crisis that followed aborted the development plan.

Third, the Shah also failed to receive the amount of U.S. economic aid he demanded. He travelled to the United States for the first time in 1949 to obtain U.S. aid, but returned to Iran empty-handed. When the United States finally extended economic aid to Iran, it was only a $25 million credit from the Export-Import Bank; the Shah had hoped for at least six times that amount. The U.S. ambassador, Grady, believed that had the United States "come in quickly and with adequate amounts," the oil nationalization crusade, which was already under way by 1951, would have been averted.[21]

The Shah's negotiations with AIOC also faced total defeat. His government produced the so-called Gas-Golshayan agreement, which was roundly rejected by the Majlis. The oil nationalization crusade was led by Musaddeq and a handful of other National Front deputies in the Majlis, and was widely supported by the Iranian people from all walks of life. It was viewed as a nationalist struggle against British dominance in Iran implemented through the AIOC. The Iranian oil industry was nationalized by the Majlis in 1951. The Shah accepted the fait accompli. His government had opposed the nationalization formula as an alternative to his government's proposed supplementary agreement with the company, but it had lost the contest of wills dramatically.

The nationalization of the Iranian oil industry, however, was largely symbolic of Iran's new popular movement asserting itself for the second time in the twentieth century. As the constitutional revolutionary movement, it aimed at the limitation of the powers of the monarch and the elimination of foreign dominance. The first nationalist movement had been aborted as a result of the British-favored coup d'état of 1921 engineered by Colonel Reza Khan. The coup and the rule of Reza Shah had been preceded by: the Anglo-Russian division of Iran into spheres of influence in 1907; the termination of the Shuster mission and the destruction of the Majlis in 1911 under Russian pressures; the battle of foreign troops on Iranian soil in World War I; and the concomitant domestic ideological, ethnic, tribal, and political divisions, and economic destitution.

The second popular movement, as its antecedent, was supported by heterogeneous sociopolitical forces. The modern-educated elements of the middle class led the popular movement, but it was also supported by such religious leaders as the Ayatollah Kashani, and the Bazaari merchants. These disparate forces had little in common other than their combined opposition to the Shah. As their historical antecedents during the Constitutional Revolution, they were otherwise divided along personal, ideological, and political lines. The main divisions were between the nationalist and religious conceptions of a legitimate political system in Iran, and between these conceptions and communist ideology. Within these broad categories, however, there were numerous divisions along personal, factional, and political lines.

These divisions were reflected in the attitudes of various groups toward both the Shah's government and the United States even before nationalization and especially afterwards. For example, the so-called Toiler's Party of Dr. Muzaffar Baqa'i vigorously opposed the Shah's prime minister, Razmara. The popular perception was that he was both the Shah's strongman and a U.S. favorite. When Ambassador Grady arrived in Tehran, Baqa'i warned him against supporting Razmara's government. He wrote in his party's organ, *Shahed*, "Dear Mr. Ambassador, we have learned that you are an enlightened and capable statesman. We should like to suggest to you not to interfere in our internal affairs. . . . The insistent pressure of American Embassy for installing dictatorial military governments in Iran is contrary to the mutual interest of our two countries. In the name of the Iranian people, we expect you to remember throughout the term of your duty in Iran that you represent a nation that claims to be freedom-loving."[22]

Other factions in Iran, however, did not believe in such methods of denunciation of the Shah's government. An unsuccessful attempt against the Shah's own life was made in 1949, and Prime Minister Razmara was murdered by a member of the terrorist Muslim fundamentalist group, *Fada'eyan-e Islam*, shortly before the Majlis nationalized the oil industry. This extremist group had surfaced in 1946. Its relationship with the Ayatollah Kashani is still unclear,[23] but it is known that when the Ayatollah became the speaker of the Majlis he arranged for the release of Khalil Tahmasebi, Razmara's assassin; the Ayatollah himself had been exiled in 1949 after the attempt against the Shah's life.

After the oil nationalization, however, the divisions among the various factions of the opposition deepened. For example, Kashani was at first a firm supporter of Musaddeq, but later turned against him. To cite another example, the Tudeh Party had at first also supported Musaddeq's crusade against the British, but it also turned against him subsequently. In both instances, the divisions surfaced after Musaddeq accepted President Truman's offer of mediation between Iran and the British in the oil nationalization dispute. Of the two, the Tudeh's opposition to the U.S. mediation was far more vociferous. Even before Harriman arrived in Tehran, the party demanded that Musaddeq reject the president's offer of mediation, and declared boldly, "Harriman must not come to Iran. We condemn any kind of interference by American imperialists in Iran's internal affairs with all severity."[24] Kashani's opposition to Harriman's mediation apparently took more the form of sabotaging Musaddeq's discussions with the president's envoy. Harriman told me that during the course of his talks with Musaddeq he found out that Kashani was vetoing the results of his conversation with Musaddeq behind the scene.[25]

Yet as the oil nationalization dispute with Britain continued, Musaddeq increasingly lost support among the nationalist and religious forces and gained the backing of the Tudeh Party. The ideological and political differences between him and the Tudeh on the one hand, and between him and the Soviet Union on the other had been long demonstrated. But the failure of the Harriman mission and many other attempts at negotiations, and the defection of many of Musaddeq's friends under deteriorating conditions made him politically vulnerable to the Tudeh pressures. Musaddeq himself was regarded partly responsible for his gradual isolation. He was unable to compromise. To him and his supporters, the absolute control of the oil industry was a moral duty. They struggled, in effect, for Iranian "self-determination," as they saw the dispute with Britain. He and his close associates, Allahyar Saleh and Dr. Ali Shaygan, reflected this perception of the issue within the U.N. Security Council, and the International Court of Justice. The choice for Musaddeq himself was between "submission" (*enqiyad*) to the British dominance, and "independence" (*esteqlal*) from it.

Washington perceived the situation increasingly from the perspective of the Cold War. During the early phase of the oil nationalization dispute, the U.S. and British positions had been dissimilar. Washington pursued the path of mediation and negotiation, advised against the show of force by Britain, insisted on the AIOC's acceptance of the principle of 50–50 profit sharing, and invited Musaddeq to the White House for discussions. London opposed the takeover of the oil industry, sued the purchasers of Iranian oil, and imposed an "economic blockade" on Iran. But as the Iranian internal economic situation deteriorated, as the Tudeh Party gained strength, and as Musaddeq insisted on 100 percent implementation of the acts of nationalization, the U.S. concern with Iranian domestic politics grew. Once the Republican Administration took office in Washington, and the Conservative government took power in London, the U.S. and British positions drew closer. The United States accepted Eden's proposition that the choice was between the Shah and Musaddeq, and not between a "communist coup" and Musaddeq.

By the summer of 1953 the Shah's position had been seriously undermined. The Majlis was dominated by the pro-Musaddeq forces; the Shah had lost a bid for installing a pro-Shah government under Prime Minister Ahmad Qavam, and instead agreed to Musaddeq's demand for the control of the Ministry of War in July 1952; and a Majlis committee of eight deputies (*komiteh-ye hasht nafari*) tried to strip the Shah of all of his power as the commander-in-chief, and place the military under civilian control of the Cabinet. Musaddeq also decreased the size and activities of the U.S. military mission that the Shah had laboriously built up as the principal means of deepening

U.S. protection for, and as the main pillar of, his regime before Musaddeq had become prime minister. By then also, the Tudeh Party was flexing its muscle belligerently against the Shah and the United States, and was also pressuring Musaddeq to adopt an even more uncompromising policy toward them both. It demanded the rupture of all diplomatic discussions with the United States and the "expulsion of American spies and destruction of their espionage organizations throughout the country."[26] It also demanded the destruction of the Shah's regime and the institution of monarchy. Its student slogans were "Death to the Shah" (*marg bar Shah*), and "Down with the monarchy" (*barchideh bad in saltanat*).[27]

In light of all this, Washington had already decided that Musaddeq should be overthrown and his government should be replaced by one under the control of the Shah as a means of preventing the threat of a "communist coup d'état." With the approval of Secretary of State John Foster Dulles, Kermit Roosevelt surreptitiously met the Shah and told him of the CIA's "Ajax" plan for a coup, which had the approval of both Churchill and Eisenhower.[28] Stripped of details, the Shah left the country temporarily, leaving behind a "royal order" (*dastkhat*) that dismissed Musaddeq and appointed in his place Fazlollah Zahedi to the post of prime minister. The coup plan was fully realized on August 19, 1953. It was aided by ample U.S. funds in Iranian currency, by several Iranian agents, by part of the Iranian army, by several alienated religious leaders, and by the pro-Shah crowds and their paid leaders. Kashani, who had broken up with Musaddeq, played "a minor role in mobilizing the crowds of south Tehran,"[29] and Shams Qanatabadi, another pro-Shah religious figure, had been involved in discussions with the U.S. Ambassador Loy Henderson before the coup, according to Soviet sources.[30]

The Shah felt that his decade-long courtship of the United States finally paid off handsomely; the United States helped him save his throne, and the Tudeh communist party and its Soviet supporters had to abandon momentarily their dream of establishing the "People's Republic of Iran." Ruhollah Musavi Khomeini's wartime vision of the "Government of God" (*hokoumat-e haq*) in Iran was also momentarily spoiled, as was the nationalist goal of Musaddeq and his supporters for a liberal-democratic and nonaligned Iran in which the Shah would reign rather than rule.

THE FIRST BLANK CHECK

Did the U.S. covert intervention help its national interest? Washington would have said "yes" confidently. Its British-supported action had averted a perceived "communist coup d'etat;" Iran was a "strategic prize." It was denied to the Soviet Union in the Cold War.

From the hindsight of the Iranian Revolution a quarter century later, one might indeed be tempted to find the "roots" of the revolution in this single act of covert U.S. intervention. But in so doing, one would overlook the more crucial aspect of the problem of U.S. intervention. By this intervention, the United States not only identified itself with a regime of dubious legitimacy, but worse, it abandoned its own influence leverage over the Shah's regime willfully and shortsightedly. In recognizing the new Shah's government in 1941, the British government had demanded, and received inter alia, the Shah's future observance of the Constitution of Iran. The United States not only failed to seek any such assurances from the Shah, but when he volunteered to Kermit Roosevelt that, among others, he "owed his throne" to the United States, Roosevelt told him, "... Iran owes me—us, the Americans and the British who sent me—absolutely nothing." The Shah thanked Roosevelt and took special note of his statement "that there is no obligation. We accept and understand it fully."[31]

Even this blank check endorsement of the Shah's regime, however, does not establish the "original sin" of U.S. policy failure in Iran conclusively. It only marked the beginning of a quarter century of close U.S. relationship with the Shah's regime, which will have to be examined empirically over a period of time before it can be assessed in a broader perspective more objectively. Toward that end, I will first discuss four major issue areas in that relationship during 1954-77, before I take up the Iranian revolutionary situation during 1978-79 in Chapter 6, and the U.S. role in that situation in Chapter 7. The conclusion will then take up the problems of an assessment.

NOTES

1. For this theme, which I developed years before the Iranian Revolution, see Rouhollah K. Ramazani, *Iran's Foreign Policy, 1941-1973: A Study of Foreign Policy in Modernizing Nations* (Charlottesville: University Press of Virginia, 1975), esp. pp. 25-178.

2. U.S. Department of State, *Foreign Relations of the United States*, 1941, vol. 3 (Washington, D.C.: U.S. Government Printing Office, 1959), p. 462 (hereafter cited as *Foreign Relations of U.S.*).

3. See Haj Ruhollah Musavi Khomeini, *Kashf-e Assrar* (Tehran: Chapkhaneh-ye Eslamiyeh, 1944), pp. 221–34. At the time Khomeini was not recognized as an Ayatollah. The word Haj before his name indicates a person who has been on a pilgrimage to Mecca. His work mentioned here was, in fact, a refutation of a tract by Ali Akbar Hokmizadeh, under the title of *Assrar-e Hezar Saleh.*

4. *Foreign Relations of U.S.*, 1941, vol. 3, pp. 470–71.

5. See Sir Henry Rawlinson, *England and Russia in the East* (London: J. Murray, 1875), p. 31.

6. See Hamid Algar, *Religion and State in Iran, 1785–1906: The Role of the Ulama in the Qajar Period* (Berkeley and Los Angeles: University of California Press, 1969), p. 177.

7. See *Foreign Relations of U.S.*, 1882, pp. 1016–17.

8. See Mehdi Heravi, *Iranian-American Diplomacy* (New York: Theo. Gaus' Sons, 1969), p. 13.

9. See U.S. Congress, *Congressional Record*, 47th Cong., 1st sess., vol. 13 (Washington, D.C.: U.S. Government Printing Office, 1882), pp. 6846–47.

10. Mehdi Kianfar, *Siyasat-e Amrika dar Iran* (Tehran: Chapkhaneh-ye Elmi, 1949), pp. 47–53.

11. For details see Nikki R. Keddie, *Religion and Rebellion in Iran: The Tobacco Protest of 1891–1892* (London: Frank Cass, 1966). See also Keddie's "Iran: Change in Islam; Islam and Change," *International Journal of Middle East Studies* 2 (July 1980): 527–42.

12. This point about the lower classes is often overlooked in the literature on the Constitutional Revolution because of the emphasis placed on the role of the *ulama*, the Western-educated intellectuals, and the Bazaar merchants. For details see H. Mudeer Hallaj, *Nehzat-e Iran ya Tarikh-e Mashrutiyyat* (Tehran: Bongah-e Matboo'ati-ye Afshari, 1934), p. 17. This slender firsthand report of the Constitutional Revolution includes especially revealing information about the revolutionaries taking refuge in the British legation.

13. See Robert A. McDaniel, *The Shuster Mission and the Persian Constitutional Revolution* (Minneapolis: Bibliotheca Islamica, 1974), esp. pp. 190–210.

14. See L. P. Elwell-Sutton, "Reza Shah the Great: Founder of the Pahlavi Dynasty," in George Lenczowski, ed., *Iran under the Pahlavis* (Stanford: Hoover Institution Press, 1978), pp. 1–50.

15. *Foreign Relations of U.S.*, 1944, vol. 5, pp. 470–71.

16. Ibid., pp. 462–63.

17. Ibid., vol. 7, pp. 336–47.

18. Truman's claim in 1957 seems to have gone largely unnoticed because it appeared in an article (*New York Times*, August 25, 1957) that was concerned with the Syrian crisis and the role of the United States vis-à-vis the Soviet Union.

19. Cited in George Lenczowski, *Russia and the West in Iran, 1918–1948* (Ithaca, N.Y.: Cornell University Press, 1949), pp. 310–11.

20. *Foreign Relations of U.S.*, 1946, vol. 7, p. 520n.

21. Henry F. Grady, "What Went Wrong in Iran?" *Saturday Evening Post*, January 5, 1952, p. 57.

22. Author's translation from the original in *Shahed*, Tir 11, 1329.

23. See Shahrough Akhavi, *Religion and Politics in Contemporary Iran: Clergy-State Relations in the Pahlavi Period* (Albany: State University of New York Press, 1980), pp. 60–61.

24. See *Besoy-e Ayandeh*, Tir 20, 1330.

25. Author's interview with Harriman, December 1979.

26. *Besoy-e Ayandeh*, February 29, 1953.

27. Ibid., March 3, 1953.

28. For details see Kermit Roosevelt, *Countercoup: The Struggle for the Control of Iran* (New York: McGraw-Hill, n.d.).

29. Akhavi, *Contemporary Iran*, p. 69.

30. *Current Digest of the Soviet Press*, September 19, 1953, p. 20.

31. See Roosevelt, *Countercoup*, p. 291.

2

OIL INFLUENCE

Between the overthrow of the Musaddeq government and the outbreak of the Iranian Revolution, the principal issue areas in United States-Iran relationship are related to oil, security and arms, economic development, and political continuity and change. I shall take up these issue areas in this and the next three chapters in that order. These four issue areas are inextricably intertwined. They are divided because influence is issue specific as indicated in the introduction to this study. For example, in reality the United States-Iran disagreement over the oil price issue interplayed with their differences over the arms transfer issue. These disagreements in turn affected debate between the Shah's regime and the United States over the Iranian economic development issues. In turn, all of these issues were intimately related to the overriding problems of political continuity and change. Let us first look at the issues and developments related to oil.

U.S. OIL INTEREST

The overthrow of the Musaddeq government was followed immediately by the move to settle the oil nationalization dispute between Iran and Britain. The Shah's government was relatively powerless. Economically, the country was nearly bankrupt. The virtual closing down of the Iranian oil industry during the nationalization dispute, the inability of the Musaddeq government to sell Iranian oil in the cartel-controlled world markets, the refusal of the Eisenhower Administration to give the Musaddeq government any financial aid, and the British economic boycott against Iran meant that the Shah's government was in no real position to bargain effectively with the Western governments and their oil companies on an equal footing. President Eisenhower's grant of $45 million to the government of General Zahedi (September 1953) fell far short of the Iranian estimate of its need for $300 million. The aid, however, was intended to induce the Zahedi government to move quickly toward a settlement with Britain.

Nor was the Shah politically and psychologically capable of driving a hard bargain. The economic bankruptcy was matched by political chaos. The disparate sociopolitical forces that had been let loose after the downfall of the Shah's father had radicalized. The Tudeh Party, as seen, boldly demanded not only the overthrow of the Shah's regime, but also the destruction of the monarchy. The Shah could not, and did not, consolidate power overnight. It took him almost another decade after 1953 to suppress his opponents effectively. Psychologically, too, the Shah was in a weak position. He knew that he owed his throne to Washington, a liability that cast a dark shadow on his claim to legitimacy, despite the so-called mystique of the monarchy. Both power and authority had to be won.

Yet neither political consolidation nor economic rehabilitation could be envisaged without oil revenues; they constituted the backbone of the Iranian economy. The very reentry of Iranian oil supplies into the world markets posed serious problems. The shutdown of the Iranian oil industry had been followed by stepped-up production in other Middle Eastern oilfields, and the buildup of new refineries in Germany, Britain, Australia, and Aden. What abetted the Iranian oil industry was the rapid rise in world oil consumption. That made the reabsorption of Iranian oil supplies possible. But complicated arrangements had to be worked out among the seven big oil companies, and between them and the U.S. and Iranian governments in order to get the Iranian oil supplies flowing into the world markets again.

An agreement was signed in August 1954. It created a new company, known as the Consortium. Significantly, the Consortium included five U.S. companies, each allotted 8 percent of the shares. The participation of the U.S. companies involved a deal between them and the U.S. government. Opinion about the nature of the deal is still divided. According to some observers, the National Security Council assured the majors that their participation in the Consortium would not subject them to prosecution under U.S. antitrust law.[1] Others, however, believe that the United States government pressed for the companies' entrance into the Consortium by offering to prevent any effective prosecution of the antitrust suit that had already been pending against them in the Justice Department. The deal, anyway, gave the United States "a new and malleable form of influence over the Iranian government and over Middle Eastern politics in general."[2] This is largely a one-sided observation.

Several years after the agreement was signed, the Shah said that "its most important result was the termination, once and for all, of the British monopolistic hold over Iran's oil industry."[3] British Petroleum's share in the Consortium was now confined to 40 percent of the total, although it equalled the 40 percent total shares of the five U.S. companies. The Shah did not really like the Consortium arrangement but was unable to do much about it at that particular moment. Nevertheless, he let President Eisenhower, Ambassador Henderson, and Herbert Hoover know about his reservations. In signing the agreement, he intimated that he was satisfied with the agreement "under the circumstances." He also allowed severe public criticism of the agreement in the otherwise docile houses of Parliament. The agreement was attacked there for giving Iran only 50 percent of the profits, for its 25-year duration, for the too generous compensation granted to British Petroleum for claimed losses, and for its having been imposed on the country.[4] The critics of the agreement claimed that in reality the Iranian oil industry was "denationalized," despite the legal euphemism of the provisions of the agreement to the contrary. The Consortium in effect controlled oil production and prices as had the Anglo-Iranian Oil Company during the previous decades.

IRAN, OPEC, AND THE CONSORTIUM

Oil production and price issues affected United States-Iran relationships directly and indirectly throughout the 1960s and the 1970s. Although the issues were fundamentally the same, the circumstances were constantly changing. Protesting the unilateral decision of the Western oil companies to reduce posted prices for Middle Eastern crude oil in August 1960, Iran joined Venezuela, Iraq, Kuwait, and Saudi Arabia (with Qatar joining later) to set up the Organization of Petroleum Exporting Countries (OPEC). OPEC nations believed that their 50–50 profit sharing was threatened by the cuts in posted prices. Their overriding objective at the time was to safeguard, and if possible improve, their income per barrel. Toward that end, in 1962 OPEC demanded the restoration of posted prices in the Middle East to the levels prevailing before August 1960. But the organization recommended to its members to take up disputed issues directly with the company or companies with which they were individually involved.

The Iran-Consortium relationship during the 1960s went through two major phases. First, in launching his land and other reform programs, euphemistically called the "White Revolution," the Shah increased pressure on the Consortium for greater production. The resulting "supplementary agreement" in 1964, however, did not satisfy the Shah's appetite for increased oil revenues. In 1966, for example, the director of the National Iranian Oil Company (NIOC) complained to the representatives of the Consortium that the "restriction that is being imposed upon the normal growth of production in Iran in order to enable the fulfillment of other plans elsewhere is most deplorable and I feel it my duty to remind you, Gentlemen, that overlooking Iran's vital interest in this regard is causing grave concern in my country."[5] He specifically attacked the Consortium's planned increase of only 9 to 10 percent in offtake from Iran, despite the newly proven reserves in the Karun-Marun field. Low oil revenues meant reduced power for the Shah's regime at home and abroad.

Second, the Shah's pressures on the Consortium for higher oil revenues increased substantially in 1968–69, as circumstances improved his bargaining position at the time. By the late 1960s, the Shah felt a greater sense of self-confidence. Domestically, his control over the forces of political opposition had increased substantially since 1954, especially after the bloody suppression of the opposition in 1963 and the exile of Ayatollah Ruhollah Khomeini in the following year. Domestically, also, the Shah had by then weathered not only the economic setbacks of the early 1960s, but also his regime had maintained a spectacular rate of economic growth, averaging for years about 11 percent annually.

External factors had also helped the Shah's sense of self-confidence. U.S. economic aid was discontinued in 1967 as a sign of Washington's recognition of Iran's rapid economic development. U.S. military aid was also discontinued in 1969 partly in recognition of the Iranian ability to purchase military hardware with its own increasing oil revenues.

The Shah's growing sense of power and influence was reinforced especially by two other major international developments. First, the "normalization" of Soviet-Iranian relations, which had begun in earnest in the mid–1960s, led to unprecedented economic and commercial ties with Moscow. The acrimonious atmosphere of Soviet-Iranian relations of the 1940s and 1950s was considerably reversed. Second, in 1968 the British announced their historic decision to withdraw their forces from the Persian Gulf region in 1971. Instead of filling the power vacuum left by the British, the United States decided to rely on Iran, under the Nixon Doctrine (1969), for the protection of security and stability in the Persian Gulf region. This factor in particular emboldened the Shah in his relationship with the Consortium. For almost three decades he had sought and developed U.S. protection for his regime. Now Washington was seeking the protection of U.S. interests by his regime. The effect of this perception revealed itself immediately in his attitude toward the Consortium. He told it in 1969 that Iran was no longer prepared to accept the company's mere offer to do its best to reach the amount of revenue demanded by the Iranian government. "I can not build the future of my country on promises," he stated. "What I say is absolutely clear. I say this is our oil—pump it. If not, we pump it ourselves."[6]

TEHRAN AGREEMENT

Although the above factors enhanced the Shah's ability to press the Consortium to meet his demands for ever-larger revenues, none had the dramatic effect of the increased worldwide demand for Middle Eastern oil. By 1970 the oil industry had been transformed from a buyer's to a seller's market. The Organization of European Cooperation and Development (OECD) estimated that by the mid–1980s Saudi Arabia, for example, would have to produce 20 million barrels a day to satisfy world demand. In 1970 the State Department estimated that by 1980 the United States would consume 24 million barrels of oil a day, that domestic production would cover only half of this, and that two-thirds or more of the imports (about 35 percent of total consumption) would, of necessity, come from the Eastern Hemisphere.[7] The Shah's sternest warning to the Consortium in 1970 produced an agreement on November 16. This agreement, however, like the 1969 settlement and others before it, failed to satisfy the Shah. The sharp increase in world oil demand seemed to promise not only Iran, but all other Persian Gulf oil-producing nations an unprecedented leverage in influence.

That leverage was dramatically applied for the first time collectively in 1971 under the Shah's prodding. The historic Tehran agreement between the Persian Gulf states of OPEC and 22 major Western oil concerns was signed by the Iranian, Iraqi, and Saudi Arabian representatives for their own countries, and on behalf of Kuwait, Qatar, and Abu Dhabi. The price of the Persian Gulf crude oil would increase an average of 46 cents per barrel, and a 2.5 percent additional increase per year was envisaged for the purpose of offsetting inflation in the West.

Iranian jubilation over the Tehran agreement was dampened almost immediately. President Nixon decided on August 15, 1971 to devaluate the dollar. While admitting that the de facto devaluation of the dollar meant loss of revenues to such oil-producing countries as Iran, the Consortium argued that the Tehran agreement's provision for 2.5 percent increase against inflation would automatically compensate for the loss. The Shah's regime remained unconvinced; the Tehran agreement had simply not foreseen any such contingency in the international monetary system.

OIL NATIONALIZATION

The Shah's pent-up resentment partly led him to the decision to "nationalize" the Iranian oil industry. The 1954 agreement had been concluded for an initial period of 25 years; it was to expire in 1979. But the Shah said in January 1973 that he would not renew it. This decision brought Iran the closest to the realization of Dr. Musaddeq's dream of nationalization of the oil industry, but it was to be done through negotiations rather than unilateral action. The Shah personally negotiated the St. Moritz sales and purchases agreement, which annulled the 1954 contract, thus giving Iran full control of the oil industry (*hakemiyat-e mutlaq*). In presenting the agreement to the Majlis for ratification, Prime Minister Hoveyda told the deputies that "we may say that the Nationalization Act has been implemented in its fullest sense after a lapse of twenty-three years, thus realizing our long-cherished national objective."[8] Although the Consortium did deliver all the remaining ownership and operations to NIOC, now as a purchaser only, it received, in return, the promise of guaranteed amounts of crude oil and refined products at a discount of 22 cents a barrel. More precisely, although Iran finally managed to control the production and price of its own oil, its "oil power" was still limited for two major reasons. First, it continued to need the expertise of the advanced industrialized countries to extract maximum benefits from its oil industry. For this reason, the St. Moritz agreement provided for the formation of an Oil Service Company of Iran (OSCO). Second, the Consortium was really more than just a "purchaser" of Iranian oil; it was to lift Iranian oil until NIOC could develop its own marketing capacity. This power in particular still lay with the oil giants and the Western industrialized countries.

Nevertheless, the Shah's bold action was received with alarm in Washington. The United States feared the potential spillover effects of the Iranian decision on the other Persian Gulf oil-producing countries such as Saudi Arabia, Kuwait, Qatar, and Abu Dhabi. These nations had agreed with the oil companies that their share of control of the oil industry would increase from a mere 25 percent in 1973 to only 51 percent by 1983. According to the *New York Times* (January 30, 1973), the Iranian action "was a new blow to Western oil companies which have already suffered nationalization on concessions in Libya and Iraq and have been forced to give Persian Gulf producers the right to acquire majority control of existing private operations by 1983. The Shah's move to obtain 100 percent control over the output of the Western consortium is seen as a threat to the recently negotiated participation accords."

The Shah's action, however, was partly the result of Washington's own reliance on the Shah's regime in the Persian Gulf. By the time he nationalized the oil industry in 1973, he was in control of the Persian Gulf oil lanes. He swiftly moved to capture the three strategic islands of Abu Musa and the two Tunbs in 1971, when the British forces moved out of the region after some 150 years of imperial presence. In the following year, President Nixon promised to sell the Shah any conventional weapons he wanted. The Shah's relentless pressure for higher oil prices was partly, if not largely, fueled by his insatiable appetite for ever more sophisticated arms purchases from the United States.

OIL POWER

The Arab-Israeli war of October 1973, the Arab oil embargo, and the explosion of oil prices transformed OPEC into the biggest single macroeconomic force in the world. The Arab oil embargo was imposed in response to the United States' resupplying Israel with arms during the war. The U.S. action in turn was in response to the Soviet resupplying of the Arab states. The embargo decision was made by the Organization of Arab Petroleum Exporting Countries (OAPEC), in which Iran took no part. But the fourfold price increase was decided by OPEC; that was a decision in which Iran played a leading role.

The OPEC decision to increase oil prices, however, was initially based on economic grounds only. Saudi Arabia linked its oil prices to the settlement of the Arab-Israeli conflict for the first time in 1976. At this time, when the OPEC nations split into two camps over the percentage of oil price increases, Saudi Arabia (with the United Arab Emirates) adopted a lower percentage. But Sheikh Zaki Yamani, Saudi Arabia's oil minister, warned the West, especially the United States, that Saudi Arabia expected a show of appreciation with responsive measures in both the Arab-Israeli conflict and the North-South negotiations between industrialized and developing countries.[9] Lower oil prices and higher production were used as a means of putting U.S. pressure on Israel.

Iran's putative oil power seemed to increase dramatically after the fourfold rise of oil prices in 1973. Throughout the life of the oil industry, Iran's oil revenues had been meager. Even after the oil agreement of 1954, throughout the 1950s and 1960s, the Iranian oil revenues never reached the $1 billion mark. Only after the 1971 Tehran agreement did oil revenues pass that level. Nevertheless, Iran's oil income was minuscule in contrast with the dramatic post-1973 increases. In 1972, for example, it amounted to $2.3 million. But in 1974 it jumped spectacularly to $22 billion. In 1973, when Iran's revenues rose to $5.6 billion, the total OPEC receipts were $23 billion. But in 1974 they rose to around $90 billion, which was the largest transfer of capital from one group of nations to another.

OIL PURCHASE ISSUE

Iran's financial power, however, was immediately beset by serious self-imposed limits. Its oil revenues fell from $22 billion in 1974 to around $20 billion in 1977. As a result, the Iranian government was forced to propose the first deficit budget since the price increases of 1973. In 1976 its estimated revenues fell $2.4 billion below its expenditures. The Iranian government blamed the shortfall exclusively on the slackening worldwide demand for oil because of recession. But the record clearly shows that the Iranian crude oil was vastly overpriced in a weak market. As compared with Saudi Arabia, the Shah argued, Iran's much larger population and development expenditures demanded that it steadfastly maintain maximum oil prices. But as compared with Iraq, this argument made no real sense. Iraq was also a populous country with large-scale expenditures as well. Yet it quietly cut prices and increased its output. The truth is that the Shah's grandiose and wasteful economic development plans, especially vast arms purchases, would have created the cash flow problem even under better market conditions. We shall discuss these problems later. It is enough to indicate here that Iran's defense expenditures jumped from $1.4 billion in 1972 to $7.8 billion in 1975–76. More than half of this latter figure represented U.S. arms sales to Iran.

Faced with the widening gap between ambitious goals and limited means, the Shah's regime sought to pressure the United States to get the oil companies to increase the volume of oil they took from Iran. The oil companies were buying considerably less than they had agreed to in 1973 when a new sales and purchases agreement had replaced the old 1954 Consortium agreement, as seen before. The Shah argued that the reduced take of Iranian crude oil would adversely affect the country's five-year development plan (1973–78), might require a reduction in its foreign aid, and jeopardize a multibillion dollar economic agreement between Iran and the United States.[10] The oil companies, however, stuck to their position, contending that Iran's oil was highly overpriced. The U.S. government preferred direct negotiations between Iran and the companies.

OIL PRICE ISSUE

The United States-Iran relationship in the oil issue area, however, extended beyond the Iran-Consortium dispute. It also involved direct United States-Iran relations, the North-South relationship and relations among OPEC members as well. As contrasted with the U.S. media, the United States government was extremely careful about public criticism of the Shah's oil-pricing policies. This was particularly true of Secretary of State Henry Kissinger. He considered the Shah's regime one of the most important allies and friends of the United States and a major political stabilizer in the Persian Gulf and the adjacent regions. But other U.S. officials did not keep quiet about the Shah's hawkish oil-pricing policy. For example, Secretary of Treasury William E. Simon characterized the Shah as a "nut."

On two quite separate occasions, the disagreement between Tehran and Washington over the oil price issue surfaced. First, in November 1974 when Kissinger and the Shah conducted extensive talks on a wide variety of subjects, including the oil price issue, they refused to admit that they had discussed it. But it became clear, nevertheless, that Kissinger disagreed with one of the Shah's favorite plans for easing the energy crisis. The Shah repeated his proposal for the establishment of an index that would relate the price of oil to the prices of commodities that the oil producers imported from the industrialized nations. While declining to discuss the specifics of the indexing plan with the press, Kissinger said in Tehran on November 2, 1974: "Obviously, it is in neither side's interest to build an institutionalized system that accentuates the tendencies toward" inflation. The Shah, however, brushed aside the point by asking the press rhetorically: "We have had inflation in the world when oil was cheap. How do they [the critics] respond to this?"[11]

The second occasion of open disagreement between Washington and Tehran was prompted by Kissinger's allusion to the possibility of the use of force in the relations of the Persian Gulf oil producers and the United States. In a well-publicized interview in *Business Week* in January 1975, Kissinger replied to a question on whether he would consider military action on oil prices: "A very dangerous course. We should have learned from Vietnam that it is easier to get into a war than to get out of it. I am not saying that there is no circumstance where we would not use force. But it is one thing to use it in the case of dispute over price, it's another where there is some actual strangulation of the industrialized world."[12] A storm of criticism was raised by the "strangulation" thesis, although no one really knew what it exactly meant. Kissinger subsequently tried to clarify what he had meant by saying that there would have to be "an overt move of an extremely drastic, dramatic, and aggressive nature before this contingency could ever be considered." In another press conference, he also said that such a contingency "could arise only if warfare were originated against the United States. I don't foresee this."[13] These statements seemed to rule out any use of force over oil prices. Nevertheless, Kissinger's remarks about the use of force were deeply resented, even if they meant that the United States would resort to it only in case of the reimposition of an Arab oil embargo. More cocky than ever, the Shah himself said that oil prices would continue to rise unless soaring costs of Western commodities were curbed. The oil-producing nations would be ready to talk if the consuming countries wished to cooperate. But, he added, "if it is a policy of confrontation we will take the appropriate measures. Disguised dictation will not work."[14]

NORTH-SOUTH DIALOGUE

As the situation developed, however, United States-Iranian disagreement over oil prices were partly submerged in the larger context of the so-called North-South dialogue. The dialogue itself began as a response to the French proposal to convene an international conference on energy among OPEC members, the industrialized countries, and the developing nations that did not produce oil. The first attempt at such a dialogue in Paris in April 1975 failed miserably. OPEC leaders had accepted the French invitation on condition that the conference's agenda would include the overall issues of raw materials and development rather than energy only, but the industrialized states, led by the United States, wished to confine the dialogue to energy problems exclusively. Subsequently, the Conference on International Economic Cooperation (CIEC) was created in accordance with a United Nations resolution of September 1975; it consisted of 27 members, 19 from developing countries, and 8 from the developed nations. Iran joined the group of 19. The CIEC worked through four commissions, including one on energy, over a period of 18 months without any significant results. A close observer of the North-South dialogue wrote that the CIEC came to a "battered and confused end" (June 3, 1977) on all issues including energy; in addition, the central issue related to energy—the relationship between the price of oil and its supply by OPEC members—"remained totally unresolved."[15] The basic interests of the oil-producing states and the industrialized oil-consuming states continued to diverge as the latter group sought stability of prices and availability of supplies, and the former wanted Western help in industrializing, placing investments, and stopping the erosion of their petrodollars by inflation.

OPEC SPLIT

Within OPEC, however, the United States found a faithful ally in Saudi Arabia in its duel with Iran and other members of the organization, which pushed for higher oil prices. Because of the Arab oil embargo, Iran's oil exports to the United States had increased to 696,000 barrels a day in 1974, but as a result of the lifting of the embargo they dropped to 550,000 in 1975, or 8.3 percent of total U.S. crude oil imports. Even without this drop, the U.S. oil imports from Saudi Arabia far exceeded the imports from Iran. The oil-pricing policy of Saudi Arabia, the world's leading oil exporter, had a far greater overall impact on the international economy than that of Iran, the second largest oil exporter at the time. Whichever way one may look at it, Saudi Arabia's relatively moderate oil-pricing policy could redound to the advantage of the United States as well as other major industrialized oil-consuming nations, and, of course, the resource-poor Third World countries as well. The disagreement between the two leading oil exporters over oil prices at Doha (Qatar) in December 1976 split OPEC members. Saudi Arabia raised its oil price by only 5 percent in contrast with a two-stage increase of 15 percent favored by Iran and ten other OPEC nations; the United Arab Emirates alone followed the Saudi policy. Washington did not miss the opportunity to hint at its displeasure with the Iranian pricing policy, but did so indirectly. It characterized the Saudi Arabian moderate position as "statesmanlike." President Ford labelled Saudi Arabia a "responsible" OPEC member, which did not go along with the "irresponsible" ones pushing for higher oil prices.[16] The OPEC split was perceived in Washington too jubilantly; the Saudi Arabian explicit linking of its oil-pricing policy and the settlement of the Arab-Israeli conflict and North-South differences was largely overlooked.

Washington's direct or indirect chiding of the Shah's regime, however, had little effect on the Shah's appetite for greater oil revenues. Iran's own unreasonably overpriced oil—in a market that was saturated at the time with the kind of heavy crude oil that Iran produced—was pushing its crude oil out of the market. The bulk of the Iranian oil was taken by the companies involved in the sales and purchase agreement, about 4.5 million barrels per day. But NIOC also sold oil directly to other oil companies. They were the ones that protested the high Iranian prices and reduced their purchases from a scheduled 1.2 million barrels to 693,000 daily. NIOC officials themselves revealed in January 1977 that Iran expected sales in that year to run about 10 percent below expected levels, causing about $6 million per day loss in revenues.

OIL FOR ARMS

Nevertheless, the Shah continued adamantly to overprice Iranian oil. He wanted increasingly larger revenues to finance his grandiose development projects, food subsidies, and particularly his astronomical arms purchases. The latter objective was accorded the highest priority. Between 1972 and 1975 Iran had placed orders for more than $10 billion worth of military equipment from the United States, and planned an estimated $10 billion from 1975 to 1980. For this reason Iran tried to barter its oil for U.S. arms. The swap would have amounted to a multibillion dollar deal involving U.S. arms manufacturers. General Dynamics Corporation, the Boeing Company, and Northrop Corporation confirmed that they had been involved in prolonged negotiations in 1976. General Dynamics' F-16 warplanes were the particular object of the Shah's barter deal. We shall explore Iran's arms purchase policy later. For now it is sufficient to note that such a deal would have theoretically involved U.S. arms manufacturers in the oil business through oil brokers. But there were serious limits on Iran's ability to do so. For example, in order to move its oil to world markets, it would have had to cut its oil prices, which would have been found out by other OPEC nations no matter how cleverly camouflaged under the barter cloak. This would have damaged Iran's credentials with other OPEC members favoring higher oil prices.

The U.S. government would object to any such barter deal anyway. Washington was displeased with the publicity that the media was giving to the prospective deal, and considered it contrary to the U.S. national interest in lowering oil prices. Iran's ability to sell as much oil as it pleased through barter, and hence reduce its cash flow problem, would have redounded to the disadvantage of the United States no matter how profitable it would be to arms manufacturers. Increased sale of oil by Iran would not have served U.S. purposes because it would have taken "the pressure off Iran" to refrain from seeking further price increases by OPEC.[17] The idea of Iranian oil for U.S. arms had been around for quite some time, but Washington had always been wary of it. The negotiations with arms manufacturers in 1976 did not get very far either; the success of such negotiations would have defeated the U.S. purpose of keeping the pressure on the Shah's regime to soften its hard-line stand on oil prices.

What prompted the Shah's abrupt shift away from overpricing Iranian oil? There was no single cause. His own claim of compassion prompting his change in policy was actually related to necessity, since the world faced an oil glut at the time. But this economic factor alone does not adequately explain the Shah's change. His tenacious overpricing of oil had proven unsound economically, but that did not make much difference in the Shah's policy. Many observers, if not all, have suggested that the Shah was probably motivated by his interest in buying more sophisticated weapons from the United States. We shall take up this question at the end of the next chapter after we have had a chance to examine the development of security and arms relationship between the two countries.

OIL BALANCE SHEET

In an influence balance sheet on the United States-Iran oil relationship over a quarter century, the United States looks quite good. Against the backdrop of the U.S. oil companies' failure in the early 1920s and the 1940s, the U.S. oil interests finally got a foothold in the Iranian oilfields, helped the resumption and continuation of the flow of "embargo-proof" Iranian oil supplies to the markets of its West European allies and friends, and to its own markets as well. The assured access to Iranian oil was considered beneficial to the industrial democracies not only in economic terms, but also in political and strategic terms; the defense of the Western alliance was considered strengthened.

On the other hand, however, the unprecedented activities of U.S. oil companies unavoidably increased the general U.S. involvement in Iran, with all its attendant hazards of being eventually resented and rejected, as it eventually was. The increased U.S. imports of Iranian oil subjected it and other major oil consumers to the oil overpricing policy of the Shah's regime; and the new U.S. stake in Iranian oil resources, the backbone of Iran's economy, meant added U.S. involvement in other aspects of the basically unstable Iranian economy and especially its fragile political system.

On the Iranian side, the Shah's regime managed, mainly through U.S. help, to resume oil sales and earn increasing oil revenues, use the revenues for military and economic modernization and other purposes, terminate the historical monopolistic British control of the Iranian oil industry, and, above all, insure, for a quarter century, revenues necessary for the survival of the regime.

On the other hand, the involvement of the exclusive Western interests in Iranian oil through the Consortium, and OSCO operations in Iran, fueled popular resentment against perceived economic dominance of Iran by the West. The termination of British monopoly was largely seen as the diversification and intensification of Iran's dependency on the West, rather than its elimination. The takeover of the Consortium did not, and could not, necessarily entail complete Iranian influence over the oil companies and the industrial nations of the West because of Iran's technical and marketing limitations. Above all, the Shah's ways of using Iran's single most important perishable natural resource was deeply resented. Oil revenues were used for grandiose economic projects, massive arms purchases, and enriching corrupt elements of the royal family and some corrupt officials at a time when the gap between the rich and the poor was widening.

NOTES

1. See Robert Engler, *The Politics of Oil* (New York: Macmillan, 1961), p. 207.

2. Frances Fitzgerald, "Giving the Shah Everything He Wants," *Harper's Magazine*, November 1974, pp. 55–82.

3. Mohammad Reza Shah, *Mission for My Country* (New York: McGraw-Hill, 1961), p. 112.

4. For details see Rouhollah K. Ramazani, *Iran's Foreign Policy, 1941–1973: A Study of Foreign Policy in Modernizing Nations* (Charlottesville: University Press of Virginia, 1975), pp. 269–71.

5. For the text see *Mid-East Commerce*, November 1966, p. 36.

6. Quoted in *Kayhan* (Daily English) May 11, 1969.

7. See James E. Atkins, "The Oil Crisis: This Time the Wolf Is Here," *Foreign Affairs* 51, no. 3 (April 1973): 462–90.

8. For the text of his statement, see *Kayhan* (Weekly English), July 28, 1973.

9. *Washington Post*, December 18, 1976; and *New York Times*, December 18, 1976.

10. *New York Times*, February 14, 1976.

11. Ibid., November 3, 1974.

12. U.S. Department of State, Bureau of Public Affairs, *Business Week*, January 13, 1975, p. 4.

13. U.S. Department of State, *Press Conference of the Secretary of State*, January 28, 1975.

14. *Kayhan* (international edition), January 25, 1975.

15. For details see Jahangir Amuzegar, "A Requiem For the North-South Conference," *Foreign Affairs* 56, no. 1 (October 1977): 136–59.

16. *New York Times*, December 18, 1976.

17. Ibid., May 15, 1976.

3
SECURITY AND
ARMS TRANSFER ISSUES

Even before the settlement of the oil nationalization dispute, President Eisenhower and the Shah envisaged an alliance relationship. To the president, Dr. Musaddeq had been a "semi-invalid" who had carried on a "fanatical campaign" against the British, but the Shah was a ruler with whose alliance "we may really give a serious defeat to Russian intentions" in the Middle East.[1] Kermit Roosevelt reported to the president, after the successful overthrow of the Musaddeq government, that the Shah was convinced that with U.S. help Iran could become "a significant link in the Free World's defense." This was no surprise against the backdrop of the Shah's longstanding search for a U.S. alliance.[2] But only now did the opportunity finally seem to be at hand. Secretary John Foster Dulles regarded neutralism as "obsolete" and "immoral." He had no need to convince the Shah of that, but could not have approached the Iranian leadership for participation in a United States-sponsored alliance system when he visited the Middle East in May 1953; Musaddeq was then in power. That obstacle had now been removed and the door seemed to be wide open for an alliance between Iran and the United States.

THE ALLIANCE ISSUE

The Shah's regime joined the Baghdad Pact Organization in 1955, but it complained from the beginning about U.S. nonparticipation in the organization. Washington did not believe it would be prudent to join the alliance between Iran, Turkey, Pakistan, Iraq, and Britain.

U.S. participation might aggravate the Baghdad-Cairo cold war. It might also antagonize Israel since Iraq was a member of the alliance. Iran, on the other hand, feared that U.S. nonparticipation might mean no effective defense against the Soviet Union, might put unacceptable limits on U.S. economic and particularly military aid to Iran, and might leave a dangerous power vacuum in the Middle East. The British power was in decline and the perceived rise of Soviet influence in Egypt concerned Tehran and Washington. The Tehran-Moscow cold war, which had begun in earnest in 1947 when Iran rejected the Soviet bid for oil concessions in Iran, and the Washington-Moscow cold war in the Middle East in general converged sufficiently to temper the differences between the United States and the Shah over the issue of U.S. alliance participation.

After the Iraqi Revolution in 1958 and the defection of Iraq from the alliance the following year, the Shah's regime sought once again to press Washington to join the alliance system, which was then labelled the Central Treaty Organization (CENTO). The fact that the United States had decided to join the military committee of the organization made little difference to the Shah. Ambassador James P. Richards, special representative of President Eisenhower, went to Iran to get the Iranian endorsement of the Eisenhower Doctrine, which was a joint resolution of the Congress promising aid to any Middle Eastern country threatened by "international communism." Iran endorsed the doctrine, welcomed the U.S. promise of increased military and economic assistance, and applauded the decision of Washington to participate in several CENTO committees. But it still insisted that "full participation" by the United States was needed to give the alliance "moral and military strength."[3]

Having been unable to press Washington to join the alliance, the Shah welcomed the Soviet overtures for a 50-year nonaggression pact partly as a means of inducing Washington to come through with a better commitment to Iran's defense. Tehran entered into negotiations with Moscow, but the latter's asking price for a nonaggression pact was seen to be too high. The Soviet Union demanded Iran's withdrawal from the CENTO alliance. The Shah's regime rejected the Soviet demand amidst the rise of unprecedented hostility between Tehran and Moscow. At the same time, the Shah's government continued negotiations with the United States for a commitment to come to Iran's assistance in case of an armed attack. Washington, however, was not willing to make any treaty commitment. It persuaded Iran to accept an executive agreement instead. Three such agreements were signed in 1959 with Iran, Pakistan, and Turkey under the authority of the joint resolution of the Congress known as the Eisenhower Doctrine. The United States regarded as "vital to its national interest" Iran's territorial integrity and political indépendence, under the terms of the agreement. The United States also promised to come to Iran's assistance "in case of aggression against Iran." But this promise did not mean any automatic U.S. defense of Iran. Iran's disappointment was only slightly tempered by the U.S. pledge to continue economic and military assistance. It resented the strings attached to U.S. aid—Washington called for effective "economic development" by the Shah's regime.

The Shah's frustration with the alliance peaked during the Kennedy Administration. While the president acknowledged that had it not been for the Shah's leadership the Middle East would have long ago "collapsed" before the Soviet Union, he did not even mention further military aid to Iran when the Shah visited the president in Washington in April 1962. Instead, he emphasized the necessity of "further acceleration of economic development in Iran."[4] This emphasis ran squarely counter to the Shah's long-cherished view that the sine qua non of Iranian economic development was external and internal military security. In keeping with this belief, he had never tired of trying to acquire U.S. military assistance, although the main reason for pushing for military strength was political control. But Kennedy's advisors believed that all that military assistance had produced was an Iranian army that resembled "the proverbial man who was too heavy to do any light work and too light to do any heavy work." It was neither adequate for border incidents and internal security, nor of any use in an all-out war.[5]

On the surface, the Shah recovered from the shock of the Kennedy treatment when President Johnson took office. The new president endorsed a program in 1964 that enabled Iran to purchase $200 million worth of U.S. military equipment, but the Shah paid a heavy price for it. The Pentagon pressed for, and acquired, immunity from the Iranian criminal jurisdiction for U.S. military personnel and their dependents in Iran.[6] From the U.S. perspective this was not an unusual practice. The United States had Status of Forces Agreements with many other states. But from the Iranian nationalist and religious perspective, the U.S. privileges amounted to the restoration of the historically hated capitulatory regime. Such a regime had been imposed on Iran by Russia after a disastrous war in 1826–28. It had been abolished a century later. The depth of Iranian resentment was evident even in the otherwise complacent Parliament where 61 votes were cast against the relevant bill. The passage of the measure insured U.S. immunity against Iranian criminal jurisdiction in traffic accidents under Iranian laws, but the cost of the ill will that it generated far surpassed the benefits. The Ayatollah Ruhollah Khomeini, as we shall see, condemned the relevant law as "the document of the enslavement of the Iranian nation" (sanad-e bardegi-e Iran). This perception of U.S. domination was nurtured over the years until the seizure of power by the revolutionary forces. It was embodied in the constitution of the new Islamic Republic of Iran as a supreme cause of the revolution.

"SPECIAL RELATIONSHIP"

As contrasted with the 1950s, the balance of influence began to shift increasingly in favor of Iran during the 1960s and peaked in the 1970s. As noted, between the mid-1950s and the mid-1960s, the Shah's regime had been unable to obtain either a U.S. treaty commitment for automatic defense of Iran against armed attack or to receive the promise of large-scale U.S. military aid. Subsequently, however, a complex of interconnected developments added a new significance to the Iranian geographic location and rich oil resources.

Domestically, the Shah's regime felt an increasing sense of self-confidence both politically and economically. Politically, the processes of consolidation of power that began in the 1950s, partly through the suppression of opposition, reached a new peak in the 1960s. As we shall see, the attempted destruction of secular opposition in the 1950s was repeated in the early 1960s. But in the latter period the religious opposition was also attacked, which led to the exile of the Ayatollah Khomeini in 1964. The Shah's rapprochement with the Soviet Union at the time aided his regime's ability to force the religious and secular opposition underground.

Economically, too, the fortunes of the Shah's regime improved significantly. Despite the increased oil revenues and continued U.S. economic aid in the 1950s and early 1960s, the Iranian economy, as we shall see, had been in the grip of rising prices, falling foreign exchange reserves, pervasive waste, inefficiency, and widely acknowledged corruption. But the picture began to change dramatically, at least in terms of economic growth. For years before the fourfold increase in oil prices in 1973, Iran's increase in GNP in real terms averaged above 11 percent, a development that prompted the usually discriminating *New York Times* to declare that Iran had reached "the take-off point." It was a development that prompted the United States to terminate direct economic assistance to Iran in 1967, ostensibly because of Iran's "continuing progress," to borrow President Johnson's words. Actually, however, it was because of the increasing U.S. financial burden resulting from the deepening involvement in the Vietnam War.

On the United States' side, the domestic situation contrasted sharply with Iran's. The war in Southeast Asia was producing the impulse toward retrenchment at a time when the Iranian domestic political and economic developments were encouraging Iranian self-assertion. The war in Vietnam that cost the United States about $25 billion a year and more lives than in any previous armed conflict in U.S. history needs no repetition here. But the public mood of self-flagellation and an intensive aversion to the exercise of U.S. military power that it produced had profound effects on the nature and extent of U.S. reliance on the Shah's regime.

Regional developments also enhanced the Iranian ability to influence U.S. security and arms transfer policies. As a pro-Western and, on the surface, a tranquil regional power, Iran could expand its role beyond the mere preservation of its own independence. In South Asia, the Indo-Pakistani wars of 1965 and 1971 had the effect of intensifying the Iranian desire for self-reliance in the face of perceived U.S. failure to come to the aid of Pakistan. The Shah's 1973 commitment to the preservation of Pakistan's territorial integrity was a function of these developments, as were his subsequent efforts to mediate repeatedly between Pakistan and India and Pakistan and Afghanistan toward the settlement of their chronic disputes.

In the Middle East, the role of the Shah's regime could also aid U.S. objectives. Before the Arab-Israeli war of 1967, Iran had been viewed merely as a U.S. ally, and together with Israel, as a counterforce to "anti-U.S." Arab regimes led by President Nasser. After the war, the Shah's regime had been valued more highly as a counterweight to the expansion of Soviet power in the eastern Mediterranean, Egypt, and Syria. The spectacular Israeli victory in the Six-Day War had certainly damaged the Nasser regime, but Iran felt that it had to condemn the Israeli occupation of Arab lands. Discreet rapprochement with Israel had to be balanced by public support of the Arab states. In this respect, the U.S. and Iranian positions diverged, but they significantly converged in opposing the expansion of Soviet power.

In the eastern Mediterranean, the Soviet naval power had been increased in the early 1960s largely in response to the U.S. Polaris A-1 and A-2 missile systems. The former could bring Moscow and Leningrad under counterattack, and the latter could reach the major industrial centers of the Ukraine, the Baku oilfields, and parts of Soviet Central Asia from submarines deployed in the eastern Mediterranean. But the Soviet naval and ground presence surged only after the Arab-Israeli war of 1967. At that time the Soviets obtained air "facilities" at Mansura, Jiyanklis, Inchas, Cairo West, and other sites as well as naval "bases" at Mersa Matruh, Alexandria, and Port Said in Egypt, and at Latakia in Syria for support of the Soviet Mediterranean Squadron. Moscow's influence gained particularly in Egypt where between 80 and 100 percent of Cairo's lost army and air force equipment was replaced by the Soviet Union with shipments worth about $3 billion.[7]

Washington valued Iran as a major source of support for its peacemaking efforts after the Arab-Israeli October War of 1973. The Cairo-Tehran and Damascus-Tehran cold wars of the 1950s and the 1960s were abandoned especially after the war, although Iran had resumed diplomatic relations with Egypt in 1970, after a ten-year break. Relative Arab success in the war, the surge of Arab self-confidence, the favorable U.S. reappraisal of the Arab states, Egypt's reduced dependence on the Soviet Union and reorientation toward the United States, and the prospects of the reopening of the Suez Canal spurred Tehran to press forward its prewar cultivation of friendship among the Middle East Arab states to get their support for Iran's Persian Gulf policy. Iran offered substantial financial aid to Syria and particularly Egypt in 1974–75, continued the flow of oil supplies to Israel, offered to facilitate Henry Kissinger's peace mission in the Sinai I and Sinai II disengagements, sent peacekeeping forces to the Arab-Israeli zone of conflict as part of the United Nations Disengagement Observer Force, and supported the Camp David accords and the Israeli-Egyptian peace treaty.[8]

Another development in the Middle East that enhanced Iran's ability to influence U.S. policy behavior was Washington's deepened reliance on the Central Intelligence Agency's strategic-weapons monitoring system in Iran when Turkey closed down its sites after the U.S. arms embargo in 1974. The highly secret listening posts were hardly known to the public until after the Iranian Revolution. The two main functions of the posts were the monitoring of Soviet ballistic missile launches, and the eavesdropping on radio conversations by Soviet military aircraft, tanks, and field units.[9] The importance of the first function for the verification of strategic arms limitation agreements between the United States and the Soviet Union was well recognized by the Nixon, Ford, and Carter Administrations. Two U.S. monitoring stations were located near the Soviet borders. Most military and intelligence experts expressed doubts whether any course of action could easily make up for these sites if they were ever destroyed. We shall see what happened to them after the revolution.

The single most important regional development, however, that deepened U.S. reliance on Iran and hence increased Iranian influence over the United States was the departure of the British forces from the Persian Gulf region, the U.S. reluctance to act as the British legatee, and the eagerness of the Shah's regime to play a leading role in the region. Iran has always been keenly interested in the Persian Gulf region by virtue of stretching its maritime boundaries along the entire eastern shore of the Persian Gulf, and straddling the strategic Strait of Hormuz. But because of its inability to project power beyond its own land boundaries in competition with West European maritime powers, Iran had to remain satisfied with its inferior status in modern times despite its memory of the Iranian domination of the Persian Gulf in the heyday of its ancient past. But with the collapse of Pax Britannica after one and a half centuries, Iran's opportunity finally arrived. That is, at least, the way the Shah saw the Persian Gulf prospects.

The U.S. reluctance to fill the power vacuum on the one hand, and the desire to see it filled by a friend and ally on the other, made the Iranian opportunity realizable under the Nixon Doctrine. According to Henry Kissinger, "There was no possibility of assigning any American forces to the Indian Ocean in the midst of the Vietnam War and its attendant trauma. Congress would have tolerated no such commitment; the public would not have supported it. Fortunately, Iran was willing to play this role."[10] To sharpen the meaning of Kissinger's words, we must recall the contrasting moods of self-assertion in the Shah's Iran and self-flagellation in the United States. When the British decided to withdraw from the Gulf region, the U.S. public was agonizing over the reported massacre at the village of Mylai, and when the British forces actually withdrew from the region and Iran captured the three strategic islands of Abu Musa and the two Tunbs at the entrance of the Persian Gulf, many in the U.S. public were dismayed over the handling of the Vietnam War as revealed by the so-called Pentagon Papers.

Finally, two global developments boosted Iran's influence. First, the U.S. pursuit of détente turned out to redound to the advantage of the Shah's regime in a peculiar way. The Shah disingenuously worried about the implications of a Soviet-United States summit in Moscow. Were the superpowers trying to agree to divide the world between themselves, as Britain and Russia had divided Iran into spheres of influence in 1907? The Shah, of course, knew better; President Nixon had characterized him as a "world statesman." But the Shah was really after something else. The professed worry was intended to induce the president to promise the Shah what he had always wanted—sophisticated arms from his favorite U.S. arsenals. The president fell for the ploy. The Shah was an "old friend" and ally of the United States, and now the United States-annointed "policeman" of the Persian Gulf. Nixon affirmed the United States-Iran alliance, and promised the Shah in May 1972 whatever advanced conventional U.S. weapons he wanted. He made this controversial promise to the Shah in Tehran on his way back from the Moscow summit meeting.

The president's decision and the ensuing military sales were critically examined in a staff report submitted to the U.S. Senate Committee on Foreign Relations in 1976. With respect to the decision itself, the study inferred that "the 1972 decision was based upon broad geostrategic and political considerations rather than exacting calculations about the balance of military power in the Persian Gulf. When arms decisions are made at the highest levels, the probability that potential future policy and programmatic problems will take a back seat to perceived tangible political benefits is increased."[11] With respect to Iran's position, the study's criticism was directed at the problems of logistics, maintenance, training, etc., that Iran already faced, and expressed concern about Iran's plans to purchase large quantities of sophisticated weapons in the future, despite past difficulties.

The Shah was not going to let this criticism pass without a response. He was fully aware of the growing attack on his large-scale arms purchases and hawkish oil-pricing policy from the U.S. public and Congress. But he was determined to continue to buy more sophisticated arms from the United States. He lashed back with his usual threat: "If you supply us with what we need," he told U.S. journalists in Iran, "O.K., we are very happy. . . . If your sources are not available to us, there are many other sources in the world just waiting for us to go and shop in their stores." In an apparent response to the Senate study's concern that increasing U.S. involvement in Iranian military programs might make the U.S. military personnel "hostages" in an armed conflict, the Shah said rhetorically: "Hostages? In what sense? If my country is occupied completely? Then 34 million Iranians will be hostages too. If they [the hypothetical invaders] have ordinary relations—I mean diplomatic relations—with you they cannot take them hostages."[12]

The president's decision became the subject of heated debate, especially after the Iranian Revolution. There were those who considered it as a primary cause of the Iranian malaise that led to the revolution. There were others, especially Henry Kissinger, who disputed the assertion that the president's decision had been "open-ended." In any event, as the Senate study clearly indicated, the "ensuing problems might never have occurred but for the hike in oil prices in 1973 which gave Iran the means to buy *far more* arms than had been anticipated at the time of the decision."[13]

This brings us to the second global development that seemed to help shift the balance of influence in Iran's favor. As noted in the previous chapter, the increase in world oil demand enabled Iran to lead other Persian Gulf oil-producing countries in extracting unprecedented concessions from the Western oil companies under the Tehran agreement in 1971. But the Shah also took advantage of the increased demand for oil supplies to wrest control of the Iranian oil industry from the Consortium. This happened to take place only months before the outbreak of the Arab-Israeli October 1973 war, the Arab oil embargo, and the explosion of oil prices. Because of this sovereign control over its oil industry, Iran seemed to be in a better position to take advantage of higher oil prices than, let us say, Saudi Arabia which had chosen the path of a more gradual control through "participation" rather than "nationalization." But as noted in the previous chapter, as long as Iran had to depend on the technical and marketing capabilities of the Western oil companies and countries, Iranian oil influence was not necessarily that much greater than the Saudis' although "nationalization" was symbolically very important in Iran. The Iraqi nationalization of its oil industry in 1972 had also been a source of new pressure on Iran. Even after Iran took control of its oil industry, the Iraqis contended that Iran was not the "full master" of its own oil resources. The contention was presumably based on Iran's new sales and purchases agreement with the Consortium.

The increase in Iran's ability to influence the United States' foreign policy behavior, therefore, was not merely a function of its geographic location and oil resources as such. Rather, it was a product of the dynamic interplay of domestic, regional, and global developments. These variables made the constants of Iranian geographic location and oil resources all the more significant to the United States.

Despite all these sources of increase in the influence of the Shah's regime, the indications were that the influence was largely ephemeral. As domestic disturbances increased, the Shah's self-confidence began to sink, and consequently his pressure on Washington for a more clear-cut commitment to Iran's defense mounted. He may well have raised the issue with President Carter during his last visit to Washington in 1977. The cycles of mounting unrest in 1978 increased the Iranian pressures on Washington, but the Carter Administration, as all the other administrations in the two previous decades, was not willing to consider a stronger formal alliance with Iran. A leading U.S. scholar on Iran sympathized with the Iranian concern, and expressed his view on it in an Iranian-sponsored conference in Washington. He called for a U.S. "reaffirmation" of the United States-Iran alliance, a proposition that I found implausible. "Reaffirmation of the U.S. alliance with Iran," I said, "would smack of a return to the 1950's when allies were, in effect, dependent clients of the United States"; and the climate of opinion in the United States would not favor any such reaffirmation because it might produce an adverse impact on the larger U.S. interest in détente.[14] In the same year, John C. Stetson, U.S. secretary of the air force, declined to comment on the nature of the U.S. commitment to the defense of Iran, saying only that the exact interpretation of "various written understandings" between Tehran and Washington would be up to "international lawyers."[15] The Shah's 1941 dream of a real U.S. alliance was still unfulfilled in 1978.

U.S. MILITARY SALES

Regardless of the unresolved alliance issue, the most prominent issue in the security relationship between the United States and Iran concerned the transfer of sophisticated arms. As contrasted with the alliance issue, the Shah's regime was on the whole quite successful in acquiring U.S. arms. As noted in Chapter 1, the Shah's interest in U.S. military training dated back to 1943 and in military equipment to 1947. The 1943 agreement was the foundation of the U.S. Military Mission to the Iranian Gendarmerie (GENMISH) until 1976, and the 1947 agreement set up the U.S. Army Mission Headquarters (ARMISH), which in 1958 was consolidated with the Military Advisory Group (MAAG). Hence, long before the overthrow of the Musaddeq regime, the basis for a tradition of military relationship between Iran and the United States had been established in tandem with the Shah's singleminded determination to deepen the U.S. involvement in Iran. But given the Shah's deep interest in military relations with the United States, as contrasted with any other type of relationship, he tended to view the success of his arms acquisition as the acid test of U.S. confidence in his regime and himself personally. For this important reason, the failure to obtain clear-cut U.S. commitment to the defense of Iran was tolerable only as long as the arms flow continued, expanded, and included ever more sophisticated weapons.

The value of arms purchases contracted, not actually delivered, over a period of 22 years before the explosion of oil prices in 1973 as contrasted with subsequent years shows the enormous impact of the oil revenues on Iran's arms-purchasing ability. During the entire period from 1950 through 1972, purchase agreements amounted to only about $1.5 million, while from 1973 through 1977 they rose to a staggering total of over $11 billion. In the first year after the dramatic increase in oil prices, the value of arms transactions amounted to twice the total value of all arms contracted during the previous 22 years (see Table 1).

Far from being discouraging, the Nixon Administration seemed to encourage Iran's huge arms purchases. For example, in spite of the fall in Iranian oil revenues after 1974, Kissinger announced in Tehran on August 7, 1976 that the United States would sell Iran $10 billion worth of military equipment from 1975 through 1980 as part of a total trade of $50 billion during the same period. The projected

TABLE 1

U.S. Military Sales to Iran: 1950-80
(dollars in thousands)

Fiscal Year	Military Sales Agreements	Military Sales Deliveries
Cumulative		
1950-70	790,525	365,473
1971	354,613	78,566
1972	455,615	214,807
1973	2,133,680	245,293
1974	3,935,069	648,527
1975	1,290,509	985,822
1976	1,558,797	1,890,913
1977	2,760,650	2,416,591
1978	913,494	1,669,142
1979	35,862	1,413,752
1980	0	0
Cumulative		
1950-80	14,228,814	9,928,886

Source: *Foreign Military Sales and Military Assistance Facts; December 1980*, Data Management Division, Comptroller, U.S. Department of Defense, Security Assistance Agency (DSAA).

sales were overtaken by the Iranian Revolution and did not therefore materialize. But the point is that the Shah's well-known insatiable appetite for arms was whetted by the behavior of the Nixon Administration, not to mention the pressures of several private arms contractors. The secretary of state kept justifying U.S. arms sales primarily in broad strategic terms without regard to their adverse economic, social, psychological, and political effects. "If one looks at the threats," he said, "the potential threats, that Iran faces and the armaments of its neighbors and the role Iran has, its effort at self-defense is strongly in the American interest and is not a favor we do for Iran."[16] In spite of his well-known fondness for "linkages," Kissinger refused to link the U.S. arms sales to oil prices in a way that would discourage the Shah's hard-line oil-pricing policy. The justification for this attitude was reportedly that he "did not want the Shah to call his bluff, and then have to sell the arms anyway."[17]

He used strategic rationale to continue burdensome sophisticated arms sales to Iran. He reportedly assured the Shah of Iran's importance to the United States as a regional power, and pledged that "it would have continuing access to the most advanced conventional arms."[18]

Nor did the Carter Administration do much more to discourage the Shah's unbridled arms purchases. All the fanfare of the 1976 campaign about limiting arms sales seemed forgotten, at least in the decision to sell seven Airborne Warning and Control System planes (AWACS) to Iran in 1977. Secretary Cyrus Vance argued before the House International Relations Committee that the president's exception in this case was based on the grounds that the Soviet Union and Soviet-supplied Iraq had in the past "constituted threats to Iran and could do so once again. The combined arsenals of these neighbors are, of course, far larger than that of Iran. Iraq alone has MIG-23's, supersonic Blinder bombers, surface-to-surface missiles, and superior air defense. AWACS will thus help answer specific identifiable Iranian security concerns, and maintain the balance against the actual—or, equally important—the threatened use of force by its neighbors."[19] These considerations may well have been important in making the decision to sell, but reportedly "the key reason given for the Pentagon's action was that the Air Force, which is sponsoring the program, wanted to sell the planes abroad to spread its research and development costs."[20] This reason was confirmed by a report from Bonn after the overthrow of the Shah's regime. NATO officials warned that Iran's cancellation of the AWACS could threaten adoption of the system by the Atlantic alliance because of a loss of $1.3 billion for the seven planes ordered by Iran before the "Islamic Revolution."[21]

ARMS, AGENTS, AND PRICES

The United States-Iran arms transfer relationship did not always develop smoothly. The military relations of successive administrations with the Shah's regime were taxed often by various differences. The disputes in the arms transfer issue area, as in the oil issue area, did not, however, concern merely governmental relations; they involved private U.S. companies as well. The complications stemmed more from the United States' than the Iranian side. The Iranian decision making was quite simple. The Shah made all the decisions, most particularly in the security field. He was reputedly knowledgeable in technical military matters. He accorded the modernization of the air force the highest priority, and was himself a trained pilot. The implementation of arms purchases decisions was left to such officers as General Toufanian and General Azhari, but they received guidance from such U.S. advisors as Eric F. von Marbod, a high official of the U.S. Defense Department in Iran beginning in 1976.

On the United States' side, however, things were far more complicated. The overall clashes in foreign affairs between the executive and legislative branches could hardly find better textbook examples than in the Iranian arms transactions field. For example, John C. Culver, Democrat of Iowa, was joined by other senators such as Alan Cranston, Democrat of California, Patrick J. Leahy, Democrat of Vermont, William Proxmire, Democrat of Wisconsin, and others to block the sale of AWACS. The differences between the White House and the Congress were compounded by interservice rivalries, and interdepartmental disagreements on the one hand, and the promotional activities of private manufacturers and their eager lobbyists on the other. The main controversial issues involved the transfer of advanced weapon systems at the peak of Iranian arms purchases. Two major issues, in particular, emerge from a survey of the record.

One of the issues festered for years, and reached the proportions of an international scandal. In 1974, two years after President Nixon's assurances to the Shah that the F-14—the most advanced aircraft available to the U.S. forces—would be sold to Iran, the Shah decided to purchase the fighter planes worth $2.2 billion from Grumman Corporation. Eighteen months after probing the foreign activities of United States-based corporations, the Senate Multinational Subcommittee opened its hearings into high-level foreign bribery and payoffs in September 1976. The investigation showed that the Pentagon did not learn until mid–1975 that Grumman Corporation had retained agents two years earlier to help negotiate Iran's purchases of 80 F-14 aircraft, that it had paid $6 million to sale agents despite the Shah's repeated objections to the use of such middlemen, and that, according to Senator Frank Church, the chairman of the subcommittee, the Pentagon's arms sales program was without cohesive direction, which often deteriorated into a series of "*ad hoc* responses."[22] More specifically, the senator expressed concern over the arms deal because Grumman began its F-14 sales operation in Iran before the U.S. government had decided that it was in the national interest for the advanced aircraft to be sold.

Amid the revelations of the Senate, the Shah's government accomplished two objectives simultaneously: to recover the hidden fees paid by Grumman to the agents, and, more important, to display a theatrical sense of outrage against bribery at a time when massive corruption in the royal family and the ruling elite was under attack by the Shah's opponents. In bold letters, the Iranian newspaper, *Kayhan*, for example, said, "We Won't be Robbed, Iran Warns Grumman," featuring the justified charges made by General Hassan Toufanian, Iran's vice minister of war, against Grumman. He said that Iran would insist on receiving some $28 million paid or pledged to agents in violation of "contractual understandings with Iran."[23] Finally, Grumman announced a "compromise" settlement of Iran's claims for the commissions the company had agreed to pay to agents. In the meantime, one of the so-called Lavi brothers, the Iranian-born agents who resided in the United States and were denounced by the Iranian government, instituted a suit in the State Supreme Court in Manhattan against Grumman and others for $114.6 million in the international struggle for fee payments!

A second issue that occurred in connection with various transactions was the price of U.S. arms sold to Iran. The case of the destroyer sale symbolized the increasing tensions in the United States-Iran arms relationship. Iran had been encouraged by the Pentagon to buy six Spruance-class destroyers. It placed two orders for them in 1973 and 1974. These were among the most advanced ships in the U.S. Navy. The Shah had extended Iran's "security perimeter" beyond the Persian Gulf into the Gulf of Oman and the northwest quadrant of the Indian Ocean in 1972. His dream of transforming Iran into a major regional maritime power was symbolized by plans to construct a huge naval base at Chahbahar on the Arabian Sea, between the Pakistani border and the strategic Strait of Hormuz. The Iranian objective of establishing a naval presence in the Indian Ocean seemed threatened, when in 1976 the Defense Department told Iran of a 50 percent increase in the price of the destroyers, costing at the time a total of $2 billion. The Iranian reaction was indignant. The Shah's government threatened to cut back its arms purchases. The Pentagon wanted to sell other advanced weapons to Iran, including the F-18L lightweight fighter planes under development at the time by the navy. In the end, however, the Carter Administration decided against the sale of the planes, in keeping with its new policy of cutting back on conventional arms sales. The decision meant a potential loss of billions of dollars for the Northrop Corporation, a major defense contractor. And the Iranian Revolution overtook the dispute over the increase in the price of the destroyers.

SECURITY BALANCE SHEET

To sum up, the United States seemed to get a great deal out of its security relations with the Shah's regime. It managed to involve strategically located Iran in an alliance system along the northern tier of the Middle East during the Cold War, without itself becoming sucked into it too deeply before or after the Vietnam War. It maintained the security and stability of the Persian Gulf region by using Iran as a surrogate for nearly a decade without committing U.S. troops to the defense of the region. It helped the U.S. balance-of-payments problem by selling Iran billions of dollars worth of weapons and military training, and maintained in power for a quarter century a friendly regime that it had helped to install.

On the debit side, however, the historical goodwill of the politically aware Iranians toward the United States was seriously damaged by: (1) the United States' covert intervention in returning the Shah to the throne during the Eisenhower Administration; (2) its perceived imposition of the status of forces agreement on Iran during the Johnson Administration; (3) its unbridled, vast military sales to, and military presence in, Iran during the Nixon, Ford, and Carter Administrations; and (4), above all, its overly close identification with the increasingly authoritarian and repressive regime of the Shah, particularly in the security field, during all these administrations.

The Shah's regime also seemed to benefit considerably in its security relations with the United States. The Shah recovered his throne with covert U.S. aid, he consolidated his own power at home with U.S. security and arms aid, he kept under the control of the central government multiple ethnic, cultural, and racial groups, and enjoyed a sense of personal and national security.

On the debit side, however, whatever legitimacy the Shah might have enjoyed before, or even right after, the forcible overthrow of the Musaddeq government was eroded by: (1) the Shah's recovery of his throne with covert U.S. aid; (2) his overly close identification with the United States, especially in the role of a U.S. "policeman" in the Persian Gulf; (3) his squandering of Iran's oil revenues on massive arms purchases, and hosting numerous private U.S. arms contractors and thousands of U.S. military personnel; (4) the popular perception of his total submission to U.S. dominance and dictation, especially under the so-called status of forces agreement; and (5) above all, his cooperation with the Central Intelligence Agency in matters of Iranian internal security.

NOTES

1. Dwight D. Eisenhower, *Mandate for Change*, 1953-1956 (Garden City, N.Y.: Doubleday, 1963), pp. 164-66.

2. See Chapter 1 of this study.

3. *New York Times*, May 28, 1957.

4. For the text see U.S., President, *Public Papers of the Presidents of the United States, John F. Kennedy*, 1962 (Washington, D.C.: U.S. Government Printing Office, 1963), pp. 315, 323.

5. Theodore Sorenson, *Kennedy* (New York: Harper & Row, 1965), p. 628n.

6. For details see Rouhollah K. Ramazani, *Iran's Foreign Policy, 1941-1973: A Study of Foreign Policy in Modernizing Nations* (Charlottesville: University Press of Virginia), pp. 361-64.

7. For details see Rouhollah K. Ramazani, *The Persian Gulf and the Strait of Hormuz* (The Netherlands: Sijthoff & Noordhoff, 1979), pp. 37-38.

8. See Rouhollah K. Ramazani, "Emerging Patterns of Regional Relations in Iranian Foreign Policy," *ORBIS* xviii, no. 3 (Winter 1975): 1043-69; and Ramazani's "Iran and the United States: An Experiment in Enduring Friendship," *The Middle East Journal* 30, no. 3 (Summer 1976): 322-34.

9. See *New York Times*, January 18, 21, and March 1, 1979.

10. Henry A. Kissinger, *White House Years* (Boston: Little Brown, 1979), pp. 1263-64.

11. See U.S., Congress, *U.S. Military Sales to Iran*, A Staff Report to the Subcommittee on Foreign Assistance of the Committee on Foreign Relations, U.S. Senate (Washington, D.C.: U.S. Government Printing Office, 1976), p. 53.

12. *Kayhan* (Weekly English), August 14, 1976.

13. U.S., Congress, *U.S. Military Sales to Iran.*

14. My statement was in response to Professor George Lenczowski. See Abbas Amirie and Hamilton A. Twitchell, eds., *Iran in the 1980's* (Tehran: Institute for International Political and Economic Studies, 1978), pp. 373-77.

15. *Kayhan*, April 30, 1978.

16. *New York Times*, August 8, 1976.

17. Ibid., November 11, 1976.

18. Ibid.

19. U.S. Department of State, *Secretary of State*, January 28, 1977.

20. *New York Times*, July 12, 1977.

21. Ibid., February 18, 1979.

22. Ibid., September 11, 1976.

23. *Kayhan*, February 21, 1976.

$$4$$

ECONOMIC DEVELOPMENT ISSUES

The United States-Iran relationship during the Shah's regime extended beyond the issue of oil in the economic field. As the backbone of the Iranian economy, however, all other economic activities, including those in the United States-Iran relationship, were significantly affected by the vicissitudes of the Iranian oil revenues. As a result of the oil nationalization crisis of 1951–53 and the consequent stoppage in Iran's oil revenues, the United States extended $45 million emergency aid to the Shah's regime in order to bolster the bankrupt economy until the flow of oil to world markets could be resumed. But this was a bitter reminder of the Shah's prenationalization failure to obtain the desired amount of U.S. aid despite all perceived wartime promises. During the entire period between the arrival of U.S. forces in Iran in 1942 and the overthrow of the Musaddeq government in 1953, the United States' total aid to Iran consisted of only $25 million in loans and $16 million in grants. After his return to the throne, the Shah had asked for about $300 million, but he got only the $45 million in emergency aid.

THE AID ISSUE

The U.S. economic aid issue persisted and festered after the emergency aid. The newly forged alliance relationship between Iran and the United States provided the basic framework of the increasing Iranian pressures for economic assistance during the 1950s. On the whole, the Eisenhower Administration was forthcoming. It was also reluctant to demand that Iran embark on economic reforms in return for U.S. aid, mainly due to the administration's overall concern with the military dimension of the alliance. The Eisenhower Administration extended over $600 million in economic aid and another nearly $4.5 million in military aid to Iran after the overthrow of the Musaddeq government. The Shah's government never ceased to complain about the paucity of U.S. aid despite its rise. That was, of course, an integral part of the Persian Bazaar tradition; neither government allowed the haggling to hurt its basic alliance however. Nor did the Eisenhower Administration try to link its economic and military assistance to progress in Iran's economic reforms, although such reciprocation was sometimes intimated, as in 1957–58.

The Kennedy Administration, however, did not hesitate to link U.S. assistance to the progress made in Iran's social and economic reform measures. The president not only opposed further U.S. military aid to Iran, as seen, but also refused to extend U.S. funds in supporting the Iranian budget. President Eisenhower had been reluctant to pressure the Shah's regime for basic reforms despite severe congressional criticism of U.S. aid programs in Iran as early as 1956.[1] But the Kennedy Administration favored the appointment of a "reform government" led by Dr. Ali Amini, whom the Shah disliked. He had served in the governments of Musaddeq and General Zahedi as minister and as ambassador to the United States. The administration believed that short of basic social and economic reforms further aid to Iran would be like "pouring money down a rat hole." Neither increasing oil revenues, nor substantial U.S. assistance in the past seemed to have helped the Iranian economy. A reform-minded government, it was believed, might be able to do some good. As it turned out, however, the Amini government did not have a real chance to realize its ideas on anticorruption and social and economic reform programs. Amini resigned after a brief tenure (May 1961–July 1962). The "United States refusal to give further budgetary support," according to the *New York Times*, "was a factor in Dr. Amini's resignation."[2]

The Johnson Administration altogether terminated U.S. assistance to Iran in 1967, but for reasons totally different from the Kennedy Administration's reluctance to aid the Shah's regime. The termination was due mainly to changes in Iran's economic and political conditions in the face of the increasing U.S. burdens in the Vietnam War. Economically, the pressures on the Iranian economy began to ease by the mid-1960s. The economic problems of the late 1950s and early 1960s had been fueled by, inter alia, increasing imports unrelated to demands, excessive dependence on funds from abroad, disproportionate and unnecessary increases in capital investment in the building industry, etc. The principal factors that helped improve the Iranian economic situation included the increase in oil revenues as a result of the supplementary agreement of 1964–65 with the Consortium, the prior "stabilization" program of the Amini government, the cumulative effects of Iranian economic development efforts in general, and the limited but beneficial effects of the launching of the Shah's highly publicized reform programs in 1962–63, which was labelled the "White Revolution."

Politically, the Shah's opponents were brutally suppressed in June 1963. His harsh tactics terminated not only the domestic political crisis of the 1960–63 period, but it crowned the process of consolidation of the Shah's authoritarian control that had only begun after the downfall of the Musaddeq government in 1953. Although the Shah launched his reform programs before the suppression of the 1963 religio-political uprising, he could hardly have pushed them through without further control over the government.

Furthermore, the Soviet Union's withdrawal of support from the opponents of the Shah's regime helped the Shah both in consolidating political control and in launching his reform programs, as shown elsewhere.[3] Iran promised Moscow in late 1962 that it would not allow the establishment of foreign missile bases on its territory. Almost overnight, the Shah's hitherto "rotten monarchical" regime became a "pioneer" in land reforms in the eyes of the Kremlin. And suddenly, the Shah's opponents who had been morally supported by Soviet propaganda were dropped for being "reactionary."

The Johnson Administration discontinued the tradition of economic and military aid to Iran largely because of Iran's relative political quiet and economic strength by 1967. But Washington cited only economic reasons for its action. In terminating the aid, President Johnson said, "We are celebrating an achievement—not an ending. This is a milestone in Iran's continuing progress and in our increasingly close relations." Secretary Rusk spelled out what the president's message meant. He said, for example, that in ten years Iran's industrial production had increased 88 percent; its exports by more than a third; its GNP increased 11.8 percent in 1965 and 9.5 percent in 1966.[4] U.S. economic and military assistance, from inception to termination, amounted to over $1 billion. By terminating the aid program, the United States was not really denying itself a major instrument of influence. As noted earlier, except for a brief attempt by the Kennedy Administration, the Eisenhower and Johnson Administrations were, on balance, reluctant to use U.S. aid as leverage on the Shah's regime. The Johnson Administration quickly resumed the military aid to Iran that had been suspended by President Kennedy.

THE TRADE ISSUE

U.S. trade with Iran had to overcome the traditional problems of state control of the economy and the direction of Iranian trade. Reza Shah had established a state monopoly on Iran's commerce not only in order to cope with worldwide conditions of depression, but also as a means of reducing the historical domination of Russia over the nonoil trade of Iran.[5] By the time of his abdication in 1941, he had managed to make Germany Iran's principal nonoil trade partner. The new Shah's interest in establishing a major trade partnership with the United States dated back to 1943,[6] but only after the overthrow of the Musaddeq government did the United States-Iran trade relationship begin to develop significantly. The foundation of that development, and, for that matter, of all United States-Iran economic relations, was established formally by the unprecedented Treaty of Amity and Economic Relations and Consular Rights, signed on August 15, 1955.[7]

The subsequent expansion of trade, however, was tied mainly to the increase in Iranian oil revenues. These increases took place largely in the mid-, and especially late, 1960s. But it was the Tehran Agreement (1971) that had a major impact on the expansion of Iran's trade with the United States before the explosion of oil prices in 1973. For example, according to the IMF figures, the value of Iran's total exports to the United States was only slightly over $89 million, and of imports over $196 million in 1969, but after the Tehran Agreement, it increased to nearly $3.5 billion and $614 million respectively in 1972. After the spectacular 1973 oil price increases, the value of both exports and imports rose dramatically until it reached $15.5 billion and over $4 billion respectively in 1978, the year before the Shah's downfall.

If we calculate the value of Iran's exports to, and imports from, the United States during the same years, as percentages of Iran's total foreign trade, we arrive at the following revealing figures: Iran's exports to the United States in 1969 were merely 4 percent of its total foreign exports; in 1972, they rose to about 5 percent, and then rose increasingly after 1973, reaching 13 percent in 1978. To take up Iran's imports from the United States, the great imbalance between the two becomes amply clear: in 1969 the Iranian imports from the United States were 14 percent of its total imports, which rose dramatically to 22 percent in 1972, and 20 percent in 1978 (see Table 2).

The Shah's regime always complained about the imbalance in its trade with the United States. Stripped of the preeminence of oil in Iran's exports and arms in its imports, the balance of trade favored the United States consistently. Iranian complaints grew louder with the overall expansion of trade. For example, the Iranian Prime Minister Hoveyda complained to U.S. businessmen in 1975 that the Iranian imports from the United States in 1973 amounted to $487 million, while the nonoil exports to the United States amounted to only $54 million. In 1974 the imports nearly tripled, reaching the $1.3 billion mark, while the nonoil exports amounted to only $46 million. He then expressed "Iran's profound concern over the efforts made by certain American quarters to deprive Iran, as an OPEC member, of the advantages of the general program for preferential trade relations with the United States. Our concern does not stem from our expectations concerning that program, rather it is more because of the manner in which a friendly country is being treated as a country whose trade relations with the United States at present is way out of balance."[8]

Henry Kissinger's projected total trade between Iran and the United States from 1975 through 1980 would have increased Iran's exports to the United States. Iran would have sold the United States a total of $16 billion worth of goods, of which $12 billion would have been oil. The remaining $4 billion over six years would have averaged significantly larger than the nonoil exports of only $46 million in 1974. But the United States-Iran Joint Commission, through which a more balanced trade relationship was to be made possible, was established too late. Such a commission had been established between the United States and the Soviet Union as early as 1972 and between the United States and Egypt in 1973. By the time Henry Kissinger was making these projections in 1976, Iran's deteriorating economic conditions could not have improved significantly through increases in Iran's exports to the United States. Furthermore, oil and arms would have still dominated and distorted the

TABLE 2

United States-Iran Trade
(figures in millions of dollars)

Year	Exports			Imports		
	World	U.S.	%	World	U.S.	%
1938[a]	153.0	3.3	2.15	57.9	4.9	8.46
1948[a]	589.8	25.8	4.37	130.8	38.7	29.58
1954[a]	140.1	19.5	13.91	213.3	50.8	23.81
1958[b]	879.1	41.9	4.76	411.5	72.2	17.55
1963[c]	919.1	46.1	5.01	522.6	89.7	17.16
1968[d]	1,869.7	74.8	4.00	1,393.0	239.3	17.17
1972[e]	4,158.0	199.0	4.78	2,770.0	614.0	22.16
1973[e]	6,314.0	344.0	5.44	3,379.0	474.0	14.02
1974[e]	18,877.0	2,133.0	11.29	5,426.0	974.0	17.95
1975[e]	18,249.0	1,398.0	7.66	10,346.0	2,051.0	19.82
1976[e]	20,534.0	1,483.0	7.22	12,887.0	2,133.0	16.55
1977[e]	21,618.0	2,768.0	12.80	15,974.0	3,004.0	18.80
1978[e]	22,070.0	2,876.0	13.03	19,964.0	4,053.0	20.30
1979[e]	19,872.0	2,707.3	13.62	9,738.0	1,121.7	11.51
1980[f]	13,680.0	322.0	2.35	10,545.0	25.0	0.23

Sources

[a]*Direction of International Trade*, 64th annual issue, statistical papers, series T, vol. 9, no. 10, joint publication of the United Nations and the IMF/IBRD, New York, 1958.

[b]*Direction of International Trade*, 66th annual issue, statistical papers, series T, vol. 11, no. 9, United Nations, New York, 1960.

[c]*Direction of Trade*, 1963–67 annual issues, (supplement to the IFS), IMF/IBRD, Washington, D.C., 1969.

[d]*Direction of Trade*, 1968–72 annual issues, IMF/IBRD, Washington, D.C., 1973.

[e]*Direction of Trade Yearbook*, 1979, IMF/IBRD, Washington, D.C., 1980.

[f]*Direction of Trade Statistics* (monthly), May 1981, IMF/IBRD, Washington, D.C., 1981.

very structure of the United States-Iran trade relationship. Out of the projected total trade of $50 billion over the six-year period, $24 billion worth would have been set aside for oil and arms in almost equal amounts. In any event, the revolutionary events overtook the projected deal.

THE NUCLEAR ISSUE

Like almost every other issue, the nuclear issue in the United States-Iran relationship loomed large mainly after the explosion of oil prices in 1973. But as all other issues, it must be viewed in the perspective of the 25-year relationship of the Shah's regime with the United States, after the overthrow of the Musaddeq government. Unlike the other issues, the nuclear issue had no long history. The first agreement between the two countries for cooperation in civil uses of atomic energy was signed on March 5, 1957 for an initial period of five years.[9] Iran would gain reactor technology, and the United States would share it within the framework of its atoms-for-peace program. But the Shah used the agreement also because it was prestigious both at home and abroad. When other agreements were signed in the 1960s in order to continue to expand the nuclear relationship, the United States emphasized the Iranian responsibility to use any relevant material and equipment "solely for civil purposes." More specifically, the United States prohibited Iran from using any nuclear material for "atomic weapons, or for research on or development of atomic weapons, or for any other military purposes."[10]

The increased oil revenues, after the Arab-Israeli war of 1973, made it possible for the Shah to develop grandiose plans about nuclear energy as about everything else. But two other factors loomed large in the Shah's mind in the nuclear case. One was the nightmare of Iran's projected decline in oil production during the 1980s and the exhaustion of its oil reserves during the 1990s. Iran's reserves are significantly limited as contrasted, for example, with those of Saudi Arabia and Iraq. To the Shah, these dim energy prospects meant, among other things, an absolute need for utilization of nuclear and other sources of energy, such as solar, as substitutes for oil. But the prestige of nuclear power reactors always had a special fascination for the Shah as revealed, for example, by the personal pride he took in the announcement of the first United States-Iran nuclear agreement, mentioned above, at the opening ceremony of the U.S. atoms-for-peace exhibit at Tehran on March 6, 1957.

The other factor that spurred the Shah's grandiose plans for nuclear energy development was the surprise Indian nuclear explosion of May 18, 1974. Quite apart from its repeated written commitments to the United States to use nuclear material solely for civil uses, the Shah's regime had signed the Nonproliferation Treaty (NPT), and had called for a nuclear-free zone in the Middle East as early as 1969. It called for such a zone again on July 12, 1974 in the United Nations after the Indian nuclear explosion. The Indian feat was regarded as conclusive evidence of the close link between civilian and military uses of nuclear energy technology. The Israeli use of the plutonium produced in the Dimona reactor, Tel Aviv's refusal to sign the NPT, and the United States' offer of nuclear power reactors to Egypt and Israel were now seen in the light of the Indian experiment. Iranian leaders asked in private if their country, under the circumstances, should be denied the option of becoming a nuclear power. But publicly the Shah had made it clear on many occasions that it was, to borrow his words, "a cardinal point" of Iran's national policy not to produce nuclear weapons.

Regardless of the Shah's intentions, his nuclear energy plans were the wildest of all his ambitions. With respect to the peaceful uses of nuclear energy, his government argued that its plans were designed to help Iran meet its energy requirements for electricity, prolong the life of its oil reserves "from 25 to 250 years," and conserve oil for the development of the petrochemical industry. Secretary Henry Kissinger and Hushang Ansari, the Iranian minister of finance and economic affairs, on March 4, 1975 signed a protocol for general cooperation at the end of the second session of the United States-Iran Joint Committee in Tehran. It was announced, during the following day, that the Iranian Atomic Energy Organization was to place orders with the United States for the purchase of eight nuclear reactors with an aggregate of 8,000 megawatts to generate electricity and for water desalination.[11] Given Iran's agreements with France and West Germany for four additional reactors, Iran would have had a total of 32,400 megawatts by the year 1995. By then India would have had only 3,500 megawatts, and Pakistan 9,000 to 10,000 megawatts by the year 2000. The cost of the eight U.S. reactors would have been about $7 billion over a ten-year period. But according to a reputable Iranian source, the entire Iranian nuclear program of 20 reactors was likely to cost "much more than the $30 billion envisaged—possibly three times as much."[12]

Just as the Indian nuclear explosion provoked the Shah's interest in nuclear energy, it deepened U.S. concern about safeguards. The NPT safety standards did not seem adequate since the International Atomic Energy Agency (IAEA) lacked sufficient inspectors, and was incapable of seeking out clandestine plants. Extreme precautions were, indeed, called for. The Shah's regime was interested in having a nuclear fuel reprocessing plant built in Iran. Most countries that have had nuclear power generating plants do not have their own reprocessing facilities. The danger of producing nuclear explosives increases with the possession of such facilities, unless they are somehow controlled. Iranian officials argued that adequate safeguards existed without additional ones being required by the United States; Iran was a member of the IAEA and a signatory of the NPT. Washington, however, disagreed, demanding a more positive control mechanism of a multinational or at least binational nature, involving a Western industrial power such as France or West Germany.[13]

In spite of the fact that an agreement was finally initialed by the United States and Iran in August 1977, the U.S. Congress had the power to disapprove it. But as it turned out, the Iranian officials themselves began to have doubts about the wisdom of the Shah's grandiose nuclear plans. The doubts, however, were mainly due to mounting political unrest and economic dislocation facing the nation in 1978. The opponents of the Shah would have found nuclear plants highly visible targets for sabotage. They argued that Iran could build a power program around its vast natural gas reserves for about one-tenth of the cost.[14] According to a reliable international energy expert, Iran was one of the major gas exporters of the world in 1974, when its share of world exports was 8 percent (to the USSR); but more importantly, he believed, Iran possessed "nearly half of the Middle East's gas."[15] The Middle East possessed 24 percent of the world's total gas reserves.

ECONOMIC REFORMS

The previous discussions have in one way or another touched on the issue of economic reforms in the United States-Iran relationship. In effect, of all the issues this is the one with the longest historical tradition. Even before the establishment of United States-Iran diplomatic relations, it may be recalled, the early U.S. missionaries who arrived in Azerbaijan had a greater interest in establishing modern schools, hospitals, and the printing press. To be sure, they went to Iran to proselytize, but their failure to convert Iranian Muslims to Christianity did not stop them from other activities. The U.S. Christian missionaries in Iran did not become—as did those from Britain, Holland, and France who went to other Muslim lands—the fore-. runners of colonial and imperial European rule.[16] On the contrary, they were the predecessors of the more secular-minded U.S. reformists, such as Morgan Shuster, Arthur Millspaugh, and many others, who were invited by the Iranians to come to their help. As seen, this national pattern of involving U.S. citizens in Iran was increased by the young Shah in every field of activity long before the covert U.S. intervention in Iran. When the Shah first envisaged an economic development plan for Iran after World War II, it may be recalled, he invited U.S. companies for advice.

The 1953 intervention raised the U.S. stakes in the Shah. But no commitment to reforms was sought by the United States or given by the Shah, as we have seen. Strategic considerations that led to his restoration to the throne dominated U.S. policy toward the Shah throughout the Eisenhower Administration. Against this background, the Kennedy Administration's determined pressure for reforms was clearly unprecedented. Long before the Iranian Revolution, this U.S. pressure in combination with such other factors as Soviet-Iranian relations, the Iraqi Revolution, and domestic economic and political pressures, contributed to the Shah's decision to launch his reform programs. Two points need mentioning in the interest of better understanding these reforms.

First, the partially United States-induced reforms of the Shah's regime should not be allowed to obscure their real meaning in the perspective of Iranian history. The goal of social and economic reforms emerged in the context of a fundamental interaction between the Iranian society and the West, but the Iranian Constitutional Revolution legitimized the goal, along with such other basic aspirations as independence and national integration.[17] The constitutionalists themselves hired Morgan Shuster to help their goal of financial and economic reforms. But this fundamental goal was overshadowed throughout the decades by the primacy accorded to the goal of Iran's independence from foreign control. In spite of all his reforms, Reza Shah accorded Iran's independence the highest priority. His reforms hardly touched the basic structural problems of Iranian society. Nor did his son address these problems in spite of his repeated expressions of interest in land reform before the 1960s. Even Musaddeq made it absolutely clear that his highest priority was Iran's emancipation from British domination, not land reform. The Shah's land reform program, as the first principle of his social and economic reforms, was, therefore, unprecedented in Iran's modern history.

But was it any good? A satisfactory answer cannot be offered by delving solely into the Shah's motivation. One distinguished observer, for example, says: "Land reform in 1962 was not really intended to improve agricultural production. It was a political manoeuvre designed to bring the rural masses into the political spectrum and to curb the influence of the large landlords."[18] This may well have been one of the Shah's motivations, but there were also other political motives. He also wanted to undermine the secular political opposition (mainly the National Front and the Tudeh Party), and, as importantly, to curb the unprecedented onslaught of the Soviet propaganda agitation against his regime.

The answer must be twofold in terms of its actual effects. As most land reforms in history, it failed to improve agricultural production. The Iranian failure, however, went far beyond the adverse effects of the fragmentation of land holdings on agricultural production. It stemmed from the persistent failure of the regime, before and after the launching of the land reform program, to accord agricultural production a high priority in its planning of economic development until it was too late to do any good. It also stemmed from such grotesque creations as farm corporations, presumably designed to remedy the adverse effects of fragmented small holdings, but actually threatening to destroy individual initiative and freedom of action of the peasants. As early as 1947, when the Shah wanted to launch Iran's first development plan, the seven-year development plan, the obsession of the elite with industrial over agricultural development and social services was at least noted perceptively by Max Thornburg, as seen in Chapter 1. Hence, the primacy of politics in Iran's economic development was nothing new in the 1960s. Nor was it novel in 1947; it had always been true since the beginnings of modernization in the nineteenth century.

Yet even politically motivated change can be somewhat beneficial. In spite of all its motivational, economic, marketing, and many other drawbacks, the Shah's land distribution was the first major social reform attempted in Iran's modern history. The rationale for that act was freedom for the peasants. After visiting numerous villages in the

1960s, I was "told repeatedly by farmers of widely scattered villages of their great sense of 'freedom' [*hess-e azadi*], although complaining about the weight of their new responsibilities, paucity of government credits and their chronic indebtedness."[19] The threat to that freedom mounted in the 1970s, but the cardinal fact remains that the United States-induced land reform of the Shah destroyed the millennial serfdom of the peasantry (*zarain*) in Iran. As the Iranian saying goes, "God willing, even the enemy can be the source of good" (*'adou shavad sabab-e khair aggar khoda khahad*). Even the Shah's politically motivated land reform did some good!

The second point to be made in the interest of a more balanced perspective is about the overall performance of the Iranian economy before and after the fourfold increase in oil prices in 1973. The worst effect of the Iranian Revolution on scholarship has been the tendency of some observers to pontificate on the basis of hindsight. By any fair standards of measurement, the Iranian economy performed reasonably well, in spite of many problems, during the Third (1962–67) and Fourth (1968–73) National Development Plans. These plans, according to a distinguished and objective U.S. economist, "channelled a huge amount of public development funds—204.6 billion rials [$2.73 billion] and 506.8 billion [$6.75 billion] respectively—into the various sectors of the economy. In addition private enterprise, actively encouraged by the government, invested some two-thirds to three-quarters as much as the public sector during the two plans. The result was a real rate of growth in the period 1960–72 of over 9 percent per annum, a figure matched by a bare handful of countries."[20] As seen, it was in the light of such a performance that the Johnson Administration terminated the U.S. aid program to Iran, and the *New York Times* thought Iran had reached the "take-off" point.

ECONOMIC DEVELOPMENT

The explosion of oil prices in 1973 transformed the Iranian "black gold" (*talay-e siyah*) into a "black blight" (*balay-e siyah*). The contribution of oil income to the Iranian economy had been insubstantial in the 1960s despite its overall importance.[21] But its contribution to total Iranian revenues in the 1970s reached an extraordinary level; it was 87 percent in the 1974–75 Iranian calendar year, according to Prime Minister Hoveyda. Moreover, the flood of oil revenues magnified every weakness in the Iranian social and economic system ranging, for example, from an inordinate emphasis on economic growth to the pace of growth, and the magnitude of corruption within and outside the royal family and the government. In my last interview with Prime Minister Hoveyda, in the presence of his minister of science and higher education, in 1975 in Tehran, I was astounded by the obsession of both with the rate of GNP. This was at a time when Iranian food production, for example, was rising by only 7 percent a year, while consumption was increasing by 22 percent, costing the country about $500 million a year for food imports. U.S. frankfurters were pouring into the Iranian supermarkets when the traditional Iranian mutton was becoming a scarce commodity. This was at a time when about 300 private U.S. firms, including 40 U.S. arms contractors, and many thousands of U.S. citizens and scores of U.S. universities were becoming involved in the social and economic fabric of the Iranian society with all the social and cultural problems attending the large and ubiquitous U.S. military and economic presence in Iran. Yet the technocrats were bragging about Iran's real GNP at 34 percent in 1973–74 and 42 percent in 1974–75, discounting the rate of inflation.

In a flush of overconfidence because of increased oil revenues, the Shah's government amended its budget for the 1974–75 Iranian year and revised its fifth national development plan (1973–78). Prime Minister Hoveyda told the Iranian Parliament on December 1, 1974 that his amended bill was three times the budget originally envisaged for that year, represented "the impressive achievements" that had already been made, and showed "the rapid pace of our economic and social progress." With respect to the revised development plan, he said, "the need for the revision was felt when Iran's oil revenues increased on an unprecedented scale, and when Iran made outstanding gains with regard to international cooperation."[22] In reacting to these changes, to the extremely ambitious scope and fast pace of economic development, and to the growing gap between the rich and the poor, U.S. observers, at the International Conference held at Persepolis in 1975, warned the Iranian technocrats not to overheat their economy.

The Iranian planners, however, argued endlessly that: (1) the overheating problem was not as great as it would seem, considering the sudden rise of income from $5 to $20 billion; (2) the determination of "absorptive capacity" of the economy was a difficult "empirical problem"; and (3) Iran had been "bold," but not necessarily "adventurous" in plotting its economic development. Regarding the maldistribution of wealth, they argued, inter alia, that they were aware of the problem, were working toward solving it by a variety of means, including the allowance of workers' purchasing of shares in factories up to 49 percent, and there was real difficulty in avoiding imbalances of this kind in the current stage of Iran's economic development.[23]

All these arguments, however, became academic. The bubble of oil affluence burst. Oil revenues fell because of lower demand and hence production. By June 1975 the handwriting was on the wall. By August Iranians were looking for international lenders. It was also rumored that about $400 million credits had been extended to Iran by U.S. banks. In February 1976 the Iranian minister of state for planning and budget, Dr. Abdol Majid Majidi, said that Iran should henceforth look for a "modest rate" of growth. Between the spring of 1975 and 1976 the GNP dropped 60 percent. The government was now forced to scale down its ambitious projects because of an anticipated deficit of $2.4 billion in the following year's budget, which was the largest deficit in Iran's history. The government was also forced to cut back its $69.6 billion fifth national development plan (1973–78) in order to belatedly cool off the economy and fight inflation, which was running at more than 20 percent at the time. The watchword of the days of illusory affluence, "growth," was now accompanied by "bottlenecks," indicating, most of all, the shortage of manpower, electric power, and infrastructural installations such as ports, roads, and railroad networks. A group of businessmen told Ambassador William H. Sullivan in May 1977, "The greatest service you could perform is to really speak frankly to the Shah, but you can't. You'd be declared persona non grata at once."[24]

The Shah himself seemed to get caught up in the rhetoric of the day. He hated "bottlenecks," talked about lower growth rates, retreated from his mass subsidization of social idleness in the name of social welfare, and called for hard work and increased productivity. But he never admitted that most root causes of the economic and social problems facing the nation were the result of his misguided policies. In his inauguration address to the twenty-fourth session of the Majlis and the seventh session of the Senate on October 6, 1976, his first and last candid statement before the Parliament, he said, "Because of these same incredible improvements we are now facing a number of problems, including a shortage of capacity of ports, a deficiency in road capacity, and an almost runaway increase in wages and salaries in the private sector in all occupations."[25]

The Shah's new prime minister was appointed on August 7, 1977. Jamshid Amuzegar tried to sharply curtail the massive program of industrial development. He coined a new slogan, "leave the people's work to the people." In introducing his first and last budget for the year beginning March 21, 1978 to the Majlis, he called for a "rational and balanced economic and social growth," for elimination of waste, imbalances, and bottlenecks, and for strengthening the economic infrastructure. These and similar ideas were presumably based on the recognition of the nation's inability to absorb the annual 20 percent growth rate of the previous years. Shifting away from a nationalized industry to the encouragement of private industry, however, was a dubious proposition. There were serious doubts about the ability of the Iranian private business community to undertake such a task in heavy industry. The prime minister's emphasis on increasing agricultural productivity was also 30 years too late, if dated from Iran's first development plan launched in 1947. The means to cope with this formidable problem were not at hand.

ECONOMIC BALANCE SHEET

The United States-Iran influence balance sheet in the economic area is integrally intertwined with the balance sheets pertaining to oil and arms examined in the two previous chapters and to politics to be discussed in the following chapter.

To consider the United States first, Washington's economic relations with the Shah's regime over a quarter century redounded to its benefit in acquiring a new and expanding market for U.S. nonmilitary exports. The United States consistently enjoyed a favorable balance of trade with Iran in the nonoil sector. Besides many U.S. arms contractors, hundreds of private companies did lucrative business with Iran. U.S. private investment ranked first among all other foreign powers. Furthermore, as the job market in the United States deteriorated, many thousands of U.S. citizens found work opportunities in Iran, and scores of U.S. universities and colleges sought financial solvency with Iranian aid.

The U.S. influence on Iran's economic reforms was limited. The only major instance in which U.S. aid was used effectively as a leverage to induce reforms in Iran was during the brief Kennedy

Administration. The U.S. influence was either not exercised to induce major socioeconomic reforms, or when used failed to produce the desired results. Especially after the explosion of oil prices, the Shah's regime was resistant to U.S. pressures. In fact, the Shah resented advice from any quarters when he needed it most. He overheated the economy until it was too late to prevent its adverse social, economic, cultural, political, and psychological consequences. The belated cutbacks of expenditures were mainly the result of Iran's own initiative. The United States remained skeptical about the efficacy of even Amuzegar's stringent efforts. The Shah's belated goal of self-sufficiency was preposterous. After 30 years of neglect of agriculture, he claimed to want to remedy it only when economic and social disaster had struck.

On balance, however, the United States was reluctant to press the Shah's regime too hard for basic reforms or a more balanced and rational approach to economic development. For more than a quarter century, strategic and selfish economic considerations prevailed over the U.S. concern for basic social and economic reforms in Iran; all cannot be blamed on the Shah alone. Iran was regarded as a "strategic prize." As such, its perceived "stability" was not to be jeopardized, which really meant that the status quo must be preserved. Relations between Washington and Tehran were amicable most of the time. Except for private and independent observers on both sides, basic social and economic change was more a matter of rhetoric than actual consistent policy.

Economic relations with the United States were viewed by the Shah primarily in terms of their political and military dividends. Between the mid-1950s and mid-1960s, the Shah's regime benefitted enormously from U.S. economic assistance, which helped the nation's economy and the Shah's hold on power. But the Shah's strategic leverage never got him the amount of economic assistance he desired. The termination of the U.S. aid program in 1967 meant little loss to the Shah's regime. Oil revenues were increasing and the Iranian economy was relatively robust at the time. The Shah's regime benefitted also from U.S. technical and managerial training. The massive infusion of capital into the economy, however, spun it out of control; the shortage of skilled manpower, like all other shortages and bottlenecks, was grossly magnified. Money was not a panacea after all.

Iran's nonoil trade with the United States was always at a disadvantage. But the traditional imbalance seemed glaring in the 1970s as

Iran's ambitious industrialization projects, its preference for U.S. commodities and services, its decreasing agricultural productivity, and its rising real income increased the imports of machinery, capital goods, food, and consumer goods. In spite of attempts at diversification of trade, the United States attained the rank of a major trade partner, generally after West Germany and Japan, and retained it until the fall of the Shah's regime.

All told, the United States-Iran economic relationship had a bias against genuine and fundamental change. Each side will blame it on the other for many years to come, but objectively, both sides must share the blame. This kind of concept of "special relationship" is a ready-made recipe for destructive revolutionary change. It is basically a bankrupt concept because it fails to allow for a sustained and coherent strategy of socioeconomic change that would benefit a Third World society.

NOTES

1. See the voluminous report of the International Operations Subcommittee of the Committee on Government Operations of the House of Representatives, in U.S., Congress, House, Subcommittee of the Committee on Government Operations, *Hearings*, 84th Cong., 2d sess., 1956.

2. *New York Times*, July 26, 1962.

3. U.S., Department of State, *Bulletin* 57 (December 18, 1976): 825-27.

4. U.S., Department of State, *Bulletin* 57 (December 18, 1976): 825-27.

5. For the Iranian foreign trade situation during the rule of Reza Shah, see Rouhollah K. Ramazani, *The Foreign Policy of Iran, 1500-1941: A Developing Nation in World Affairs* (Charlottesville: University Press of Virginia, 1966), especially pp. 171-241.

6. For details see my *Iran's Foreign Policy, 1941-1973*, pp. 86-90.

7. For the text of this treaty see U.S., Department of State, *Treaties and Other International Agreements* 8, TIAS no. 3853 (1955): 899-932.

8. For the text of his speech see FBIS, Daily Report, *Middle East & Africa* 5 (October 24, 1975).

9. For the text of the agreement see U.N., Secretariat, *Treaty Series* 342, no. 4898 (1959): 29-41.

10. This quotation is taken from the March 18, 1969 agreement the text of which is in U.S., Department of State, *United States Treaties and Other International Agreements* 20, pt. 2, TIAS no. 6726 (March 18, 1969): 4841-44.

11. See FBIS, Daily Report, *Middle East & Africa* 5 (March 6, 1975).

12. *New York Times*, May 30, 1979.

13. Ibid., May 17, 1976.

14. Ibid., October 23, 1978.

15. The expert in question is Melvin A. Conant; see U.S., Congress, Senate, *Geopolitics of Energy*, Committee on Interior and Insular Affairs, 95th Cong., 1st sess. (Washington, D.C.: U.S. Government Printing Office, 1977), p. 70.

16. For an account of such missionaries, see G. H. Jansen, *Militant Islam* (New York: Harper & Row, 1979), pp. 49-86.

17. See Rouhollah K. Ramazani, "Iran's 'White Revolution': A Study in Political Development," *International Journal of Middle East Studies* 5 (1974): 124-39.

18. See Robert Graham, *Iran: The Illusion of Power* (London: Groom Helm, 1978), pp. 208-09.

19. See Rouhollah K. Ramazani, "Iran's Changing Foreign Policy: A Preliminary Discussion," *The Middle East Journal* 24, no. 4 (Autumn 1970): 421-37.

20. See Charles Issawi, "The Iranian Economy 1925-1975: Fifty Years of Economic Development," in George Lenczowski, ed., *Iran under the Pahlavis* (Stanford: Hoover Institution Press, 1978), pp. 129-66.

21. Charles Issawi says that "the direct contribution of oil was not very great: its share in gross domestic product (GDP) was only one-tenth in 1960 and still below one-fifth in 1972; and its contribution to growth of GDP was under one-quarter; and its foreign exchange contribution was not very large when measured against GNP or population." See ibid., p. 163.

22. See FBIS, Daily Report, *Middle East & Africa* 5 (December 4, 1974).

23. See Rouhollah K. Ramazani, "Iran and the United States: An Experiment in Enduring Friendship," *The Middle East Journal* 30, no. 3 (Summer 1976): 322-34.

24. *New York Times*, May 30, 1977.

25. FBIS, Daily Report, *Middle East & Africa* 5 (October 7, 1976).

5

THE U.S. CLOSE IDENTIFICATION WITH THE SHAH, AND THE CHALLENGE OF THE FORCES OF OPPOSITION

The political issue area in the United States-Iran relationship before the Iranian Revolution was the most crucial of all areas so far examined. In reality and in perception, the development of the relationship between the Shah and the United States over the decades was inseparable from Iranian domestic politics. As seen, the Shah courted increasing U.S. involvement in Iran for nearly a decade after his accession to the throne in 1941 partially to bolster his nascent regime against the challenge of domestic political opposition, including the nationalists, the communists, and the Muslim fundamentalists. As also seen, the covert U.S. intervention in 1953 resulted in the Shah's return to power, and the beginning of the process of consolidation of royal power.

We shall see in this chapter how that process continued throughout the period between 1954 and the start of the Iranian Revolution, and how it was challenged by the forces of opposition either openly or underground. Furthermore, during this period, just as before, the development of the United States-Iran relationship was intertwined with Iran's domestic politics. In fact, as that relationship became increasingly close, the U.S. involvement in Iran grew in reality and in perception. For example, U.S. aid to the creation of the Iranian SAVAK, U.S. pressure for social and economic reforms during the Kennedy Administration, and finally, the Carter Administration's campaign for "political liberalization" increasingly intermeshed Iranian sociopolitical developments with the Tehran-Washington relationship. This growing identification of the interests of the Shah's regime with those of the United States made the challenge of the opposition to the regime also a challenge to the U.S. influence in Iran.

THE SHAH'S SUPPRESSION OF THE OPPOSITION: THE FIRST TWO DECADES

Restored to the throne, the Shah sought to consolidate power by crushing the forces of opposition during the entire Eisenhower Administration without any serious concern with Washington's reaction. Dr. Musaddeq was put on trial for treason and sentenced to death. His life was spared but he was confined to his home for the rest of his life. His foreign minister, Hussein Fatemi, was executed, and other leading National Frontists were hunted, harassed, arrested, and jailed. Several other Cabinet ministers, such as the internationally renowned jurist Dr. Ali Shaygan, were put in jail.

The repression of the Tudeh Party members exceeded that of all other opposition groups. The party's network in the army was smashed in 1954. Of the captured officers, 27 were executed, 134 were imprisoned for life, 119 were sentenced to 15 years' imprisonment with hard labor, and 115 were placed in solitary confinement. The overwhelming number of the captives were young men. None ranked higher than colonel and the largest single group included first lieutenants.[1] Three years later, Khosrow Ruzbeh (the "Lenin" of Iran) was finally captured and executed.

The main instrument of the Shah's political repression was the *Sazeman-e Ettela'at va Amniyat-e Keshvar*, or SAVAK. Years later, William Colby, former director of the CIA, reportedly said that "the CIA created SAVAK . . . and taught it proper methods of intelligence."[2] Kermit Roosevelt added that "certain Israeli friends discreetly joined the CIA in helping to organize and give guidance to a new Iranian security service."[3] Israeli intelligence, Mossad, and the CIA most probably did teach the Iranian service the "proper methods," but in an overwhelmingly illiterate society with a long tradition of authoritarian government, such methods were bound to be abused, as they actually were, in brutal ways. The Shah's regime did not gouge out thousands of eyes and erect a pyramid of skulls, as did Agha Muhammad Shah of the Qajar dynasty, but it used modern methods to mete out such gruesome punishment as electric shock, tearing out fingernails and toenails, rape, and genital torture. SAVAK did not confine itself to meting out cruel physical punishment. It also engaged in censorship, shadowing, harassment, and other activities, especially against intellectual dissidents.

Although SAVAK's surveillance of potential sources of dissidence included the Shi'i clergy, during the 1950s the relationship of the regime with leading clerics was, on the whole, more accommodative than conflictual. Ayatollah Sayyed Abol-Qasim Kashani, the activist Muslim leader of the Musaddeq era who was suspected of close ties with the terrorist *Fada'eyan-e Islam* group, was shunned and sank quickly into oblivion. The religious leader Ayatollah Burujerdi "maintained contacts with high government officials"[4] until the late 1950s. He and Ayatollah Behbehani of Tehran supported the Shah's regime on some issues but opposed him on others. They shared the Shah's concern with the Tudeh Party, with the perceived communist orientation of the Iraqi revolutionary regime, and with the Soviet Union. For example, in the wake of the breakdown of Soviet-Iranian negotiations for a long-term nonaggression pact in 1959, mentioned before, Premier Nikita Khrushchev attacked the Shah personally and unleashed an unprecedentedly violent Soviet propaganda campaign against Iran. He charged that the Shah was transforming Iran into "an American military base" by signing the 1959 agreement with the United States, and asked rhetorically: "Whom then, in actual fact, does the Shah of Iran fear? He does not fear us, but fears his own people...."[5] When Khrushchev repeated his verbal attack on the Shah, the regime spread the rumor that the Shah was leaving the country, and the crowds pleaded with Ayatollah Behbehani to accompany them to the palace to ask the Shah to remain.[6] The "tactical alliance" between the Shah and the religious leaders, however, broke down quickly over other issues, as we shall see below.

Tensions between Washington and Tehran surfaced for the first time during the Kennedy Administration over the issue of U.S. arms and economic and social reforms. The pervasive corruption, economic waste, and other factors had worried Washington before the Kennedy Administration took office. It was reported in the *Christian Science Monitor* in January 1960 that the U.S. government had made a crucial decision to contact the National Frontists as an alternative to the Shah's government just in case it was overthrown. The State Department denied the report categorically. Late during the Eisenhower, and certainly during the Kennedy Administration, there was a surge of U.S. concern with social and economic reforms in developing countries. Political liberalization was of a lesser concern. As is well known, President Kennedy's "alliance for progress" in Latin America emphasized social and economic change. Certainly in U.S. policy toward Iran, Washington's stress was on social and economic modernization.

Kennedy favored Dr. Ali Amini for the post of prime minister. Amini was regarded with favor in Washington in the hope that, as a reputedly competent economist, he would be able to improve Iran's social and economic conditions. Many years later, Armin Meyer, a former U.S. ambassador to Iran, denied that he had said to an audience in Washington that the United States had "imposed" a prime minister in Iran, but he did acknowledge that "there was a linkage between our extension of assistance and what we hoped to see done in Iran."[7] Although he was saying this in criticism of U.S. policy, the Shah's government used this statement to vent its unhappiness with the Carter Administration's human rights policy, as we shall see. Regardless of whether or not Amini was imposed on the Shah's regime, one thing seems clear: Amini's Qajar background, reformist ideas, family ties with Dr. Musaddeq, appeal to the National Front, and other factors did not endear him to the Shah. The king hated him.

Moscow also despised Amini. The Soviets went out of their way to denounce the prime minister's land reform policy. But that policy was attacked not only by the pro-Soviet Tudeh Party but also by such disaffected clerics as Ayatollah Mahmoud Taleqani and Ayatollah Ruhollah Khomeini. It was attacked even by Ayatollah Burujerdi who had had good relations with the Shah's government earlier. The land reform was opposed by the *ulama*, religious leaders, partly because it threatened their vested interests. But it was opposed by most of them for two other reasons as well: it would cut the revenues of the lands held by the clergy and used for religious educational purposes. It would also contradict their belief in the sanctity of private property under Islamic Law.[8] The clergy also resented the Shah's attempt to cast his land reform program in Islamic terms. In a major speech in the holy city of Qom the Shah said:

> If the Muslim community adapts itself to the requirements of modern times in the glorious spirit of Islam, it will find new power and victory. Our society continues to be in need of religious and moral principles, and those *ulama* who have either cooperated with, or have remained unopposed to, the land reform program are indubitably our religious

leaders. But those others who have expressed opposition to it would seem to be preoccupied with the appearance rather than the substance of the religion. We trust that Allah will guide those in positions of leadership to the Right Path, and that by the blessings of this sacred shrine they will serve Islam, the Shah and their country.[9]

The land reform issue was the catalyst that brought into the open clerical opposition to the Shah's overall repressive policies and the perceived U.S. dominance of Iran through its alliance with the Shah. In addition to the clerics, the National Frontists opposed those policies. They supported a major teachers' strike in May 1961 when Abdol Hussain Khan'ali, a leader of the striking teachers, was killed. Such Nationalist Front leaders as Baqer Kazemi, Allahyar Saleh, and Karim Sanjabi demanded "liberty and democracy" and "an independent national" foreign policy. These demands finally led to mass demonstrations in Tehran University in January 1962, which were brutally crushed. The Shah had already dissolved the Majlis without indicating a date for new elections, contrary to the constitution. He then ordered the Amini government in November 1961 to implement a May 1960 land law, and after the fall of the Amini government in July 1962 he sought to legitimize his decreed six-point reform program (the "White Revolution") by a referendum in January 1963 in the absence of the Parliament.

The opposition was led by several eminent religious leaders. Riots broke out in several cities in June 1963. The regime charged that they were instigated by "the elements of Black Reaction." They were put down ruthlessly by the Shah's armed forces, resulting in at least 1,000 dead in Tehran alone. Ayatollah Ruhollah Khomeini of Qom, Ayatollah Qomi of Mashad, and Ayatollah Mahallati of Shiraz were arrested. Despite its many shortcomings, land reform did destroy the ancient serfdom of Iran. But quite apart from its economic, technical, and other drawbacks, it was marred from its inception by the political circumstances under which it was undertaken. It simply lacked political legitimacy; it was decreed from above, and it was perceived to be the product of U.S. dictation. Just as the 1953 overthrow of Musaddeq was perceived as the "American coup," this was seen as the "American revolution." President Kennedy's enthusiastic endorsement of the results of the January 1963 referendum conducted by the Shah's regime was premature. The referendum was not considered truly free, as the Shah promised no political liberalization to accompany or succeed his social and economic reform plans. Once again, the United States failed to pressure the Shah to undertake political reforms when it had the opportunity to do so. In August 1953, as seen, the Shah had been assured that he had "no obligation" toward the United States. And now, a decade later, the Shah's repressive regime was hailed for its planned economic reforms. In both instances the United States had the power to press for political reforms, but it failed to do so because it accorded the highest priority to short-term strategic considerations. The immediate result of this second failure was the Shah's brutal and bloody suppression of the June 1963 uprising. The price of both failures was high. Whatever misguided policies the Shah pursued subsequently, including even greater repression than in the 1950s, were bound to be perceived to have U.S. support. As if Kennedy's premature endorsement of the Shah's "White Revolution" had not been enough for further Iranian alienation from the United States, another unfortunate move—this time by the Johnson Administration—capped the whole process of misappraisal of the Iranian situation.

The Pentagon's pressure for diplomatic immunities for U.S. military personnel in Iran was the new instance of U.S. misappraisal of the Iranian situation. President Johnson reversed Kennedy's decision to press for social and economic reforms by withholding U.S. arms. In 1964 Washington extended a $200 million credit for the purchase of U.S. military equipment. This had to be approved by the Iranian Parliament. In the meantime, Iran and the United States were discussing the Pentagon's demand for a "status of forces agreement" with Iran. The Shah's favorable decision on this agreement happened to come up for parliamentary approval at the same time that the bill for accepting the U.S. aid for military purchases was being considered. In the eyes of the public, the two issues became linked. Coming in the wake of the United States-supported "White Revolution" and the June 1963 disaster, this seemed to be another U.S. plot. More important, against the background of Iran's bitter historical memory of immunities enjoyed by foreign nationals on its soil, the U.S. demand seemed to smack of the imposition of U.S. extraterritorial rights on the country. The Russians had extracted such privileges from Iran at the end of a war in 1826-28. Other foreign powers had used the Russian model subsequently. The "capitulatory system," as it was called, was finally abolished in 1928.

The perceived U.S. challenge to Iranian independence was taken up by Ayatollah Khomeini. He used it to roundly condemn the Shah's regime and the United States. The unfortunate timing of the U.S. demand, and the Shah's compliance with it, played squarely into the Ayatollah's hands. In a stinging declaration, he characterized the relevant bill passed by the Parliament as "the document of the enslavement of the Iranian nation" since, he charged, it placed the "Iranian nation under American bondage." He then warned:

> I declare that this shameful vote of the Houses of the Parliament is contrary to Islam and the Koran and hence illegal; it is contrary to the will of the Islamic nation; the Majlis deputies are not representatives of the nation, they reflect the power of the bayonet. . . . The world must realize that all the difficulties faced by the Iranian nation and the Muslim peoples are because of aliens, because of America. The Muslim nations hate aliens in general and Americans in particular. The misfortunes of the Islamic governments stem from foreign interference in their destiny. It is America that supports Israel and its friends; it is America that gives Israel power to displace the Muslim Arabs; it is America that imposes the parliamentary deputies on the Iranian nation; it is America that considers Islam and the Holy Koran detrimental to its interest and is determined to remove them; it is America that considers the Islamic clergy as the obstacle to its exploitation [of Iran and other Muslim countries], and feels it must cause them pain, imprisonment and insult; it is America that pressures the Majlis and the Iranian government to approve and implement such a bill; it is America that treats the Islamic nation barbarously. It is incumbent on the Iranian nation to tear up these chains. . . . [10]

The Shah's regime exiled the Ayatollah, who first resided in Turkey briefly and then in Iraq for almost 15 years before returning to Iran. His exile marked the end of the 1960–64 crises. Had he not been forced to leave the country he would have continued to oppose the regime's policies openly. Contrary to the claim of the Shah's regime, he never promised to keep quiet about political events in Iran after he was released in 1963. He told his students in Najaf years later that the regime had lied about his pledge.

Khomeini's exile also marked the beginning of the Shah's road to absolute power. The Parliament, which had been dissolved on May 9, 1961, was finally reopened on October 6, 1964. The Milyyun-Mardom party—a facade of a two-party system that had been established in 1957—was now replaced by a new two-party system, which was actually dominated by the Iran Novin Party, the heir to Premier Ali Mansur's "Progressive Center." The composition of the new Parliament was quite different. The traditional forces, such as the landed aristocracy, the tribal nobility, the army, and the royal family, which had dominated governmental structures in the past, seemed to be less in evidence in the new Majlis. But the Parliament, as the new party system, was completely subservient to the throne.

The number of alienated social forces had increased by the mid-1960s as contrasted with the mid-1950s. The support of the landed aristocracy had been undermined. The tactical alliance of the clergy with the royal court had been broken, even before the death of Ayatollah Burujerdi in 1961. He had opposed the Shah's plan for land reform as early as 1959, and the subsequent events in 1960–64 gave rise to an unprecedented clerical defiance of the Shah's regime and the United States. Never before had the clergy been so united in its opposition to the monarchy. Nor had the regime ever had such a mortal enemy as it did in Khomeini. His exile did not settle the deeper historical, ideological, cultural, social, psychological, and intellectual conflicts underlying the Shah's relations with the Shi'i clergy. Only six months after the June 1963 uprising, I wrote the following statement, which seems particularly aporopriate in the light of the Iranian Revolution about 15 years later:

> An apparent lull returned to the Iranian political scene after much bloodshed and destruction of millions of dollars worth of public and private property. But the fundamental problem that lay at the heart of the riots continues to haunt the Iranian society and politics. . . . It seldom seems realized in Iran that the persisting traditional attitude toward the relations of religion to the state can not be decreed out of existence. The change in these spheres will require of the Iranian people a rethinking of the whole structure of their life and culture, and the rebuilding of their universe and their identity in it. This is the most difficult task confronting all modernizing societies, Islamic or otherwise. It is the most difficult task because it does not lend itself to solutions decreed from above.[11]

I was equally skeptical about the continued support of the army and the peasantry for the Shah's regime. The Shah "believes that he can stay in power," I wrote in 1966, "with the support of two other segments of society. One is the army, a traditional source of monarchical support, recently armed with American equipment and reinforced by the hated security police [SAVAK]. The other is the peasantry, which is being wooed through the distribution of land. Both these groups are of doubtful reliability. The Shah believes that the army is loyal to him, but there have been serious indications to the contrary. The reliability of the peasantry's support is equally doubtful. It is by no means certain that this traditionally ignorant and isolated class will soon become politically aware and articulate citizenry, participating in politics. If they do, the Shah has no guarantee of their support."[12]

RADICALIZATION OF THE OPPOSITION

The effects of the Shah's suppression of domestic opposition interplayed with dynamic developments in the Iranian external environment. The result, in retrospect, was that various elements of the opposition became even more radicalized in their ideologies and methods of combatting the Shah's regime. This is no place to delve into all the relevant effects of the changing external environment on ideological and tactical radicalization of the opposition. The Cuban revolution, the Algerian revolution, the student radical movements in Europe and the United States, the war in Vietnam, and other factors were probably influential, but three regional developments in particular stand out.

First, the Palestinian revolution had a considerable effect. It inspired the confidence of disaffected groups throughout the Middle East. They, too, could rise up against their perceived enemies. The June war of 1967 damaged President Nasser's image, but the Palestinians appeared to pick up the challenge posed by Israel. The perceived transformation of the Palestinian nationalist movement into a revolutionary armed struggle after the June war seemed to provide both a model and a source of logistical and material support. In the wake of the war, few scholars paid attention to the potential impact of this model on the entire region. We have no direct evidence of the impact of the Palestinian movement on Ayatollah Khomeini's ideas and activities. But one can infer from statements by the Lebanese Shi'i leader, Imam Musa Sadr, who was close to the Ayatollah, that Khomeini must have considered the Palestinian upsurge a development favorable to his struggle against the Shah.[13] Among other things, Imam Musa Sadr believed that the rising star of the Palestinians was a good omen for the Muslim world, for Iran, and for the destitute Shi'i Muslim population of Lebanon, which was of great concern to him. In retrospect, it seems clear that he had in mind the possibility of collaboration between the anti-Shah dissidents of Iran and the Palestinians.

Second, the British withdrawal from Aden in 1967 and the Persian Gulf in 1971 facilitated the earliest contacts between the Iranian underground opposition and the Palestinians. The *Sazeman-e Mujaheddin-e Khalq-e Iran* (Organization of Freedom Fighters of the Iranian People) has revealed that the *Mujaheddin* failed to establish contacts with the Palestinians through the office of the Palestine Liberation Organization (PLO) in France. But they succeeded subsequently through the Palestinian elements scattered around the Persian Gulf region. The *Mujaheddin* conducted frequent clandestine visits to Qatar and Abu Dhabi where they made initial contact with the Palestinians, despite tight security precautions taken by the emirates. Subsequently, the *Mujaheddin* received training not only in Palestinian camps in Lebanon and Syria, but some members of the group, such as Reza Reza'i, a Central Committee member, and Mas'ud Rajavi, a founder of the organization, reputedly fought against King Hussein's forces and in support of the Palestinians in September 1970. The *Mujaheddin* also established ties of "solidarity" with the Popular Front for the Liberation of Oman.[14]

A third major development that intensified cooperation between the Iranian underground dissidents and the Palestinians was the Arab-Israeli war of October 1973 and its aftermath. After the war the Shah's regime clearly increased its tactical support for the Palestinians as well as the moderate Arab states, especially Egypt, but not excluding even Syria.[15] After the Rabat conference, which designated the PLO as "the sole and legitimate" representative of the Palestinian people, the Shah's regime accepted the notion that the PLO's participation in the peacemaking process was essential to the success of the negotiations.

The Shah's ambivalent courtship of the Palestinians had no major effect on the existing alliance between the dissident Iranian groups and the Palestinians. Both sides knew that the Shah's attitude toward the Palestinian demand for "self-determination" corresponded at best with that of President Sadat, but in effect had greater affinity with the U.S. policy. The intensified cooperation between the Iranian dissidents and the Palestinians impelled the Shah finally to make public his dissatisfaction with some Palestinian factions. In an interview with the correspondent of the Beirut weekly *al-Hawadis* on December 13, 1974, he said: "We have stood and we still stand at the side of the Palestinians, despite the fact that some groups of the resistance trained Iranian saboteurs to infiltrate our territory, kill people, and blow up various installations. We know how to discriminate between the justness of the Palestine question and the wrongdoing directed against us by some Palestinians."[16]

THE FORCES OF OPPOSITION
AND THE UNITED STATES

Of the two major secular groups that were suppressed, the National Front and the Tudeh Party, the latter had suffered more repression in the 1950s. It suffered even more in the 1960s. At this time, however, the Tudeh experienced a major setback because of the opportunistic attitude of the Soviet Union toward the Shah. The improved relations between Moscow and Tehran, after the Shah made a pledge to Moscow in 1962 that Iran would not allow the establishment of foreign bases on its soil, dealt a heavy blow to the Tudeh Party from which it recovered only after the start of the revolution in Iran.

THE FREEDOM MOVEMENT

The old National Front umbrella organization suffered a major setback in the 1960–63 crisis. Some of the old-timers such as Dr. Karim Sanjabi and Dr. Shahpour Bakhtiar stayed with the organization until after the start of the revolution. Others broke away during the crisis and established the *Nehzat-e Azadi-ye Iran* (the Freedom Movement of Iran), led by Mehdi Bazargan, and joined by Ayatollah Sayyid Mahmoud Taleqani, Hassan Nazih, and others.[17] Neither the old National Front nor the Freedom Movement advocated armed resistance. The Frontists had demanded "liberty and democracy" and an "independent national" foreign policy during the 1960–63 crisis. The Freedom Movement believed in all this too, but at least some of its founders, such as Bazargan and Taleqani, supported the role of religion in politics as well. Although a lay and modern-educated man, Bazargan emphasized the importance of Islam in all his writings. He considered himself to be a "gradualist" in favor of a moderate approach to domestic and foreign-policy issues. Although he was attracted to the Western social-democratic tradition and was opposed to communism, he showed reservations about "Christian capitalists" (*kapitalist-ha-ye masihy*).[18] He believed that both Marxism and capitalism were "materialistic," but that Islam was "spiritualistic." This simplistic distinction is prevalent among Muslim apologists. The most interesting aspect of Bazargan's ideas was the emphasis on the overriding importance of self-criticism. In a society such as Iran where the prevalent tendency is to blame foreign powers and their perceived agents for all the ills of the country, Bazargan's stress on individual responsibility was refreshing. In keeping with this conviction, Bazargan did not perceive the U.S. role in Iran in the kind of negative and hostile light that the extremists did at both the left and the right ends of the spectrum in the political opposition.

GUERRILLA FORCES

Three young men broke away from the Freedom Movement in the mid-1960s, and founded the *Mujaheddin* group, mentioned previously. Some observers consider the *Mujaheddin* to be a religio-nationalist group, while others regard it as a Marxist organization. They are also regarded as the disciples of the well-known Iranian Islamicist, the late Dr. Ali Shari'ati. In a recent thesis, however, Bahman Bakhtiary has argued persuasively that before 1975 the ideology of the *Mujaheddin* and their perception of the sociopolitical conditions of Iran "reflected more Maoist-Marxist influences than Shari'ati's."[19] We shall consider Shari'ati's views briefly below. What is of interest here is the *Mujaheddin*'s rejection of the moderate views of Bazargan and the Iran Freedom Movement. This was certainly true in respect to the views of the founders of the group. They frowned upon Islamic reformism and stated in their manifesto that the Freedom Movement was composed of "religious intellectuals tied to traditional petit bourgeois faction, which from an ideological standpoint did not go beyond a mere parliamentary struggle."[20] This was an outright rejection by the youthful organization of parliamentary democracy advocated by their elders in the National Front and Freedom Movement.

More crucial, however, the radical ideology of the *Mujaheddin* was accompanied by a firm commitment to armed struggle as the only means of destroying the Shah's regime and of eliminating the U.S. influence in Iran. For example, in his defense before the Shah's military tribunal in January 1974, Sa'id Mohsen, a founder of the *Mujaheddin* organization, acknowledged that the Iranian Constitu- tional Revolution (1905–11), the nationalist movement led by Musaddeq (1951–53), and the uprising of June 1963, led by Kho- meini, all aimed at "the establishment of a just government." But he cited three main reasons for the need for armed struggle: the Shah's regime had responded to all nationalist uprisings by "killing the peo- ple"; the reformist movements had failed; and liberation movements elsewhere had succeeded because of armed struggles undertaken to "establish justice for peasants and workers."[21]

The *Mujaheddin*'s perspective on the nature of the United States- Iran relationship did not undergo any change subsequent to the 1975 split in the group. If anything, the splinter group, known as Battle Organization (*Sazeman-e Paykar*), which fully embraced Marxist- Leninist ideas, advocated a more consistently violent approach. Even the principal group, the faction led by Mas'ud Rajavi—the only one of the three original cofounders of the *Mujaheddin* organization whose life had been spared through French intercession—continued to endorse armed resistance. This organization continued to perceive the Shah as a "function of imperialism," meaning a tool of the United States. He was said to have resembled the "extremity of a limb to the body" which was dominated by a brain, the control cen- ter of which was imperialism.[22] Regardless of the rhetoric, the radical and presumably egalitarian and populist ideology of the *Mujaheddin* and their unreserved commitment to violence, made them the single most violent underground group and the principal killers of U.S. employees in Iran.

The other principal secular underground opposition group, the *Fada'eyin-e Khalq* (People's Fighters), a Marxist offshoot of the Tudeh Party, took no sanguine view of United States-Iran rela- tions during the Shah's regime either. Unlike the *Mujaheddin*, the *Fada'eyin* did not even make a pretense to Islamic piety. They, like the *Mujaheddin*, viewed every aspect of the United States-Iran relationship, particularly those related to oil, arms, and economic and political issues, as nothing but manifestations of imperialist, particularly United States', exploitation and domination of Iran with the aid of the Shah, who was considered to be Washington's lackey. Yet interestingly, the *Fada'eyin*, despite their greater Marxist ortho- doxy, in effect committed no comparable acts of violence against either the Shah's officials or U.S. official employees in Iran.

While the *Mujaheddin* received training from the *Fatah* and arms from Libya, the *Fada'eyin* established links with the Popular Front for the Liberation of Palestine (PFLP). They also established the bank account 58305 in the National Bank of Yemen in Aden.[23] It was known during the Shah's regime that George Habash, the PFLP leader, and Hamid Ashraf, a leader of the *Fada'eyin*, had been in close contact. For example, a letter from Habash to Ashraf was read at the gatherings of Iranian dissident students in the United States in Chicago, Houston, and Berkeley in 1976.[24] Hamid Ashraf, together with nine other "comrades," was ambushed on June 29, 1976 and "martyred" by the Shah's troops in the southern Mehrabad region of Tehran. The *Fada'eyin* still consider Ashraf as "an outstanding leader who guided the organization through the most difficult of circumstances with revolutionary decisiveness and communist patience."[25]

Like all groups in Iran, the *Fada'eyin* have not been immune to the ancient pattern of factionalization. They split after the revolution, with one faction vouching for affinity with the Tudeh Party. The Tudeh itself, however, was splintering into several small communist groupings such as the *Sazeman-e Vahdat-e Komonisti* (Organization of Communist Unity), and *Gorouh-e Ettehad-e Komonisti* (Group of Communist Alliance).

SHARI'ATI'S INFLUENCE

While the *Fada'eyin* and other leftist groups were seeking Marxist answers to the repressions of the Shah's regime and the perceived U.S. domination, the greatest number of Iranians, secular, religious, lay, and clerical, were listening to a vast amount of lectures in person or on tape, or were reading a torrent of books, pamphlets, etc., at home and abroad, authored by Dr. Ali Shari'ati. The Persian-French-educated intellectual did not speak directly about the United States or the Shah. It is, therefore, impossible to cite his views on the Shah's regime or the U.S. role in Iran. I believe the principal reason for this reticence was his deep concern with the larger issues of his time, the loftier questions of the relationship between mankind and God, of the existence and essence of humanity, and of the personal and spiritual dimensions of mankind. Neither his God nor his man ideal person was only Iranian or Islamic; his concern was universal (*jahanbini*). He ambitiously tried to delve into various aspects of all major religions, histories, and societies in an impossible search for the dominant intellectual and spiritual currents and thoughts. He believed he had discovered them in the primacy of "existence," "justice," and above all, "mysticism." And he saw the answer to his questions in the Islamic ideology of *tauhid* (oneness) which, he thought, brought all these three diverse currents together. This synthesis presumably provided the basis for viewing humanity from a multidimensional perspective. Shari'ati saw the relevance of his intellectual edifice to social realities, for example, in the following terms:

> As our children become socialists, their mystical sense and spirituality are lost. As they become mystics, they grow so indifferent to social problems that their very mysticism inspires loathing. As they leave both of these behind, and arrive at that existential 'I' and existential freedom, they turn into hippies, Western existentialists and worthless denizens of cafes.[26]

It will take time before Shari'ati's ideas are fully understood and his true impact on the Iranian forces of opposition during the Shah's regime is fully comprehended. Regardless of differences of opinion about his ideas, there is a consensus among scholars that his revolutionary ideology had a profound influence on the Iranian mind, an impact that may have cost him his life. He died mysteriously in London in 1977. Some observers believe that SAVAK agents killed him. Like Bazargan, he advocated self-criticism and the importance of spirituality as a distinguishing feature of Islam as contrasted with the perceived Western or Eastern materialist ways of life. But unlike Bazargan, he sought revolutionary change as the preferred approach to the basic problems of the reconstruction of "Man before God." Without ever being specific, Shari'ati rejected both the Shah's "superficial modernization" and the perceived U.S. support of it. His impact on the Iranian Revolution is believed to have been profound.

KHOMEINI TURNED REVOLUTIONARY

While in exile, Ayatollah Khomeini developed his own views about how and why Islam, as he saw it, provided the basis for not only rejecting the Shah's rule and the U.S. influence in Iran, but also for establishing a whole "new" state. Since we have already dealt with his ideas during the wartime and in the early 1960s, it would suffice here to note that those specific ideas about the Shah's regime and the United States were developed into a generalized political ideology by 1969 when his Najaf lectures were collected in his well-known *Hokoumat-e Islami* (*Islamic Government*). Specifically, he still attacked both the Shah and the United States in one breath: "We possess everything and would not need the help of America or of others if it were not for the costs of the Court and for its wasteful use of the people's money."[27] Specifically also, his basically hostile view toward monarchy was an extension of his earlier work (*Secrets Exposed*, 1943).[28] And finally, his condemnation of the notion of the separation of religion and politics was neither new in his own thinking, nor in Islamic thinking in general and Shi'i political thought in particular. Witness, for example, the violent denunciation of Prime Minister Ahmad Qavam by the Ayatollah Kashani during the well-known July 1952 crisis. He said: "The separation between religion and politics has been for centuries the program of the British. It is by this means that they have kept the Islamic peoples ignorant of their interests. Traitors who have followed British policy for centuries have now, however, overthrown the barrier of the Mossadeq government. They have replaced Mossadeq by a person [Qavam] who was reared in the arms of monarchy and despotism, and whose political life is full of treason, as has been demonstrated on a number of occasions."[29]

By 1969, however, Khomeini's views extended far beyond opposition to the monarchy. He advocated its forcible overthrow, if necessary, and replacement by an Islamic state based on Islamic law and the rule of the *Faqih* (Islamic jurisprudent). This rather concrete change must be attributed to not only the Ayatollah's own personal grudge against the Shah, but also to his perception of the tyrannical nature of the Shah's regime, the U.S. domination of Iran, and the revolutionary changes outside Iran. In 1943 he had refrained from denouncing the Iranian Constitution of 1906–07, although he demanded, above all, the full implementation of its provisions regarding the clerical review of legislative acts. But in his *Islamic Government*, first published in Najaf in 1971, he vehemently denounced it. Since the constitution recognized the institution of monarchy, he condemned it. He then viewed it as a document "borrowed from the Belgian Embassy" by Iranian "agents" of foreign powers. This was a frontal attack on the political sacred cow in Iran. Even the Tudeh Party over the decades had not dared to condemn the constitution publicly, although it had denounced the Shah and the monarchy in the 1951–53 crisis. Furthermore, Khomeini now rejected the constitution because neither its provision for the *ulama*'s supervision of the parliamentary man-made law was considered enough, nor had it ever been implemented in practice. There was simply no such tradition in favor of the direct rule of the *Faqih*, or for the control of political power by the clergy as the "vanguard" of Shi'i Muslim society. Such an ideal Islamic rule had to await, according to the doctrine of *ghaybah* (occulation), until the reappearance of the *saheb al-zaman*, the Master of the Age, or the hidden messianic Imam.[30]

But Khomeini argued that it would be "sinful" to wait for the Mahdi under such intolerable circumstances. Faced with a "pharaonic" rule that "dominates" and "corrupts," an individual Muslim:

> . . . has before him two paths, and no third to them: Either be forced to commit sinful acts, or rebel against and fight the rule of false gods, try to wipe out or at least reduce the impact of such a rule. We only have the second path open to us. We have no alternative but to work for destroying the corrupt and corrupting systems and to destroy the symbol of treason and the unjust among the rulers of the peoples. This is a duty that all Moslems wherever they may be are entrusted—a duty to create a victorious and triumphant Islamic political revolution.[31]

That revolution according to Khomeini's ideology, should result in an "Islamic Republic." He found the model for such a republic in two early historical periods of Islamic government—the age of the Prophet, and that of his cousin and son-in-law, Ali ibn Abu Talib, Islam's fourth Caliph and the Shi'i community's first Imam. He made no reference whatever to pre-Islamic Iran, except for criticizing the rule of the Ummayyed and the Abbasid dynasties based on the model of the "Persian and other emperors." Hence, the notions of "independence" and "freedom" were cast in terms of the struggle against the "colonialists" in the whole Muslim world, including, but not limited to, the Shah's regime and the United States. As early as 1944, Khomeini denounced the contemporary international system of states. The world was the abode of mankind under God. State entities were the creatures of man's limited intellect.

ATTACKS ON U.S. CITIZENS

Within Iran, the leftist secular underground groups launched the earliest acts of violence against the Shah's regime and the U.S. citizens in Iran. The *Fada'eyin*, in December 1970, directed a daring attack on a gendarme post at Siah-kal, which was their hideout in the Gilan forest near the Caspian Sea. Thirteen of the captured leaders were executed, but the fugitives of the same group assassinated the chief of the military tribunal and wounded his son in April 1971. The greatest disaster that befell the *Fada'eyin*, according to their own accounts, was the success of the Iranian security forces near the Mehrabad airport on June 29, 1976. Ten of their leaders were killed in the attack, including their revered hero Hamid Ashraf.

As mentioned before, however, most of the acts of violence were committed by the *Mujaheddin*, whose favorite targets were U.S. employees in Iran. The first major anti-U.S. operation was planned on the occasion of President Nixon's visit to Iran on his way back from the Moscow summit in May 1972. The president's press secretary attributed the premature explosion of three bombs in Tehran to "terrorist activities," saying that there was "no indication whatever" that the explosions were aimed at the president. As reported at the time, the bombing had been the work of an "urban terrorist movement that is bitterly opposed to what it regards as the Shah's autocratic domestic policies, his friendship with Israel and his pro-Western foreign policy."[32] We now know that the bombing was planned by a member of the *Mujaheddin*'s Central Committee, Kazem Zul al-Anvar, a graduate of the Agricultural College at Karaj. The so-called "Nixon Operation" was intended to protest the Shah's policies and U.S. activities in Iran, particularly the perceived U.S. assignment of the role of "regional policeman" to his regime. The plan included the murder of U.S. Air Force General Price, the bombing of the U.S. Information Service offices, the blasting of the entrance to Reza Shah's mausoleum where President Nixon was to place a wreath on his tomb, and a number of other explosions along the route of the president's motorcade "as a welcoming present from our people"![33]

This was only the start of the *Mujaheddin*'s acts of violence against U.S. citizens in Iran. A sample listing of their other acts of violence will be enough:

1. A U.S. general was wounded in an assassination attempt in 1972.
2. A U.S. Army colonel was shot to death in 1973.
3. Two U.S. colonels were killed in Tehran in 1975, including the director of plans for MAAG, Colonel Paul R. Shaffer, Jr.

4. Three U.S. civilians were ambushed and assassinated in 1976 as they drove to their jobs on a secret electronic project that Rockwell Company was carrying out for the Shah's government. In a document discovered in the aftermath of this incident, the U.S. civilians were characterized as Iran's "masters."

JIMMY CARTER, THE SHAH, AND THE OPPOSITION

Neither Tehran nor Washington tried to understand the underlying motivations for these acts of violence. They viewed them simplistically as "terrorist acts"—which, indeed, they were. But they also reflected a deeper opposition movement to the Shah and the United States. In their defense, the captured dissidents repeatedly told the Shah's secret military tribunals that they were not professional terrorists, and that they were driven to acts of violence in response to the regime's repression, corruption, torture, and killing of the regime's opponents even when they were not committing acts of violence. Amnesty International, the International Association of Democratic Jurists, and other international humanitarian organizations told Tehran of their deep concern about the torture of political prisoners.[34] Their representatives tried to witness some of the secret trials of the military tribunals and reported the regime's punishment of students, intellectuals, artists, and others for their antiregime ideas, writings, and political affiliations. But Tehran and Washington were too preoccupied with strategic considerations to take sufficient and serious note of the fervor among the ancient and modern sociopolitical forces of opposition that were clearly in evidence long before the eruption of the Iranian Revolution.

Conversely, there is no doubt that the opposition to the Shah's regime and the U.S. influence in Iran was intensified partly by the Shah's own misguided security, economic, and political policies. We have already seen some of these policies in the previous chapters. Here we shall examine some of his disastrous political policies. In 1975 he created what he called a single-party system, organized as *Hezb-e Rastakhiz-e Melli-ye Iran*, or the National Resurgence Party of Iran. He divided the Iranian people into two categories: those who believed in his regime and those who did not. Those who believed in it, he decreed, should signal their conviction by joining the single party. Those who would not join the party were divided into two categories: first, the regime's active opponents, such as the Tudeh

Party members, who would be regarded as "stateless," and would either have to go to jail or leave the country; and second, the non-joiners who were not actively opposed to the regime. They could stay in Iran, but they had to make public their "national position" and not expect anything from the regime.[35] The official explanation for this abrupt creation of a political monster was that it would allow for more "efficient" use of "human resources." The real reason was the crowning of the process of repression dating back to the coup of 1953. C. L. Sulzberger pinpointed it when he said, "Nothing Hitlerian or Communistic has been created; nothing democratic either. 'Efficiency' does not seem a reason to impose unanimity."[36]

This last act of political intolerance was all that the opponents of the regime needed. At half a dozen Iranian universities and colleges, bitter anti-Shah and anti-U.S. sentiments dominated private conversations with me.[37] The students took the absence of any U.S. criticism of the Rastakhiz Party as a sign of U.S. endorsement. This perception was an inevitable result of close U.S. identification with the Shah's regime.

The 1976 Democratic presidential campaign deeply worried the Shah. He feared the decline of U.S. support for his regime if the Democratic Party should win the elections. He "owed" his throne to the Eisenhower Administration, and had enjoyed a "special relationship" with the Nixon and Ford Administrations. President Nixon regarded him as a "world statesman," President Ford had said he was a "world senior statesman," and Henry Kissinger understood his geopolitics as no one else did. But what would happen to all his massive purchases of arms if the Democratic Party should win the elections? After all, President Kennedy had denied him arms aid, and had "imposed" Dr. Amini's "reform government" on him. The Shah, therefore, sent his scouts to the United States to study the Carter campaign firsthand and write him reports. He especially asked for estimates of Jimmy Carter's success. Carter's campaign for human rights and for limiting arms sales in particular troubled the Shah. He was the United States' single largest purchaser of arms. Arms were the politico-military backbone of his regime. They were just as important to its survival as the oil revenues that financed their purchase.

The election of President Carter upset the Shah, but gave heart to the opponents of his regime. The pattern of opposition activities changed. As seen, in the 1970–76 period the opposition had been expressed primarily by acts of violence directed against U.S. employees in Iran. In 1977, however, a new pattern of opposition began to surface. The old National Front and its sympathizers increased pressures on the regime by peaceful means. In May 1977, 54 lawyers signed a declaration protesting contemplated judicial changes that they considered harmful. In June, 40 writers signed another declaration, calling for an end to censorship. And in July, a couple of similar declarations were signed and distributed by an ever-larger number of dissidents.[38] A copy of one of these declarations, which was unsigned and was probably authored by some of the leaders of the National Front, was for the first time sent to the U.S. ambassador and others at the embassy.

In the meantime, the student opponents of the regime began to intensify their opposition at various Iranian universities, colleges, and other institutions of higher learning. The ensuing occasional disturbances peaked on October 9, 1977. The student militants, who most probably belonged to the *Mujaheddin* underground organization, issued a declaration addressed to the female students living at the University of Tehran's dormitory quarters in Amir Abad. The declaration threatened the lives of the female students if they continued to dine with male students in the same cafeteria. On the same day a group of masked student militants attacked dormitory buildings, set fire to a university bus and damaged others.[39] The incident marked only the beginning of continuing disturbances during the remainder of 1977. The unrest spread gradually to other universities and educational institutions in Tehran and the provinces. At the same time, an increasing number of students absented themselves from class meetings. The attrition was so severe at some institutions that no classes could be held for days or weeks at a time.

The Shah's regime found itself caught between increasingly open domestic opposition and a perceived lack of concern from Washington. Before the election of President Carter, the Shah pretended that he did not care about the outcome of the U.S. elections. In his words, the outcome of the presidential election "would not have the slightest effect on Iran-American relations. Iran controlled a good part of the free world's energy resources and the free world could not tolerate the loss of Iran, and any threat to Iran's vital interests would lead to war."[40] Once Jimmy Carter was elected president, however, the Shah launched a campaign of propaganda of Iranian views on human rights with the aid of the royal family, high-ranking government officials, and Rastakhiz Party leaders. A few major examples will be cited.

Prime Minister Hoveyda led the campaign. He pointed out prefatorily that: Iran's foreign trade exceeded $30 billion and much of the country's commercial and economic activities was with the United States; the two countries had many mutual interests and Iran hoped the United States would keep it that way; and "democracy to us means justice and giving the people a chance to share in the decision-making process of the country through the Rastakhiz Party."[41]

Empress Farah, who enjoyed a reputation for trying hard to attend to philanthropic activities in Iran, cast the problem of human rights into a worldwide framework at the annual meeting of the Aspen Institute for Humanistic Studies in 1977. She implied that Iran was trying hard to "couple economic with political democracy" in a way that was suitable to "its own needs and traditions."[42] Hushang Ansary, a Cabinet minister and the leader of the "Constructive Wing" of the Rastakhiz Party, asked rhetorically in July 1977: "Without freedom of expression of ideas, how can we expect thoughts to blossom and the best policy alternatives to emerge?" And Majid Majidi, also a Cabinet minister and the leader of the "Progressive Wing" of the Rastakhiz Party, claimed that "freedom of expression has been, and continues to be, an indispensible right of all Iranians. The question is how government officials interpret this right."[43] The Shah's twin sister, Princess Ashraf, repeated her brother's favorite theme to portray the Rastakhiz Party as the vehicle of "nationwide popular participation in politics" by claiming that it was an authentic Iranian institution. She told the International Conference on Human Rights during its tenth anniversary meeting in Tehran that developing countries "cannot emulate the West in the realization of human rights."[44]

In the face of mounting pressures of domestic opposition, and the perceived lukewarm attitude of Washington, the Shah launched a program of "political liberalization." For example, in July 1977, the Iranian Parliament received a bill to amend the military prosecution law. Such a move was perceived as improving the lot of Iran's political prisoners who had been tried by military courts without any real due process of law. The move was seen by the Shah's opponents, however, as a byproduct of the Shah's concern with real or anticipated pressures from President Carter.[45]

To cite another example, in August 1977, the Shah, with a great deal of fanfare, launched a program of liberalization that included the revival of three institutions for examining governmental implementation of policy decisions, toleration of more open criticism of the government in the Rastakhiz Party, and a reshuffling of the Cabinet. More noticeably, the Shah asked for the resignation of Prime Minister Hoveyda on August 6 after an unprecedentedly long tenure of service (1965–77). He appointed Jamshid Amuzegar as prime minister on August 7. The Shah admired Amuzegar partly for his longstanding service as Iran's oil minister.

Such ostensible concessions to the opposition in 1977, however, were coupled consistently with a denunciation of all dissidents as "terrorists," "communists," "Islamic Marxists," and other simplistic characterizations. Two major examples will be enough. First, in a well-publicized visit to the holy shrine of Imam Reza in Mashad on May 4, 1977, the Shah was accompanied by Empress Farah and the Crown Prince Reza. In newspaper photographs printed across the country, they were shown saying religious prayers. On the same occasion, he called upon the clergy to frustrate "ridiculous" efforts of his opponents to blur the crystal-clear distinction between materialism and faith in God, and to realize that a "few sick individuals fall upon flimsy arguments to link Islam with Marxism." He then said, "Of course, this is an instrument employed by a bunch of murderers."[46] Second, in response to the outbreak of disturbances at the University of Tehran, increasing agitations in the town of Ray, and a hunger strike by his student opponents in Paris in October 1977, the Shah asserted, "All these developments smell highly of counterrevolution, black reaction and outright treason," and warned that his opponents "want to set the country back not only to pre-revolutionary times, but also to circumstances prevalent 1,500 or 2,000 years ago."

The Shah also combined his claim to political liberalization with adamant and contradictory insistence on maintaining the notorious Rastakhiz Party. For example, he declared, on the seventy-second anniversary of the Iranian Constitutional Revolution (August 5, 1977), that "for us democracy cannot be an imported commodity from abroad because our nation with its own ancient culture and civilization knows better than anyone else what path can lead to its progress and happiness." The manifestation of Iran's "multifaceted democracy," the Shah continued, "is the all-encompassing Rastakhiz Party of the Iranian people that for the first time in Iran's Constitutional history embraces all Iranian men and women with a single ideology . . . and provides them with the opportunity to express their views and their constructive and positive criticism."[47]

The Shah's apparently self-confident rhetoric about his political liberalization and his optimistic assessment of it was taken at face value in the United States. Generally speaking, the media failed to see the 1977 signs of dissidence in the historical context of a persistent pattern of violent acts of bombing, assassination, and surveillance directed against both Iranian and U.S. officials. These facts were known worldwide. On the contrary, even when such incidents were reported, they were accompanied by such caveats as "it would be a mistake to assume that dissent is widespread."[48] Furthermore, although the forces of opposition viewed the Shah's political concessions merely as signs of weakness, the CIA continued to believe that dissidence at the time was more an "irritant" than a real challenge to the Shah under whose leadership Iran would remain stable over the next several years.

Yet beneath the Shah's confident rhetoric about the stability of his regime lay a growing sense of anxiety. He felt the need for a visit to Washington, partly to acquire new reassurances about the administration's unreserved support of his regime. His visit to Washington in November was, in all probability, prompted more by his own concern with the future of his rule than a desire to discuss with the president the F-16 purchase and oil price issues; these were of secondary importance to him at the time. He had always been the worrying type of person. He had often visited Washington to seek reassurance of continued U.S. support of his regime. His fatal illness, which was a well-guarded secret, might have aggravated his longstanding sense of personal insecurity. Ironically, his feeling of insecurity had increased with the development of closer ties with the United States and his own sense of growing power and influence, as revealed by his frequent visits to the United States. In nearly 13 years between his first visit to the United States in 1949 and his return to the throne in 1953, he had visited the White House only four times, but in the next 13 years, when his power and influence had grown, he paid Washington twice as many visits (see Table 3). The 1977 visit was not simply required for discussing outstanding issues between the two countries. There were clear indications that the Shah had begun to feel that something had basically gone wrong between him and the people of Iran. He needed to know firsthand what the president thought about him.

TABLE 3

United States-Iran Exchange of Visits: 1949-77

Visits of the Shah to the United States

November 16-20, 1949	June 12, 1968
December 13-15, 1954	March 31-April 1, 1969
June 30-July 2, 1958	October 21-23, 1969
April 11-14, 1962	July 24-25, 1973
June 5, 1964	May 15-16, 1975
August 22-24, 1967	November 14-16, 1977

Visits of U.S. Presidents to Iran

Franklin D. Roosevelt	November 27-December 2, 1943
Dwight D. Eisenhower	December 14, 1959
Richard M. Nixon	May 30-31, 1972
Jimmy Carter	December 31, 1977-January 1, 1978

Sources: U.S., Department of State, Office of the Historian, *Lists of Visits of Foreign Chiefs of States and Heads of Governments to the United States*; and *Lists of Visits of Presidents of the United States to Foreign Countries*.

Whatever assurances of support the Shah had hoped to get from the president seemed to be threatened by the opposition even before he left for the United States. The spokesman of his Ministry of Foreign Affairs, Parviz 'Adl, revealed on November 10, six days before the Shah's arrival in Washington, that the Iranian government anticipated demonstrations against the Shah in the United States. He vehemently denounced in advance the "anarchists of foreign nationalities" who planned to disrupt the Shah's visit.[49] He was right about anticipating disturbances, but he was wrong about the identity of the demonstrators. The Shah's appearance on the White House lawn with the empress, President Carter, and Mrs. Carter was marred by violent demonstrations staged by the opponents of his regime. They consisted largely of disparate forces, including the supporters of the National Front, the *Mujaheddin*, the *Fada'eyin*, and other groups with or without affiliation with the Confederation of Iranian Students.

The president characterized the special relationship between the United States and Iran in these words: "We look upon Iran's strength as an extension of our own strength and Iran looks upon our strength as an extension of theirs." The masked demonstrators, of course, defied both strengths, which they viewed as "illegitimate." Beyond that they were determined to test their own strength. Retrospectively, that test was to come in earnest in 1978-79 in the course of the Iranian revolutionary process that will be examined in the following two chapters.

POLITICAL BALANCE SHEET

On the United States' side of the political balance sheet, everything redounded to the U.S. advantage after 1953 and before the Iranian Revolution. If, indeed, the covert U.S. intervention then had been primarily motivated by strategic considerations, as repeatedly claimed, then the United States fully achieved that objective. The Shah's "stable" regime was established and totally shared U.S. strategic concerns for decades. The Carter Administration appeared to have added the new objective of "political liberalization" in U.S. policy toward Iran. Before then no U.S. administration, from Eisenhower to Carter, seems to have consistently tried to persuade the Shah to undertake a sustained and genuine program of political liberalization, including the Kennedy Administration. That administration's brief pressure on the Shah primarily concerned economic and social change, and the president offered his congratulations to the Shah prematurely, as soon as the Shah was finished with the "referendum" on his land reform program. The notion that the Kennedy Administration pressed the Shah for political democratization is empirically indefensible. Despite all the fury of President Carter's critics, even his administration was ambivalent about political liberalization in Iran, as we shall see.

The United States looks even better on the political balance sheet when its advantages are expanded to include the assignment of a regional role to Iran during the decade preceding the Iranian Revolution. Even President Carter was happy with the Shah's role as the "policeman" of the Persian Gulf, no matter what reservations he might have had about his regime. The Shah furnished embargo-proof oil, massively armed his country, made the United States his major trade partner, provided a market for lucrative U.S. investment and exports, partly in an attempt to be deserving of the U.S. epithet for Iran—"an island of stability" in the volatile Middle East. Through these policies, he aided parallel U.S. strategic and diplomatic interests in the adjacent regions of South Asia and East Africa as well.

On the debit side of the U.S. ledger, the increasing identification with the Shah's regime over the years had enormous costs. The covert U.S. intervention associated the United States with a regime whose legitimacy was in doubt even before the 1953 coup. That identification meant, in the following quarter of a century, a major share of U.S. responsibility, in the eyes of the opposition, for all the misguided policies of the Shah's regime, from the creation of the SAVAK torture chambers to the suppression of political opposition, the denial of freedom of the press and assembly, the facade of party and parliamentary systems, the pervasive corruption of the royal family, the disrespect toward religious leaders, the "imposition of capitulations," and, in short, whatever else the Shah did or failed to do as an "American king."

On the Iranian side, the Shah was initially very successful. The fact that he owed his throne partly to the United States, as he voluntarily acknowledged, did not stop him from defying the United States in the political field as in some other issues in the United States-Iran relationship. In the postcoup phase of his rule, he began to consolidate his power not only by political suppression of the opposition, but also by using his oil revenues, in partnership with the Western Consortium, to build up his arsenal, to implement grandiose economic projects, to launch his "White Revolution," and to dream ambitiously of making his domain one of the five conventional military powers of the world, of raising Iran to the economic level of West Germany and France, and to create a "great civilization" modeled after Cyrus the Great's about 2,500 years earlier.

On the debit side, every major segment of the Iranian population eventually became alienated from the Shah. His own misguided political policies, like his economic and security policies, undermined what was left of his legitimacy and authority after the coup. His tenacious hold on power did not allow him to see the threat of the opposition. His program of political liberalization before the onset of the revolution was largely cosmetic and lacked credibility. His propensity to characterize every shade of opposition as communistic or anarchistic, foreclosed any chance of accommodation with even the most moderate elements of the political opposition. The longstanding process of delegitimization to which he contributed more than anyone else, and his vain and essentially insecure personality added increasingly to his isolation from even those people who might have accepted his rule before or even after the coup. No wonder his longest-tenured prime minister, Hoveyda, confided to a friend that the Shah saw his people, when they rose in opposition to him, as a bride on whom he had spent everything, but who had all along been unfaithful!

NOTES

1. The information is drawn from Iranian government, *Ketab-e Siyah dar bareh-ye Sazeman-e Afssaran-e Tudeh* (Tehran: n.p., 1334).

2. See Kermit Roosevelt, *Countercoup: The Struggle for the Control of Iran* (New York: McGraw-Hill, n.d.), p. 9.

3. Ibid.

4. See Shahrough Akhavi, *Religion and Politics in Contemporary Iran: Clergy-State Relations in the Pahlavi Period* (Albany: State University of New York Press, 1980), p. 92.

5. See *Mizan Newsletter* 1 (March 1959): app. B, pp. 1-2.

6. See *Ettela'at Hava'i*, February 28, 1959.

7. *Washington Post*, October 23, 1977.

8. See Akhavi, Contemporary Iran, p. 95.

9. Author's translation from the text in *Farsi* in *Ettela'at Hava'i*, January 4, 1963.

10. Author's translation from the text of the declaration in *Ettela'at* (regular edition), October 26, 1980. See this same issue for the text of Khomeini's speech of October 26, 1964.

11. See Rouhollah K. Ramazani, "'Church' and State in Modernizing Society: The Case of Iran," *The American Behavioral Scientist* 7 (January 1964): 26-28.

12. See Rouhollah K. Ramazani, *The Northern Tier: Afghanistan, Iran and Turkey* (Princeton, N.J.: D. Van Nostrand, 1966), p. 104.

13. This account of Imam Musa Sadr's views is based on his conversation with me in 1967, when I was holding the Aga Khan chair of Islamic Studies at the American University of Beirut.

14. See FBIS, Daily Report, *Middle East & Africa* 5 (February 14, 1974).

15. See Rouhollah K. Ramazani, "Iran and the Arab-Israeli Conflict," *The Middle East Journal* 32, no. 4 (Autumn 1978): 413-28.

16. For the text see Beirut *al-Hawadis* in Arabic, December 13, 1974, as monitored by FBIS in *FBIS* 5 (December 13, 1974).

17. The others were Yadullah Sahabi, Mansur 'Ata'i, 'Abbas Sami'i, and Rahim 'Ata'i.

18. See Mohandes Mehdi Bazargan, *Musalman-e Ejtema'ai va Jahani* (Houston: Book Distribution Center, 1977).

19. See the M.A. thesis of Bahman Bakhtiari, *A Comparison of the Ideologies of 'Ali Shariati and the People's Mojahedin in Iran*, University of Virginia, May 1981, p. 9.

20. Ibid., p. 4.

21. For the text of Mohsen's defense before the Shah's military tribunal, see *Modafe'at-e Mojahed-e Shahid, Sa'id Mohsen* (n.p.: Iran Freedom Movement, 1977); and Sazeman-e Daneshjooyan-e Mosalman-e Irani, *Assnad-e Montashereh-ye Sazeman-e Mojahedin-e Khalq-e Iran*, vol. 1, *Modafe'at* (Willmete, Ill.: Organization of Iranian Moslem Students, 1977/78), pp. 7–30. This volume includes the text of the defense statements by other leaders of the *Mujaheddin* organization, including those of Mas'ud Rajavi, Nasser Sadeq, Mohammad Bazargani, 'Ali Mihandoost, and Mehdi Reza'i. For related publications see also Sazeman-e Mojahedin-e Khalq-e Iran, *Sharh-e Ta'siss va Tarikhche-ye Vaqaye'a Sazeman-e Mojahedin-e Khalq-e Iran Az Sal-e 1344 Ta Sal-e 1350* (Long Beach, Calif.: Anjoman-e Danesh-jooyan-e Mosalman, Amrika, 1979/80); and Rafiq Hamid Mo'meni, *Tarikh-e Jame'ah Baray-e No-javanan* (College Park, Md.: Confederation of Iranian Students, n.d.).

22. See the official organ of the People's Mojahedin Organization of Iran, *Mojahed*, April 1980, p. 27.

23. This information is drawn from Sazeman-e Cherikha-ye Fada'ey-e Khalq, *Shoresh nah Qadamha-ye Sanjideh dar Rah-e Enqelab* (West Germany: n.p., n.d.). For related publications see the organization's quarterly entitled *Kar International* published in Detroit at P. O. Box 612.

24. *Kayhan*, August 8, 1976.

25. See *Kar International*, February/April, 1979, p. 50. The date of the ambush in this source is given as 1977, but it is 1976 in the *New York Times*, June 30, 1976.

26. R. Campbell, trans., *Marxism and Other Western Fallacies: An Islamic Critique*, by Ali Shari'ati (Berkeley: Mizan Press, 1980), p. 122. Considering the numerous lectures and writings of Shari'ati in Persian, one hopes that Hamid Algar's general editorship of this and other translations will contribute to a better knowledge of Shari'ati in the Western world. See Hamid Algar's own translation, for example, of some of Shari'ati's lectures, entitled *On the Sociology of Islam* (Berkeley: Mizan Press, 1978). An excellent bibliography of Shari'ati's works in *Farsi* is included in Bahman Bakhtiari's M.A. thesis done under my own supervision at the University of Virginia. See Bahman Bakhtiari, *A Comparison of the Ideologies of 'Ali Shariati and the People's Mojahedin in Iran*, University of Virginia, Woodrow Wilson Department of Government and Foreign Affairs, 1981.

27. There has been some confusion about the identification of Khomeini's writings and lectures. Some have erroneously thought that there are two works by him, one titled *Hokomat-e Islami* and the other *Valayat-e Faqih*. In fact, however, there is only one. *Hokomat-e Islami* was published in Najaf, Iraq in 1971 based on his lectures. It was published in Tehran in 1977 by Amir Kabir Publishers under the title of *Hokomat-e Islami Ya Valayat-e Faqih*. Furthermore, besides this work and an earlier work mentioned in note 28 below, there are numerous other works by Khomeini on a variety of subjects. Hamid Algar has advertised a forthcoming translation, entitled *Islam and Revolution: Writings and Declarations of Imam Khomeini*, which will help English readers. *Hokomat-e Islami* is already available in English under the title "Islamic Government" (Washington, D.C.: n.p.). Farhang Rajaee, a doctoral candidate in the Woodrow

Wilson Department of Government and Foreign Affairs at the University of Virginia is currently working on a dissertation on Khomeini's views of international politics under my supervision.

28. See Haj Ruhollah Musavi Khomeini, *Kashf-e Assrar* (Tehran: n.p., 1944).

29. See R. K. Ramazani, "'Church' and State in Modernizing Society: The Case of Iran," *The American Behavioral Scientist* 7 (January 1964): 26–28.

30. For a solid discussion of messianism in classical Islam, see Abdulaziz Abdulhussein Sachedina, *Islamic Messianism: The Idea of the Mahdi in Twelver Shi'ism* (Albany: State University of New York Press, 1981).

31. See Ayatollah Ruhollah Khomeini, "Islamic Government" (Washington, D.C.: n.p., n.d.), p. 14.

32. *New York Times*, June 1, 1972.

33. Sazeman-e Mojahedin-e Khalq-e Iran, *Zendegi-nameh-ye Mojahedin-e Shahid, Kazem-e Zulanvar va Mostafa Javan-e Khoshdel* (Shiraz: n.p., n.d.).

34. See William J. Butler and Georges Levasseru, *Human Rights and the Legal System in Iran* (Geneva: International Commission of Jurists, March 1976).

35. See *Ettela'at*, Esfand 13, 1353, which includes the text of the Shah's first statement on the creation of the Rastakhiz Party. See also *Iran-e Novin*, *Mardom*, and *Ayandegan* of the same date for examples of government-sponsored jubilation over the news of the so-called single-party system in Iran.

36. *New York Times*, March 6, 1975.

37. I was lecturing as a U.S. professor under the auspices of the USIA in Iran during February/March 1975.

38. *Wall Street Journal*, November 4, 1977.

39. *Ettela'at*, October 13, 1977.

40. *Kayhan*, October 30, 1976.

41. Ibid., February 19, 1977.

42. Ibid., July 9, 1977.

43. Ibid., August 6, 1977.

44. *Kayhan*, June 4, 1977.

45. *New York Times*, July 3, 1977.

46. *Ettela'at*, May 7, 1977; and *Kayhan*, May 7, 1977.

47. Author's translation from *Ettela'at*, August 7, 1977.

48. See, for example, *Wall Street Journal*, November 4, 1977.

49. *Ettela'at*, November 10, 1977.

6

ROYAL INFLUENCE AND REVOLUTIONARY COUNTERINFLUENCE

The intimate interrelationship between the problems of continuity and change in Iranian society and the United States-Iran relationship has been evident throughout this study. Historically, that interrelationship went back to the very inception of Iran's initiative in establishing diplomatic relations with the United States in the nineteenth century. But only the U.S. involvement in Iran because of World War II provided the opportunity for the young Shah to court the United States to support his regime in the face of the challenges of both sociopolitical forces and foreign pressures. The successful covert U.S. intervention in support of the Shah's rule was followed by the development of a quarter century of close United States-Iran relationship in every major issue area, including the political. The underground sociopolitical opposition finally surfaced after having been suppressed in the 1963–64 crisis. For the first time in 1977, the opposition began to challenge the Shah's regime and its relationship with the United States effectively.

By 1978 that challenge made the very rule of the Shah an issue between Iran and the United States. That issue was twofold: it was an issue between the Shah and the forces of opposition, and also between the United States and the Shah's regime amidst the challenge of the opposition to both the Shah's regime and the United States' influence in Iran. This chapter will take up the contest for power and influence between the Shah's government and the opposition, and the following chapter will examine the role of the United States in the Iranian revolutionary situation.

LANDMARK UPRISINGS

Between the Qom and Tabriz uprisings in January-February 1978 and the seizure of power by the revolutionary forces in February 1979, four different prime ministers held office. The frequency in changes of government was itself symptomatic of the unprecedented nature of the underlying problems. As mentioned in the previous chapter, Prime Minister Hoveyda had been kept in his post for nearly 13 years, the longest tenure enjoyed by any prime minister in Iran's modern history. His removal from office and the appointment of Prime Minister Jamshid Amuzegar on August 7, 1977 marked the beginning of frequent changes. The Shah says that he removed Hoveyda for two reasons: one, Amuzegar could better handle foreign policy issues, which at the time preoccupied him, and two, the new prime minister had "good friends" in the United States.[1] The Shah's selection of Amuzegar was also influenced by the perceived ability of Amuzegar to handle pressing economic problems. Toward that end the prime minister terminated, inter alia, the Shah's substantial financial support of the clergy, which, in retrospect, the Shah regretted.

This action of Amuzegar, however, should not be considered either as the "cause of the clerical rebellion," or more specifically of the uprising in Qom. The Qom riots broke out much later, on January 9, 1978. The government reports implied that they were instigated by "trouble-making" (*ekhlal-gar*) theological students (*tollab*) on the occasion of the anniversary of the Shah's land reform and "emancipation" of women.[2] The facts, however, seem to be quite different. It is generally established now that the demonstrations began in the "holy city" to protest an article in a government-controlled newspaper insulting the exiled clerical leader Ayatollah Ruhollah Khomeini. Reportedly, a crowd of about 5,000 people had just come out of a large mosque and started to march to the houses of the city's ayatollahs when police opened fire on them. It was the second day of a peaceful demonstration to protest the publication of the insulting letter mentioned above. The Ayatollah Shariatmadari emphatically denied the government version of the incident. He said: "That's an absolute lie."[3] The casualties were quite high. The opposition set the figure at hundreds if not more; the Western press estimated that about 70 people were killed, and the government said that only 6 people had died, and 9 were injured. Subsequently, the Shah also said that only 6 people had been killed, and added, "There is little doubt in my mind that communist elements had infiltrated the 4,000 religious students and their supporters who took part in the protest."[4]

We shall note the persistence of this simplistic characterization of the opposition on many occasions in 1978–79. It is important to observe here that this incident was the first one in years that involved shooting by government armed forces into an unarmed crowd. In fact, the incident and the reactions to it resembled the June 5, 1963 Qom unrest of nearly 14 years before which, as seen, led to the exile of Ayatollah Khomeini. As its antecedent, this more recent uprising involved the killing of a large number of unarmed people, the destruction of public and private property by unruly elements, a defiant strike by the Tehran Bazaaris, and, above all, the site of the same "holy shrine," with all its religious and emotional symbolic impact on the masses.

From this first landmark incident of the revolution stemmed the second one in Tabriz on February 18. The timing of the protest demonstrations was to mark the end of a 40-day mourning period (*cheleh*) for the martyrs (*shohada*) of the Qom incident, according to Shi'i Muslim tradition. This set the pattern of the cycle of numerous other demonstrations. But contrary to the general impression, the demonstrations were not necessarily confined to every 40 days. My count of the demonstrations during the Amuzegar government alone exceeds 19 major disturbances. By April 1978, the demonstrations spread to about 24 cities, but none attained the significance of the Qom and Tabriz incidents in the folklore of the opposition. The Tabriz riots, verging on insurrection, posed the most serious challenge to the Shah's regime since 1963. The government-censored press once again used the favorite figure of 6 dead, at first. It later increased the number to 11.[5] Other sources listed about 100 dead and more than 300 wounded. These figures were far more accurate; they fell far short of those claimed by the opposition, and were larger than those claimed by the government.

As in the Qom incident, once again the government's overreaction was provocative. Some Shi'i Muslim leaders called for peaceful strikes and worship to commemorate those killed in Qom in January, but government officials literally locked the mourners out of the mosque (*Masjed-e Jom'eh*).[6] At first the blame was placed, once again, on "Islamic Marxists" (*Mujaheddin*) and communists, but later the Shah fired local officials for "negligence" leading to the riots.

The removal of local officials, however, occurred only on March 5 and only after the religious leaders in Azerbaijan had addressed to General Ja'far Shafqat, the head of an investigative committee of the central government, a declaration of protest on February 27.[7] The declaration squarely blamed local government officials for turning the scheduled peaceful religious procession into bloody riots by their provocative actions. The Shah himself admitted, after his downfall, that "perhaps too much force" had been used, and believed, in retrospect, that the uprisings in Tabriz "marked the beginnings of efforts to reduce my authority, to turn me into a weak and ineffectual 'constitutional' monarch, and finally to oust me."[8]

The Shah's firing of a couple of local SAVAK officials and General Eskandar Azmudeh, the hated governor-general of Eastern Azerbaijan, was more an expression of anger over their inability to foresee the Tabriz uprisings than the sign of the government's recognition of the deeper causes of the disturbances. As before, the Shah continued to simplistically label all elements of the opposition as communists and Islamic Marxists. Such elements did indeed exploit the situation to their advantage, as did other extremists, both at Qom and Tabriz, by indulging in vandalism, mindless destruction of public and private property, and other acts. But such elements did not constitute the bulk of the dissidents in the Tabriz riots. Young dissidents between the ages of 15 and 30 included a great many students and ordinary citizens, including carpenters, carpet weavers, artisans, Bazaar merchants, preachers, and others.

Nor did the Qom and Tabriz uprisings seem to have the slightest effect, in early 1978, as in 1977, on the tenacious hold of the royal myth about party politics. The government continued to insist that the Rastakhiz Party was the "vehicle of democracy" in Iran. Even three months after the Tabriz uprisings, and despite the spread of violent demonstrations to all major cities and towns of Iran, the Shah failed to distinguish between the politically aware elements who demanded the restoration of a constitutional form of government through fundamental electoral and parliamentary reforms, and the communists, Marxists, and religious extremists who sought the destruction of his regime. In a wide-ranging press conference with Iranian journalists, held on May 15, 1978, for example, the Shah dismissed the reformist dissidents' reference to the constitution as a mere facade for "collaboration with communists for the partition of Iran" (*sakhtan-e ba komonist-ha baray-e taqsim-e Iran*).[9]

Even half a year after the Qom and Tabriz uprisings, the regime failed to undertake any serious political reforms. The intervening crucial months were used instead presumably to study "the causes of the uprisings." The supposed findings of the so-called "Study Group of the Iranian Problems" (*gorouh-e barresi-e masaleh-e Iran*) seemed to criticize the Rastakhiz Party for its "weak leadership; organizational defects; superficiality of cells; lack of political education;" and other problems without ever raising any serious question about its legitimacy. The study also denounced those who charged that the dissidents of Qom and Tabriz were the "tools of foreign powers," but none of this seemed to have the slightest effect on the Shah's own apparent conviction that there was not any real difference, for example, between the followers of the National Front and the communist Tudeh Party. On Constitutional Day in 1978, the Shah delivered his favorite indictment of Musaddeq for his alleged collaboration with the communists in 1951–53.[10] This indictment was a repetition of the Shah's speech on Constitutional Day of the previous year, as discussed in the previous chapter. In the light of such persistently negative attitudes toward even the moderate nationalist elements, the removal of General Nematollah Nassiri, the head of SAVAK, the lukewarm intimation by a government that the return of Ayatollah Khomeini to Iran "would not be opposed," and the so-called ban on influence peddling by the members of the royal family lacked any real credibility among any of the opposition forces.

Nor did these well-publicized gestures of conciliation have any dampening effects on the spread of disturbances to other towns and cities after the Qom and Tabriz uprisings. Both these cities were the sites of new uprisings in the following months, as were other towns and cities such as Babol, Meshed, Shiraz, Isfahan, and, of course, repeatedly Tehran. But the real disaster finally hit in the oil port city of Abadan. On August 19 fire was set to a crowded movie theatre, full of women and children, killing at least 377 people in the worst disaster of its kind anywhere in 100 years. According to a government spokesman, the fire was set by "fanatics" and was directed against "all signs of modern living and Westernization in Iran," while others believed that it could be the work of the *Mujaheddin*. The veteran National Front leader, Dr. Karim Sanjabi, however, charged it was "a government intrigue to show foreigners that Iran is unable to have a democratic system."[11]

This charge was unfortunate and farfetched; the truth of the matter is yet to be established. What is most baffling, however, is why the Shah's regime made no attempt to avoid provocation, especially after the convulsions in Qom and Tabriz. Why did the government decide to celebrate the twenty-fifth anniversary of the Shah's return to power? August 19, 1953, the day of the Abadan fire, was the twenty-eighth of *Mordad*, the anniversary of the overthrow of Musaddeq, symbolizing to most Iranians a day of national disaster. Given the explosive political atmosphere at the time and the religiously sensitive month of Ramadan, why did the regime find it necessary to send its goose-stepping soldiers to parade in Tehran and organize pro-Shah rallies in most major cities in the country? The tenure of the Amuzegar government had already been marred by two earlier instances of demonstrated insensitivity of some officials to religious and national sentiments—the publication of the insulting letter on Ayatollah Khomeini that triggered the Qom sit-in and peaceful demonstrations, and the locking of mourners out of the *Masjed-e Jom'eh* in Tabriz, which led to the bloody disturbances there. Was this the third instance of seemingly deliberate acts of provoking more religious and nationalist sentiments against the Shah's own government? The answer lies partly in the political aftermath of the Abadan fire; the Shah removed his favorite Prime Minister Amuzegar from power on August 27.

The fall of the government marked the end of the earliest phase of the crisis in 1978 when the opportunity for meaningful compromise with the opposition might have been present. But the fallen government seems to have misperceived, when in power, the nature of the opposition as much as the Shah did. Prime Minister Amuzegar was, deservedly, an internationally respected technocrat, but his perspective failed him in assessing the nature of the crisis. He seems to have been inclined to view the sources of opposition to the Shah's regime primarily in terms of the economic ills of Iranian society. If they were remedied, he thought, then the opposition would diminish, if not disappear. The corollary of this view was a misperception of the underlying reasons for the alliance between religious and Bazaari forces. He believed that they were mainly economic, but more than economic considerations cemented their cooperation: they shared, above all, religious and political grievances against the Shah's regime. Prime Minister Amuzegar was not alone, in Iran or the United States, in believing that simple satisfaction of economic needs would lead to political stability. The Shah and most of his technocratic elite held the same view. Amuzegar should be faulted for this reason rather than the alleged mishandling of the three crucial crises discussed above. For those, the Shah and some elements of his security forces were primarily responsible.

THE SHARIF-EMAMI GOVERNMENT

Presumably as a conciliatory gesture toward the opposition, the Shah appointed Sharif-Emami to the post of prime minister. The premier said that his new government would "create an atmosphere of reconciliation of all classes of the people," and declared, as a matter of principle, respect for Shi'ism as the state religion and respect for clergymen. He promised free parliamentary elections, free activities for "legitimate" political parties, and a government campaign against "corruption and exploitation," although he expressed reservations about the "small parties" that "have no roots and grow like mushrooms" (*risheh-i nadarand va mesle qarch sabz mishavand*).[12] However, he denounced the notorious Rastakhiz Party. The Shah subsequently criticized the prime minister for this because Sharif-Emami's rebuke of the party "failed to appease the opposition, but succeeded in cutting off that party's support for his government."[13]

The fact that the Shah still did not have the slightest intention of sharing any real power with the opposition left the prime minister with no genuine opportunity to make meaningful compromises with the opposition. He, therefore, undertook certain symbolic acts such as the closing of the casinos and gambling clubs, replacing the "imperial calendar" with the Islamic solar calendar, which had been Iran's calendar until two years previously, and abolishing the post of minister of state for women's affairs. The real aim of the Shah in appointing Sharif-Emami was to continue to manipulate events in order to control power instead of facing realistically the fact of his rapidly dwindling authority. At this time, he specifically aimed at dividing the opposition, not appeasing it as is so often said, by presumably wooing its more "moderate" secular and religious elements. The inclusion of the hawkish chief of the National Gendarmerie, General Abbas Qarabaghi, as the minister of interior in the new Cabinet was intended to show that the so-called conciliatory efforts would be combined with a crackdown on the "extremist elements." The opposition vehemently rejected the Shah's so-called carrot and stick strategy.

Once again Islamic tradition provided the symbolic occasion for the opposition to show its defiance of the Shah's regime. On September 4, it launched the largest demonstration in the capital in about 25 years. The day marked the end of the holy month of Ramadan. Nearly 100,000 demonstrators joined religious processions throughout the country, shouting for the return of the Ayatollah Khomeini. The slogan, "Iran is our country, Khomeini is our leader" mingled with chants aimed at the Shah's troops, "Why do you kill your brothers?"

This demonstration proved to be only a rehearsal for an unprecedented show of influence by the opposition on September 8. As many as one million people from all walks of life poured into the streets of Tehran, heading for Jaleh Square. The Shah's security forces were stunned by the sheer size of the crowds. The demonstrators shouted slogans against the Shah and the Pahlavi dynasty, and carried banners of Khomeini. The demonstrations took place only hours after the Shah had imposed martial law in Tehran and 11 other cities in order to control growing civil disorders, but the opposition reportedly had no knowledge of the ban. The soldiers first fired warning shots over demonstrators' heads, but then "lowered their aim into the crowd."[14]

September 8 became known as "Black Friday." The Shah, after his downfall, claimed, "The violence of that Friday's demonstrations reached such a pitch of murder, pillage, and arson that the security forces had no choice but to fire."[15] This was, of course, the same kind of justification that had been offered on previous occasions, especially during the uprisings in Qom and Tabriz, for the use of brute force against unarmed civilians. His explanation of the nature of the demonstration at the time was not any different from all the previous months either. In answering a question on ABC television on September 11, he said that the uprisings were "quite amazing" to him and their impact was "unexpected." "What scares us a little," he added, was that the demonstration was "completely organized and controlled by international subversive organizations."[16]

The prime minister was severely criticized, in the Majlis on September 12, for his mishandling of the demonstrations. Four deputies of the Pan Iranist Party walked out of the chamber in protest, and the party leader, Mohsen Pezeshkpour, charged that the prime minister's "hand was blood-stained" (*dastash aloudeh ast*).[17] Dr. Ali Amini, who had only recently surfaced on the political scene, believed that the situation had clearly called for the imposition of martial law by the government, but the government by no means should have killed innocent people.[18] The government, he added, had other means of controlling or dispersing demonstrators instead of firing into the crowds. The prime minister, however, defended the government action, contending that the demonstrations would have led to a "communist rebellion" (*shouresh-e komonisti*) if it had not been forcibly controlled.[19] In a long and involved exposition to the Majlis, he attempted to prove that the communists had infiltrated the religious and secular demonstrations. If we rely on what has been published, however, his "proof" was pathetic. He cited the kinds of slogans that the demonstrators had used, and referred specifically to a pamphlet of the Tudeh Party, and to the activities of the *Mujaheddin* (without naming them) as the basis for his conviction that a communist coup had been averted as a result of the government's armed intervention.

Beyond the mishandling of the incident, the aftermath of "Black Friday" presented the government with an apparent paradox: how to reconcile the need for maintaining the martial law, and the so-called promises of political liberalization. Before the September 8 incident, a group of religious leaders, including Ayatollah Sayyed Abdulrahim Najafi, had been released from the Shah's prison. Reportedly the government had also entered into secret discussions with Ayatollah Shariatmadari, although this was denied by deputy Ahmad Bani Ahmad of Tabriz in the Majlis. But immediately after the incident, even secret contacts of the government with opposition leaders became nearly impossible. Government pressure on the opposition was actually increased, resulting, for example, in the arrest of Mehdi Bazargan, the leader of the Iranian Human Rights Committee, whose colleagues took refuge in the house of the Ayatollah Shariatmadari. The government also arrested Sheikh Yahya Nassiri Nouri, known as Alameh-ye Nouri, a prominent Shi'i clergyman accused of plotting "rebellion against the government," and incitement of people to commit arson in banks, supermarkets, movie theatres, and other public and private buildings. Another well-known cleric, Mohammad Mofateh, was also arrested and as many as 20 other clergymen went underground. Prominent secular dissidents who were either arrested or threatened included Moghaddam Maraghei and Nasser Minachi, both members of Bazargan's committee.

All these tough measures and subsequent gestures of reconciliation, such as piecemeal release of political prisoners, failed to interrupt the sustained outburst of demonstrations throughout the country. Conversely, demonstrations grew in number and violence after "Black Friday." The opposition launched eight more major demonstrations and an increasing number of strikes after that tragic incident, bringing the total of major disturbances to 12 and the strikes to 4 during the government of Sharif-Emami, before its downfall.

As the crisis deepened, the Shah began to add to his so-called policy of political liberalization a search for a "coalition government." He said later that "the Americans began to push the idea. . . . Why not bring in members of the opposition, specifically the leaders of the National Front of Mossadegh's day? Reaching out across political barriers, they said, could reestablish badly frayed national unity."[20] We shall say more about the Shah's alleged search for a coalition government later in this chapter. It is enough to say here that the idea was not significant since the Shah did not seem to have the slightest inclination to share real power. With respect to his efforts at forming a coalition government while Sharif-Emami was still prime minister, the Shah himself seems to admit his reluctance to compromise. He said, "I tried. I contacted Karim Sanjabi and several other opposition leaders. But their demands were unacceptable."[21]

THE MILITARY GOVERNMENT

After Sharif-Emami's resignation, the Shah established a military government on November 6. He blamed his decision on the opposition's refusal to join a coalition government. Logically the justification would seem questionable. If the installation of the military government reflected merely the end of the search for a coalition government, as he contended, then why did the Shah continue the search after the fall of the Sharif-Emami government? Another explanation might be sought in a well-known telephone call to the Shah by the U.S. national security advisor on November 3. According to the Shah, Zbigniew Brzezinski called him "to urge that I establish law and order first, and only then continue our democratization programs."[22] But the Shah did not mention this advice to indicate that it influenced his decision. Rather, he cited it in order to criticize the incoherence of U.S. policy. He complained that he could not acquire a confirmation of Brzezinski's advice from Ambassador William Sullivan.

Two other explanations might be advanced. First, given the Shah's view of the overriding importance of the Iranian oil revenues for all his policies over the decades, the fact that the oil industry was crippled by October 31 might be cited as the main cause of his decision. None of the previous disruptions had posed such a threat to the Iranian oil industry as did the strike of oil workers at this particular time. The normal production of 5.8 million barrels of oil a day dropped to 1.1 million. The strike marked the failure of the Shah's efforts, through the head of the NIOC and his personal confidant, Hushang Ansary, to meet the demands of the oil workers. The only way to get the workers back to work would be by the threat of dismissal backed by the use of military force.

Second, an explanation might be sought in the unprecedented violence and destruction involved in the disturbances that broke out at the University of Tehran on November 4. This incident became subsequently one of the landmark dates in the history of the revolution. On the anniversary of that date, the U.S. Embassy was seized one year later. The destruction of the Shah's statues during the November 4 disturbances must have symbolically had a traumatic effect on the Shah—the same had been done to his statues in the 1953 crisis.

There must be an element of truth in all the above explanations. But I believe the Shah's decision to establish a military government reflected a more natural reaction of the Shah to political opposition. That reaction corresponded more to Iran's own authoritarian tradition, and to the Shah's own basic sense of personal insecurity. Neither that tradition, nor that personality easily fitted the U.S. expectations of the Shah's adherence to such norms as compromise, dialogue, coalition, reconciliation, and others in dealing with the opposition. In fact, his abiding suspicion of a U.S. plot to overthrow him further prompted him to act on his own instinct, to demonstrate his strength to his Iranian opponents, his U.S. detractors, who wished to dump him, and his supporters in Washington, who kept telling him to stand firm.

The Shah's choice of officials for the military government could not have been more provocative to the opposition. This was particularly true of the two top leaders. General Gholam Reza Azhari, the chief of staff of the armed forces, who was appointed prime minister, was perceived to be too closely identified with the United States. He had received his command training at the U.S. Army General Staff College at Fort Leavenworth, Kansas, and had also received military police training in the United States. General Gholam Reza Oveisi, who was made the minister of labor in the hope that he would be able to end the oil workers' strikes, was even more disliked by the opposition. He had played a key role in the bloody suppression of the religious opposition in the historic crisis of June 1963; even worse, he had been the martial law administrator during the massacre of "Black Friday."

The methods of the military government were also perplexing. One could imagine why the head of SAVAK and Prime Minister Hoveyda, for example, were arrested. The former was a main target of the opposition, and the latter was particularly disliked by the clergy presumably for his basically secular orientation, although some believed that he was also suspected of having pro-Bahai sympathies. Others might have viewed Hoveyda as a symbol of the extravagance of a corrupt regime and the longstanding instrument of the Shah's own grandiose economic and military ambitions, which cost the nation billions of dollars, although the former prime minister himself could not be accused of personal corruption. But the arrest of Dr. Karim Sanjabi seemed to contradict the Shah's avowed intention to form a coalition government.

The royal family's own halfhearted measures during the military government continued to have no softening effect on the opposition. The Shah's surprising admission of past "mistakes" on November 6, his imposition of a "code of conduct" on his family, his wife's pilgrimage to the holy city of Najaf in Iraq—the first such visit by a member of the royal family in 25 years—and even his increase in pardoning political prisoners were regarded by the opposition either as cynical moves or simply the signs of increasing weakness. The announcement of the findings by the representatives of the U.N.-affiliated International League for Human Rights in Paris on November 23, in particular, confirmed the opposition's insistence that the Shah had failed, despite all his promises, to carry out fundamental changes in the treatment of political prisoners. The league's representatives reported that thousands of prisoners were still being held, political offenses were still being dealt with by military courts, and, above all, only the accent of torture had changed from physical to psychological methods.[23]

The regime's presumed twin objective of restoring law and order, especially in the oilfields, and forming a coalition government was not realizable. The ending of the massive strike by oil workers was regarded as the acid test of the military government's ability to restore law and order throughout the country. It was also regarded as the last alternative of the Shah in combatting the opposition. At first it appeared that the government was succeeding. More than 60 percent of oil workers returned to their jobs on November 13, a development that was considered a "setback" for the opposition. But the apparent government "victory" in the oilfield was marred immediately by the first major clash between the striking Bazaaris and the government troops since the establishment of the military government. Furthermore, the oil workers went back to a massive strike again on December 4, despite the government's threats of dismissal.

The military government's show of strength in establishing law and order suffered an even more resounding defeat outside the oilfields. In an attempt to prevent violent demonstrations, the government announced, on November 28, a total ban on "all processions in any form" during the holy month of *Muharram*. This ruling was especially directed toward the anticipated Shi'i Muslim passionate mourning of the martyrdom of Ali ibn al-Hussain, the Prophet's grandson and the third Imam of the Shi'i community, and his family (*ahl al-bayt*) in the bloody battle at Karbala (681 A.D.).[24] Azhari's persistent defense of the virtues of the Shah's regime at such a turbulent time, and particularly his impolitical claim that only 200,000 of Tehran's nearly 4.5 million people had participated in the previous months' anti-Shah demonstrations were even more provocative than his ban on religious processions per se. A few days before the critical ninth and tenth days of *Muharram*, *Tasou'a*, and *Ashura* in the Shi'i calendar, the opposition responded by organizing a demonstration by thousands of people at the symbolically important *Behesht-e Zahra* cemetery, where most of the martyrs of the opposition to the Shah are buried. The embattled military government finally struck a last-minute compromise with the opposition on December 8, reversing its earlier martial law ban on anti-Shah protest demonstrations. On December 11 the opposition brought out the largest crowds across the nation—some estimates ranged up to 7 million—and the least violent.[25]

The presumed objective of forming a coalition government was even more unrealizable during the military government than during the government of Sharif-Emami. The fundamental reason remained the same—the Shah would not share any real power with the opposition. But the subsidiary reason was no less important. The National Front elements of the opposition formed a *tactical* united front with the Ayatollah Khomeini. The Ayatollah had set up his headquarters near Paris on October 6, exactly a month before the establishment of the military government. It had used beneficially all the advantages of international communication facilities for the twin purpose of mobilizing the masses in Iran behind the Ayatollah's uncompromising demand for the destruction of the Shah's regime and the Pahlavi dynasty and the establishment of an Islamic republic. On October 28 Dr. Karim Sanjabi, the leader of the National Front, Haj Mahmoud Manian, the leader of the Bazaaris and the guilds affiliated with the Front, and Mehdian, a prominent Bazaari figure went to France for discussions with the Ayatollah.[26] The exact details of the subsequent discussions are not fully known, but it is clear that the leaders from Iran accepted the Ayatollah's overall leadership of the religious *and* political opposition.[27]

What did this mean? It meant a total change in the position of the National Front on the Shah's regime. During the Sharif-Emami premiership, Dr. Sanjabi had suggested the formation of a provisional government and the holding of free elections that presumably would have led to a constitutional monarchy. After his return from Paris, and in the course of his arrest in Tehran, in a major statement to the press on November 10 he said, "The national and Islamic movement of Iran would not agree to any kind of government with the presence of the illegal monarchical regime."[28] This position was based on a three-point statement of Dr. Sanjabi issued on November 5 at the end of his talks with Ayatollah Khomeini and Mehdi Bazargan in France. It condemned the monarchy as "illegitimate," both legally and religiously. It decried the possibility that their "National Islamic Movement of Iran" would form any coalition government while the "illegal monarchy" remained in power, and it called for a referendum to establish a national government on the basis of "Islam, democracy and independence." A statement from Bazargan's Iran Freedom Movement, similar in content, accompanied this declaration of the National Front.[29]

The military government threw Dr. Sanjabi into jail, and also

Daryush Forouher, the National Front spokesman, on November 11, barely a day after they had returned from Paris. In keeping with his divide-and-rule practice, the Shah then turned to another member of the National Front, Dr. Gholam Hussain Sadiqi. The Shah said that Sadiqi was a "patriot," but rejected his suggestion for the formation of a Regency Council, while the Shah remained in Iran, "because it implied that I was incompetent to perform my duties as a sovereign."[30] The Shah did not give any credit to Dr. Ali Amini late in the crisis on November 1.[31] The Shah still nursed the old grudge against Dr. Amini, as seen in connection with the crisis of 1960–63. After having kept Dr. Sanjabi in jail for about 26 days (the Shah says a "few days" in his book), he then turned to him to form a coalition government! He knew well that it was much too late to obtain Sanjabi's cooperation, especially in the light of the Khomeini-Sanjabi tactical alliance against his regime. Nevertheless, he simply went through the motions with no intention of sharing power. From what the Shah himself said subsequently, it is clear that he rejected Dr. Sanjabi's demand for a Regency Council and for his departure from Iran.[32] He did both later when he absolutely had no choice.

Quite apart from the Khomeini-Sanjabi common opposition to the Shah's regime at this time, the spectacular demonstrations of *Ashura*, mentioned before, had had an emboldening effect on the opposition leaders in general and Dr. Sanjabi in particular. The National Front had been the guiding force behind the peaceful demonstrations.[33] To head off any rumors about a secret deal between Dr. Sanjabi and the Shah, the National Front issued a statement on December 14, repeating confidently its position since November 5: "The national and Islamic movements of the Islamic people will never agree to any combination of government with the present illegal regime."[34]

THE BAKHTIAR GOVERNMENT

Having refused to consider any diminution of his absolute power and yet faced with the ever-present reality of dwindling authority, the Shah finally turned to Shahpour Bakhtiar, a National Front leader, to form a civilian government. Bakhtiar had said on December 20, "If the Shah agrees publicly to a reduced role and the United States declares that it would not support him if he goes back on his commitment, then I believe many opposition leaders would end their insistence that he abdicate, would join a coalition government and even accept that he remain commander-in-chief of the armed forces."[35] Even before events proved him wrong, there was no basis for such a conviction at this time in view of the opposition's well-known rejection of any deal with the Shah's regime since November 5. According to the Shah's subsequent accounts, Bakhtiar had been in contact with the Shah through former Prime Minister Amuzegar, a "trusted advisor," but this time General Nasser Moqaddam, the head of SAVAK, asked the Shah if he would see Bakhtiar. The Shah asked him to form a civilian government on December 29, but he said later that he did so "with some reluctance and under foreign pressure."[36] Although he indicated that he finally decided to appoint Bakhtiar after he was strongly endorsed by Lord George Brown, the former foreign secretary of Britain and a friend of the Shah, it is by no means certain that Brown is the source of the alleged "foreign pressure." Did he then mean U.S. pressure? We do not really know, but he probably did. He claimed that the United States had insisted on the idea of talking with the opposition, especially the National Front elements. We know this is true, but that did not necessarily mean that Washington pressed for Bakhtiar. His appointment might have even been a surprise.[37]   Actually, the U.S. was simply informed after the fact.

Having gone against the express policy of the National Front, Bakhtiar was immediately expelled from the organization. Personal rivalry between him and Dr. Sanjabi also played a part in the expulsion. Bakhtiar's real problems, however, stemmed from other factors. He generally lacked popular support, was considered to be "anti-religious," was related to the infamous General Taymour Bakhtiar, the first head of the hated SAVAK, was appointed by the Shah, and was believed to lack the support of the armed forces. From his own perspective, however, Bakhtiar had succeeded in negotiations with the Shah where Dr. Sanjabi and others before him had failed. The Shah would agree to leave the country "provisionally," and he would also agree to the formation of a Regency Council. He did not insist on the abdication of the Shah, presumably because he believed that the armed forces would split into several factions, "coup would follow coup and Iran would drift into chaos or civil war." He said it was up to the Shah to decide whether to resume the throne personally or to step aside in favor of his son. He would agree to the return of the Shah once calm prevailed in Iran, but then only as a constitutional monarch. "If he tried to come back," he said, "as an absolute ruler I will fight him with all my strength, as I always have."[38]

Bakhtiar did manage to get the Shah to leave the country on January 16, 1979. He had already established a Regency Council to perform the Shah's duties in his absence, and the Majlis approved of his Cabinet on the same day that the Shah left. In departing Iran, the Shah had very few words to say, but he managed to cling to his aspiration for "the preservation of the present system." About a week or so before his departure, he had said in an interview that he had been tempted to try to repeat the 1953 experience. At his departure, did he believe that he would ever be able to return? In his farewell remarks, he said that he was going "on vacation because I am feeling tired," and it is well known that he lingered in Egypt and Morocco after leaving Iran. Perhaps he still hoped to return. In the next chapter, we shall take up the U.S. role in his departure during the eventful first two weeks of January. It is enough to say here that the Shah later said sarcastically that "interestingly enough" the plans for his departure had been announced in Washington on January 11 by Secretary of State Cyrus Vance. More interestingly, the Shah quoted approvingly his former commander of the Iranian Air Force, General Rabi'ei, who had said that "General Huyser threw the Shah out of the country like a dead mouse."[39] The Shah blamed his ouster undoubtedly on the United States. As seen in this study, he had all along suspected the U.S. intentions toward him since the election of President Carter. His own conflicting perceptions of himself as an all-powerful sovereign but an all-powerless monarch under adverse circumstances was one aspect of his complex personality.

With the Shah's departure, the struggle with the opposition was taken up mainly by Bakhtiar. Khomeini welcomed the Shah's departure as "the first step toward complete abdication of 50 years of Pahlavi brutality." He called on his supporters to participate in a massive demonstration against the Bakhtiar government, appealed to the military and the police to support his movement and to abandon the Shah, demanded the removal of the Regency Council and the resignation of the Cabinet ministers and the members of Parliament, and requested his supporters to maintain public order. Dr. Sanjabi regarded the Shah's departure as the fulfillment of only one of the preliminary demands of the opposition, and said that the struggle would continue until the monarchy was overthrown.

The key question, however, was how the armed forces would

behave. Would they attempt a coup after the Shah's departure? Would they support the Bakhtiar government? Would they split into pro- and anti-Khomeini factions? After all, the armed forces had always been the main pillar of the Shah's support. Personal allegiance of the military commanders to the Shah could mean that a switch of loyalty to Khomeini or Bakhtiar would be resisted. The danger of division among the commanders was real by this time. The breakdown among the rank and file had already surfaced. The first case of serious breakdown was reported in mid-December following the massive and peaceful demonstrations of *Ashura*, mentioned before. At Lavizan Base, the headquarters of the Iranian ground forces, the Imperial Guard killed 12 of their officers. More significantly, the disenchantment had affected the air force, the service believed to be most ardently in favor of the Shah. Army insubordination was reported during another demonstration against the Shah in Tabriz, where a unit mutinied and joined the protestors. Just before and after the Shah's departure, in responding to Khomeini's call on the military to disobey the government, troops openly fraternized with the opposition groups, stuck red carnations into the muzzles of their rifles, and shouted "Down with the Shah."

The position of the generals, however, was not all that clear. Before January 16 it was reported that 20 of them had gone on record opposing the Shah's departure. This had troubled Bakhtiar, who had also suffered a major setback in forming his cabinet when General Feraidoun Jam, a well-regarded former chief of staff and a former brother-in-law of the Shah, reportedly turned down the post of defense minister. After the Shah's departure, the possibility of a coup, at least by those who had opposed the Shah's departure initially, took on added significance. General Abbas Qarabaghi, Iran's chief of staff of the armed forces, however, tried to discount speculations about a coup by saying categorically on January 16, "I am confident that no coup will take place," and such a possibility "is incomprehensible" (*ghair-e qabel-e tassavor ast*).[40] A few days later, he repeated the same point, saying that the military "will support the constitutional government," namely, the Bakhtiar government.[41]

Despite the military's avowed public support of the Bakhtiar government, its real position remained ambiguous. Two days after the Shah's departure, the representatives of Ayatollah Khomeini and the Iranian generals reportedly started secret negotiations about the "future of the country" apparently with the knowledge of

Bakhtiar, but without his direct involvement. And when Khomeini announced on January 20 his intention to return to Iran shortly, the negotiations acquired a special sense of urgency.[42] Both sides talked sternly about the consequences of Khomeini's return to Iran and the reaction of the military. Bakhtiar said, "martyrs who recently fell in Iran did not die so that one rotten dictatorship would be replaced by another as a new repression,"[43] and claimed that Khomeini's return could "throw the country into an unprecedented major national crisis." In a letter to Khomeini, Bakhtiar warned of an army takeover if he returned to Iran, but coupled this with an expression of his willingness to accept changes based on "democratic traditions." The latter was a clear rejection of Khomeini's previously announced plan to establish a revolutionary council and a provisional government of his own in order to push through a referendum designed to transform Iran from a monarchy into an Islamic republic.[44] On the Khomeini side, Ayatollah Mahmoud Taleqani—the religious leader of Tehran and a long-time political prisoner of the Shah, who had been released just before the *Ashura* demonstrations—said that the opposition was determined to supplant the Cabinet of Bakhtiar, and warned that the Iranian people might undertake a "holy war" against the army if it attempted a coup.[45]

Ayatollah Khomeini returned to Iran triumphantly on February 1, 1979 after a delay because of a meaningless closing down of the airports. Welcomed by millions of supporters, he lost no time in visiting the *Behesht-e Zahra* cemetery where he declared that the Shah, his father, the Parliament, and the Bakhtiar government were all "illegal." On the third day after returning he said, "we will not resort to violent means," and invited the military "for their own good and the nation's good to be with us. . . ."[46] On February 5, Khomeini named Mehdi Bazargan to head a "provisional government," and warned that anyone who opposed it would be treated "very harshly" as a violator of Islamic law.[47] Not having any alternative, Bakhtiar pretended that the new government of his old friend Bazargan was a "shadow government." At the same time, he tried to meet some of the demands of the Ayatollah Khomeini. He dismantled the hated SAVAK, arrested those in high places deemed guilty of gross corruption, and dismissed "undesirable" ambassadors abroad, including Ardeshir Zahedi in Washington.[48] His foreign minister, Ahmad Mirfendereski, declared Iran's withdrawal from the Central Treaty Organization. Other measures included slashing extravagant arms purchases from the United States and Britain, cutting off future oil supplies to Israel and South Africa, supporting the cause of the Palestinians, and renouncing any role for Iran as the "policeman" of the Persian Gulf.[49]

Despite these and other gestures, the Bakhtiar government finally fell, largely because the military withdrew its support from it on February 11, 1979. The first and only armed clashes occurred near the end of 48 hours of clashes between the armed elements of the conflicting forces. Stripped of all the underbrush of fact and fiction surrounding the revolutionary seizure of power on February 10–11, there are a number of major questions to be considered briefly. To begin with, what triggered the armed conflict? At least two major theories might be advanced. First, the violence erupted as a result of the rebellion of the air force's technical personnel (*homafars*) and a small number of pro-Khomeini officers at *Doshan Tappeh* air base, and the response of some elements of the 20,000-man Imperial Guard, led by the 5,000 "Immortals" (*sepah-e javidan*). The 220,000-man army, the 100,000-man air force, and the 22,000-man navy were *not* involved in the fighting. Over the previous three months, rebellious acts had taken place primarily in the country's air bases, and the *homafars*-cadets thesis would seem to fit the existing pattern. Second, the violence was unleashed by some elements of the extremely loyal Imperial Guard of the Shah, and the response of the *homafars* and the cadets aided by revolutionary forces and segments of the civilian population.

There is enough evidence to support tentatively either of these two major theories, but in either case two questions of larger significance remain to be considered: First, why did the *homafars* and air force cadets prove to be so rebellious all along? Second, what other major elements of the opposition would seem to have been largely involved? Reportedly, the *homafars* were relatively well-educated technicians who had received training abroad, many of them in the United States; they were not known as being particularly religious; and their favorable response to Khomeini's revolutionary call might have been partly because of alienation for not having had officer status.[50] Regarding the second question, apparently the *Fada'eyin-e Khalq* underground group was involved in the initial fighting at *Doshan Tappeh* air base on February 10, while the *Mujaheddin-e Khalq* group joined the fighting at the *Eshrat Abad* military base on February 11.[51] If so, these involvements marked the first instance in which the main guerrilla elements of the opposition waged armed struggle against the Shah's regime. As such, they also marked the first and only departure from the peaceful strategy that the opposition had pursued during the revolution until the seizure of power.

As far as is known, the decision of the military to declare itself "neutral" in the Bakhtiar-Bazargan power struggle did not include all the commanders. A day before the seizure of power began by the revolutionary forces at the *Doshan Tappeh* air base, Bazargan conceded that some of Iran's military leaders were opposed to the establishment of an Islamic republic, and then warned the senior generals not to incur the popular wrath and the "revenge of God" by reacting against his government.[52] Reportedly, Bazargan, Bakhtiar, and General Qarabaghi met with General Abdul Ali Badri, commander of the Imperial Guard, and another hard-liner General Amir Rabi'ei, commander of the air force, during the February 10–11 fighting. The latter was persuaded to join the revolution. But General Badri reportedly drew his revolver and threatened to fight anyone who acted "unconstitutionally," that is, against the Shah-appointed Bakhtiar government. Although the general finally went along with the others apparently in favor of declaring the military neutral, he was killed the following day by his fellow officers.[53]

DOMESTIC INFLUENCE BALANCE SHEET

Thus, the Shah-appointed government of Bakhtiar fell when the central pillar of the Shah's regime disintegrated. It showed the tenacious hold of historical and cultural patterns on the Iranian society. All the decades of the Shah's domestic socioeconomic co-option, political maneuvers, clever methods and tactics of divide and rule, U.S. support, and a degree of general diplomatic legitimacy in world politics were not enough to save his throne, once it became evident that not only the bases of his domestic legitimacy, but also the central element of his authority, were destroyed. As most historical Iranian monarchs, he had relied most of all on the military to maintain his rule for a time. But also as most historical Iranian monarchs, he lost his throne when he no longer enjoyed either internal legitimacy or authority.

He lost to the revolutionary forces largely because they succeeded in convincing the masses that they, rather than the Shah, had the "real" claim to legitimacy and authority, and mobilized them effectively against the Shah. No single expression was so often used by the Ayatollah Khomeini, in his campaign against the Shah, as the "illegitimate regime." He invoked all kinds of religious symbols to mobilize the alienated crowds and to goad even the modern-educated elements to accept his overall leadership, and in the end his counterinfluence prevailed over the royal influence and power. He was able to lead the deeply heterogeneous forces of the opposition against the Shah largely because they had one thing in common, their opposition to the Shah. Beyond that the tenacious problems of continuity and change haunted Iranian society. No two sociopolitical groups agreed on the basic conceptions of legitimacy, authority, and capacity in spite of the revolution.

NOTES

1. See Mohammad Reza Pahlavi, *Answer to History* (New York: Stein and Day, 1980), p. 150.
2. *Ettela'at*, July 12, 1978.
3. *Washington Post*, January 20, 1979.
4. Pahlavi, *Answer to History*, p. 153.
5. *Ettela'at*, February 21 and 23, 1978.
6. *Washington Post*, March 4, 1978.
7. *Ettela'at*, February 28, 1978.
8. Pahlavi, *Answer to History*, p.154.
9. *Ettela'at*, May 16 and 18, 1978.
10. For the text of the Shah's statement, see *Ettela'at*, May 10, 1978.
11. *Washington Post*, August 21, 1978.
12. *Ettela'at*, August 31, 1978.
13. Pahlavi, *Answer to History*, p. 160.
14. *Washington Post*, September 9, 1978.
15. Pahlavi, *Answer to History*, p. 160.
16. *Washington Post*, September 12, 1978.
17. *Ettela'at*, September 26, 1978.
18. Ibid., September 19, 1978.
19. For the text of Sharif-Emami's statement to the Majlis, see ibid.
20. Pahlavi, *Answer to History*, p. 164.
21. Ibid.
22. Ibid., p. 165.
23. *New York Times*, November 24, 1978.
24. On the religio-political significance of this battle, see Abdulaziz Abdul-hussein Sachadina, *Islamic Messianism: The Idea of the Mahdi in Twelver Shi'ism* (Albany: State University of New York Press, 1981), esp. pp. 159-60; and Michael M. J. Fischer, *Iran: From Religious Dispute to Revolution* (Cambridge, Mass.: Harvard University Press, 1980), esp. pp. 128-29.

25. *New York Times*, December 12, 1978.

26. *Ettela'at*, October 28, 1978.

27. Ibid., October 30, 1978.

28. For the text of Sanjabi's statement, see *Komiteh Baray-e Defa'a Az Hoquq-e Bashar va Pishraft-e An dar Iran*, no. 16, Day 10, 1357, pp. 99–100.

29. For the texts of both these important documents, see ibid.

30. Pahlavi, *Answer to History*, p. 168.

31. For the text of Dr. Amini's statement see *Ettela'at*, November 2, 1978.

32. Pahlavi, *Answer to History*, p. 169.

33. *New York Times*, December 15, 1978.

34. Ibid.

35. Ibid., December 23, 1978.

36. Pahlavi, *Answer to History*, p. 171.

37. *New York Times*, January 4, 1979.

38. Ibid., December 31, 1978.

39. Pahlavi, *Answer to History*, p. 173.

40. The text of Qarabaghi's interview is in *Kayhan*, January 16, 1979.

41. *New York Times*, January 23, 1979.

42. Ibid., January 21, 1979.

43. Ibid.

44. *Washington Post*, January 26, 1979.

45. *New York Times*, January 23, 1979.

46. Ibid., February 4, 1979.

47. See the February 6, 1979 editions of *Christian Science Monitor*, *New York Times*, and *Washington Post*.

48. *Christian Science Monitor*, February 8, 1979.

49. Ibid.; and *New York Times*, February 7, 1979.

50. *New York Times*, February 11, 1979.

51. *Christian Science Monitor*, February 12, 1979.

52. *Washington Post*, February 10, 1979.

53. *New York Times*, February 13, 1979.

7

THE U.S. ROLE IN THE
IRANIAN REVOLUTION AND
THE COLLAPSE OF U.S. INFLUENCE

The Iranian Revolution was intimately interrelated with the influence of a major foreign power, as were its two major historical antecedents—the Constitutional Revolution and the 1951–53 nationalist movement. The first one had aimed principally at the limitation of domestic tyranny under the Qajar monarchy and the elimination of Russian dominance in Iran, and the second one at the limitation of the Shah's powers and elimination of British power and influence in Iran. The Iranian Revolution of 1978–79 aimed at the destruction of the Shah's regime and the elimination of U.S. power and influence in Iran. What was the U.S. role in this revolution, and how did the revolutionary process affect the many years of U.S. influence in Iran?

THE U.S. ROLE: THE EARLY PHASE

On December 31, 1977 the Shah told President Carter at Niavaran Palace how highly he valued the "special relationship" (*ravabet-e khass*) between their two countries; he tried to depict its historical roots and its mutually beneficial foundations, and cited an Iranian tradition that the "first guest in the new year is an omen for that year" and that since Carter was the guest "we consider it an excellent omen."[1] The president outdid his Iranian host in the exercise of hyperbole. He told the Shah, "Iran is an island of stability in one of the more troubled areas of the world. This is a tribute to the respect the people give to you."[2] The Shah later wrote, "I have never heard a foreign statesman speak of me in quite such flattering terms as he used that evening," and quoted Carter as saying, "Our talks have been priceless, our friendship is irreplaceable, and my own gratitude is to the Shah, who in his wisdom and with his experience has been so helpful to me, a new leader."[3] Princess Ashraf, the influential twin sister of the Shah, quoted the president at greater length than his brother, but apparently did not believe a word of what the president had said. "As he spoke," she wrote later, "I looked at his pale face. I thought his smile was artificial, his eyes icy—and I hoped I could trust him."[4] But she did not, and later charged that the president's various actions led to her brother's ultimate downfall.

The president also thought that his visit with the Shah on the eve of the new year was a favorable harbinger of things to come, but it did not turn out that way for either of the two leaders. As seen, the first major disturbance of the revolution broke out at Qom on the ninth day of 1978, when the Shah's troops fired lethal weapons into unarmed crowds engaged in a peaceful demonstration. The demonstration had been provoked by the publication of an insulting letter on the Ayatollah Khomeini in the government-controlled press. As also seen, this incident was followed by three other landmark disturbances—at Tabriz, where many thousands participated and many hundreds died, at Abadan where 399 innocent people were burned to death in the Rex Cinema, and in Tehran where thousands of unarmed people lost their lives on "Black Friday." Did any of these incidents effect a change in the U.S. appraisal of the Iranian situation, most particularly the estimate of the stability of the Shah's regime? Was the intelligence community's assessment, after these incidents had taken place, any different from the previous assessments? An intelligence report during the Republican administration, made only weeks before the change of administration, asserted that Iran was likely to remain stable under the Shah over the next several years, that it would continue its commitment to the United States as long as the Shah ruled, and that the chances were good that Iran would have relatively little trouble until at least the mid-1980s. More than half a year after the change of administration, another intelligence study assumed, in August 1977, that the Shah "will be an active participant in Iranian life well into the 1980's," and that there "will be no radical change in Iranian political behavior in the near future."[5] About eight months after the start of the disturbances, a better-known intelligence study asserted in its preface that Iran "is not in a revolutionary or even a 'prerevolutionary' situation."[6] Yet by this time 20 other disturbances had occurred in scores of Iranian cities and towns, in addition to the crucial incidents at Qom, Tabriz, and Abadan.

Did the intelligence estimate of the Iranian situation change, especially after "Black Friday" when, as seen in the preceding chapter, the troops fired into the unarmed crowds during the government of Sharif-Emami? On September 28, only 20 days after this disaster, a "prognosis" asserted that the Shah "is expected to remain actively in power over the next ten years."[7] While certain reports of the intelligence community indicated that the Shah "appeared to be losing his grip, and that the social fabric of Iran was unravelling," a staff report of the Subcommittee on Evaluation on Intelligence in the U.S. House of Representatives claimed that the reports of the first nine months of 1978, on the whole, "did not suggest that disturbances had exceeded the bounds of previous crises which the Shah had weathered."[8]

The policy community was no less optimistic about the Iranian situation during the governments of Amuzegar and Sharif-Emami in 1978. The president's favorable perception of the stability of the Shah's rule and the soundness of the basic U.S. approach toward Iran would seem to have been widely shared in the U.S. policy community before the fall of the government of Sharif-Emami. Apart from its rhetorical flourish, the president's flattering New Year's Eve remarks about Iran's stability and about the Shah's legitimacy seemed unshaken by the subsequent crucial disturbances. For example, two days after the massacre on "Black Friday," he called the Shah in order to express not only his regrets at the violent incident, but also to reaffirm his hopes for political liberalization and his support for the Shah.[9] He refrained, in his subsequent remarks on Iran, from referring to his call, and the Shah completely denied having received such a call even after his downfall.[10]

To cite another major example of the president's optimistic view of Iran and the soundness of the U.S. approach, the president's remarks of October 31 are particularly informative. They were made less than a week before the fall of the government of Sharif-Emami and the establishment of the military government. They were also made at a time when the Iranian crisis had reached a new peak. The president told Crown Prince Reza, who was visiting at the White House on the occasion of his eighteenth birthday, "We are thankful for his [the Shah's] move toward democracy. We know it is opposed by some who don't like democratic principles, but his progressive administration is very valuable, I think, to the entire Western world."[11] We may recall from the previous chapter that by the time the president was sounding these optimistic notes, not only had the massacre of "Black Friday" under the "progressive administration" of Sharif-Emami crowned the previous crucial disturbances at Qom, Tabriz, and Abadan, but Iranian oil production had been crippled by strikes.

The president's persistently optimistic perception of the Iranian situation despite the overwhelming evidence to the contrary paralleled the unrealistic approach of his administration toward Iran. The main thrust of that approach was two-pronged. It aimed at "political liberalization" by the Shah, with U.S. support for the Shah presumably toward that goal. This twofold approach had developed during the first year of the Carter Administration, as seen in Chapter 5. It remained basically the same during the government of Prime Minister Hoveyda and those of Amuzegar and Sharif-Emami. As such, it favored Sharif-Emami's "conciliatory" policies toward the moderate elements of the opposition, which meant largely the National Front and the perceived moderate elements of the clergy in Iran, such as the Ayatollah Shariatmadari. The fundamental assumption underlying this twofold approach must have been that the Shah was both willing and able to compromise at least with the moderate elements of the opposition. In view of the Iranian situation in general, and the Shah's tenacious hold on power long before the crisis, that assumption seems to have been unrealistic. Furthermore, during the crisis, the Shah repeatedly refused to even consider sharing power with anyone. According to his own testimony, he simply found the demands of the opposition leaders whom he contacted "unacceptable."

THE UNITED STATES AND
THE MILITARY GOVERNMENT

Yet this twofold approach continued even after the fall of the civilian government of Sharif-Emami and the actual establishment of the military government on November 6, although the Shah appointed General Azhari as prime minister the night before. Secretary of State Cyrus Vance hurried to express U.S. support for the new military government immediately after its establishment. He said,

"We fully support the efforts of the Shah to restore order while continuing his program of liberalization."[12] The statement revealed that the administration as a whole intended to continue the two-pronged approach. It also seemed to reveal that, despite the administration's belated anxiety, the fundamental assumption that the Shah was willing and able to compromise with the opposition continued to underpin the administration's basic approach. The Department of State insisted that the military government should be seen as part of the process of liberalization! And the U.S. officials in Tehran and Washington either believed the Shah's claim that he had appointed the military government because the opposition refused to join a coalition government, or they parrotted the Shah's line without really being convinced. Ambassador William Sullivan reportedly said in Tehran on November 12, "We are aware that the political options were closing out for the Shah because opposition leaders refused to join a coalition and we told Washington what that meant."[13]

While the deepening crisis in Iran did not seem to have made the slightest change in the basic thrust of the U.S. approach toward the Shah, congressional concerns seem to have first surfaced publicly after the tragedy of "Black Friday." For example, the Senate Foreign Relations Committee reportedly held a closed session on September 15 on demonstrations in Iran, when Jack C. Miklos and Henry Precht of the Department of State's Bureau of Near Eastern and South Asian Affairs appeared before the committee. On September 27, Robert R. Bowie, the director of the CIA's National Foreign Assessment, appeared before the committee in another secret session, and according to those who heard him, he gave "an optimistic view of the situation in Iran."[14]

The president, however, finally said on November 11 that he was "not satisfied" with U.S. political intelligence; this was about ten months after the start of disturbances in Iran. Reportedly he sent a handwritten directive to Secretary of State Cyrus Vance, National Security Advisor Zbigniew Brzezinski, and the CIA director, Stansfield Turner. But implicitly the directive's criticism was reportedly "aimed mainly at Turner."[15] The president's letter also directed the three officials to sit down together and jointly recommend a specific program to improve the quality of intelligence gathering and its analysis "as soon as possible." The "intelligence failure" that prompted the president's note was attributed to two reasons: first, that the CIA's "partnership" with SAVAK had impeded the development of independent U.S. sources of reporting on Iranian internal matters; and second, that there was an "agreement" with the Shah, either explicit or tacit, that the United States would have nothing to do with his opponents in terms of contacting the opposition forces "without the Shah's knowledge."[16] Apparently the "ban" on U.S. contacts with the opposition forces had emerged as early as the mid-1960s and was not lifted until weeks after the presidential directive, although other reports indicated that the United States had initiated substantial and continuous contacts with the opposition, and had so informed the Shah.

The leak of the presidential note brought the simmering passing of blame in the Washington bureaucracy out into the open. Reportedly, within the intelligence community it was "widely believed" that Brzezinski had played a key role in "making public" the president's directive. It was also charged that he had apparently convinced the president that the failure to predict events in Iran had been largely the result of the cutback of CIA operatives, ordered by Admiral Turner in 1977.[17] The widely rumored general disagreement between Brzezinski and Vance on foreign policy issues, and their divergent philosophical standpoints also surfaced during the bitter debate on the Iranian crisis. The former allegedly refused to permit a State Department review of potential Iranian problems to be placed on the agenda for a Cabinet-level meeting.[18]

While the finger pointing and internecine squabbling in Washington continued, the military government of General Azhari was brought to its knees by the opposition during the massive, peaceful demonstrations held during the mourning processions on *Tasu'a* and *Ashura* (December 10 and especially 11). Just before these anticipated processions took place, the president seemed for the first time to be publicly uncertain about the future of the Shah. Asked by reporters if he thought that the Shah would survive, he responded, "I don't know. I hope so. This is something that is in the hands of the people of Iran."[19] At the same time, the Pentagon flew five water-cannon riot control trucks to Iran to provide emergency help for the Shah. One wonders whether the course of the revolution might have changed if the United States had sent the Shah riot control equipment after the Qom riots about a year earlier, or whether it would have stopped the Shah's security forces from firing into unarmed crowds with lethal weapons throughout the year. In any event, buoyed by the peaceful nature of the mourning processions, the president said on December 12, "I fully expect the Shah to maintain power in Iran [and] for the present problems in Iran to be resolved."[20]

A day later, administration officials were told at the White House that the Shah could not hope to maintain power. George W. Ball, a former under-Secretary of State and a well-known foreign policy analyst, reportedly presented his conclusions at a Cabinet-level meeting; they were based on a study he had started on December 4 for the National Security Council's Special Coordination Committee. His secret report apparently included various alternatives, including the role of a constitutional monarch for the Shah with a council of respected, senior political figures, or notables, naming a civilian government to rule the country.[21]

Ball's proposal was refreshing against the backdrop of the administration's unrealistic assumption that the Shah was either able or willing to share power with the opposition. But in the light of the Khomeini-Sanjabi tactical alliance of November 5, mentioned in the previous chapter, I do not believe that it would have had a chance of success even if it had been accepted; it was already too late. A day after Ball's presentation at the White House, the Shah, coincidentally, talked to Dr. Sanjabi for an hour about the formation of a coalition government. As seen, the National Front immediately issued a statement on Dr. Sanjabi's meeting with the Shah, saying that the "national and Islamic movements" would "never agree to any combination with the present illegal government." Assuming that Ball's proposal was, in effect, aimed at U.S. disengagement from total support of the Shah, by the middle of December the Ayatollah Khomeini fully commanded the masses supporting the opposition. In addition Dr. Sanjabi, Mehdi Bazargan, and the leadership of the Bazaaris and the guilds affiliated with them all had shifted too far to the side of the "Islamic movement" to consider any feasible political option other than Khomeini's.

THE UNITED STATES AND THE SHAH'S DEPARTURE

Regardless of Ball's intervention, the administration was forced by the deepending crisis to consider courses of action other than the familiar one of supporting the Shah. The military government of General Azhari had proved to be a disaster. His heart attack on December 20 provided him with a face-saving way out of an impossible job. The Shah finally appointed a civilian prime minister, Shahpour Bakhtiar—whom he despised as much as Ali Amini. He seemed to believe that both of them were imposed on him by the United States, and in both instances by Democratic administrations. As previously seen, he did not mention what "foreign pressure" was exerted on him in favor of the appointment of Bakhtiar, but he was wrong if he meant the United States.

The Bakhtiar formula envisaged the formation of a Regency Council, the appointment of a Cabinet and the approval of the Majlis before the Shah would leave the country. The first two issues before the United States, therefore, were how to deal with the prime minister-designate and how to handle the departure of the Shah. Each issue seemed to present a different set of problems.

First, with respect to Bakhtiar, Washington was hardly sanguine about the chances for survival of his government, even if it could be officially formed. His immediate expulsion from the National Front, his perceived lack of popular support, probable opposition from the Ayatollah Khomeini, and uncertainty about the support of the armed forces in particular made him seem to be a bad risk. But he was, after all, the Shah's choice. Why not transfer the longstanding U.S. support of the Shah to his prime minister, especially when the overall approach of the administration was still opposed to dealing with the Ayatollah Khomeini?

The administration prematurely decided to support Bakhtiar. It said on January 4, 1979 that it was prepared "to cooperate fully" with the Bakhtiar government whether or not the Shah remained in Iran. The recognition of the prime minister-designate in advance of the formation of his government was probably intended to shore up the support of the armed forces for him. While Bakhtiar was telling U.S. officials that his government would maintain close relations with the United States, the Ayatollah Khomeini appeared to be offering the prospects of establishing good relations with the United States and its Western allies, and of supplying them with oil. In fact, he was trying to nudge Washington into speeding up the Shah's departure, and attempting to drive a wedge between the United States government and Bakhtiar. Khomeini linked the prospects of Iran's nonaligned good relations with the United States to two conditions: withdrawal of support from the Shah, and noninterference in Iran's internal affairs. The latter meant withdrawal of support from Bakhtiar. With respect to the Shah's departure, the Ayatollah said that he would feel "no hostility" toward the nations that offered the Shah political asylum, although Iran would still "pursue the Shah by legal means."[22]

Second, regarding the Shah's departure, Washington took its time in order to avoid the impression that the administration was pushing the Shah out of the country. Ambassador William Sullivan finally received instructions from Washington to reply in the affirmative if the Shah asked whether the ambassador thought he should leave. This act of diplomacy did not mollify the Shah; he specifically resented Secretary Vance's announcement of January 11 that the Shah would be leaving Iran for a vacation "in the next few days." The secretary's remark that the Shah's move was "a sound decision," and that the administration was dealing with the Shah as a "constitutional head of state" made little difference to the Shah. "Vacation" might well mean "abdication," and the remnant of authority that he would carry with him could also be snatched away by the United States. The Shah's long-held suspicion of the administration's wish to oust him appeared to be confirmed.

The administration's decision finally to concur in the Shah's departure seemed to indicate that it had at last faced the reality of the Shah's spent legitimacy, authority, and capacity for action. But its commitment to supporting the Bakhtiar government was, once again, unrealistic. How was the United States to maintain a government in power when it had no widespread popular support in the face of the formidable forces of opposition under the leadership of the Ayatollah Khomeini? The United States could not, of course, engineer either popularity for Bakhtiar or unpopularity for Khomeini. There were serious limits on the exercise of U.S. influence in Iran. Hence, the only feasible course appeared to be to induce the armed forces to support and, if need be, to defend the Bakhtiar government against the Khomeini onslaught. Yet this posed at least two major problems, if viewed in the context of the realities of the Iranian situation. First, the armed forces had always owed allegiance to the Shah above all else. For this important reason, some 20 military commanders initially went on record as opposing the Shah's departure. Second, by the time of the Shah's departure, the breakdown within the military had already surfaced on a number of occasions. Despite these serious limits on the United States' ability to influence the military to support and defend the Bakhtiar government, the administration apparently believed that it had such a capability because of its power to cut off U.S. supplies to the military, as it reportedly had done in early January when the Iranian generals were warned against engineering a coup that "seemed imminent."[23]

Ambassador William Sullivan, however, had chosen his own direction and made different arrangements with Bazargan before the appointment of the Bakhtiar government. He claims that as early as November 9 he had told Washington that if the military government failed the United States should anticipate the fall of the Shah and should make arrangements in advance to ensure that the armed forces would remain intact by being placed under the direction of "a government that would enjoy the support of the groups that would prevail after the success of the revolution and would have the blessing of Khomeini."[24] Sullivan also claims that the U.S. influence on the Iranian military was great enough to make such an arrangement stick. In his words, "Because the United States controlled the logistics for all sophisticated elements of the armed forces, there were means to assure the implementation of these arrangements."[25] Not having had any instructions from Washington, the ambassador went ahead and made arrangements with the revolutionary leaders in Tehran. Later, when the Bakhtiar government took office, he proposed that Washington send an emissary to Khomeini in order to acquire a firsthand acceptance by Khomeini of the arrangements he had made with Bazargan. The ambassador's view of his differences with Brzezinski should be read in the original, but what interests us here is that Sullivan, too, underestimated the personalistic nature of the allegiance of the armed forces and their divisions.

The administration still had to get the armed forces of Iran to support and defend the Bakhtiar government. General Robert Huyser, deputy commander of U.S. forces in Europe and deputy to Alexander Haig, was already in Iran with a mission. According to Ambassador Sullivan, Huyser's mission "was to assist in maintaining the integrity of the armed forces and in transferring their loyalty from the departing Shah to the Bakhtiar regime."[26] The press reports, however, indicated that that was only one of his missions, and mystery still seems to surround Huyser's role in those tumultuous days. If his main tasks were what the ambassador mentioned, then the general's role was an impossible mission. The military was too divided to shift its allegiance en bloc to Bakhtiar. Furthermore, as said before, the loyalty of the military was too personal to be simply transferred from the Shah to Bakhtiar.

Largely because of the withdrawal of support from Bakhtiar by the divided military, his government fell on the second day of armed clashes between the revolutionary and government forces. In the two-day-long fighting, several hundred persons were believed killed or injured, including the veteran Middle East correspondent Joe Alex Morris, Jr. of the *Los Angeles Times.* Amidst the heavy fighting, Iranian military helicopters at *Doshan Tappeh* Air Base evacuated 50 to 75 U.S. advisors working there. This evacuation seemed to fulfill the revolutionary slogan "We will destroy Yankee power in Iran."

COLLAPSE OF THE UNITED STATES-IRAN INFLUENCE RELATIONSHIP

In less than a year of revolutionary change, the entire quarter-century structure of the United States-Iran relationship began to collapse. Let us look at this in terms of the issues in which that relationship had developed. The Oil Service Company of Iran (OSCO) had continued its work since the start of the revolutionary process in January 1978, but the oil strikes in October and November took their toll. The U.S. imports of Iranian oil had averaged about 1 million barrels a day before the revolution, which was 10 percent of total U.S. imports and about 5 percent of its consumption; it fell to about half of that amount in 1979. It had climbed from zero in 1953 when the United States was not yet involved in the Iranian oil industry. Despite the fact that U.S. oil stocks amounted to a 70-day supply in 1979, as contrasted with 54 days in 1973 during the Arab oil embargo, oil prices increased twofold. Although the U.S. imports from Iran were nowhere as substantial as those of its Western allies and Japan, oil price increases affected the United States as well as other oil-consuming countries because of the integrated nature of the world oil system and international agreements. The fall of Iranian oil production from the prerevolutionary 5.5 million barrels a day fluctuated with the vicissitudes of the oil workers' strikes; it dropped down to as little as 450,000 barrels a day in February 1979. On the day of the Shah's departure (January 16, 1979) the spot-market prices were about $3 over the basic price of approximately $13 a barrel.[27]

The oil production disruption was not merely the result of the strikes. The Iranian oil industry had about 67,000 oil workers and

500 foreign employees, including 200 U.S. workers. Over several months these foreign technicians had been harassed and threatened by the militant elements of the opposition. The main targets, however, had been the U.S. employees: on November 13, 1978 the car of George Link, the U.S. general manager of the OSCO, was firebombed, but he escaped injury. On December 23, Paul Grimm, Link's deputy, was shot to death. The assassination was attributed to the *Mujaheddin*, who had murdered a number of U.S. workers over the years during the Shah's regime, as mentioned earlier.

Besides its impact on oil interests, the revolutionary process most adversely affected the U.S. arms sales in Iran. The record, however, shows an amazing attitude of "business as usual" on the part of the United States and the Shah during the first nine months of the revolution. The disturbances at Qom and Tabriz, the tragic fire at Abadan, and the massacre on "Black Friday" did not seem to make the slightest difference in the voracious appetite of the Shah for U.S. arms or the eagerness of U.S. arms manufacturers for sales. The Shah pressed ahead with his plans for a massive naval expansion worth more than $5 billion as late as March 1978;[28] President Carter approved the sale of nearly $600 million worth of U.S. arms, including 31 Phantom jet fighters as late as July; and in the same month, the Shah told Washington that he wanted to spend $2 billion for 70 more F-14 fighter planes, as if nothing were happening in Iran. On the day of the tragic fire at Abadan and the Shah's celebration of the overthrow of the Musaddeq government in 1953, it was reported that the Carter Administration had used a ploy to sell Iran exorbitantly expensive armed frigates without violating its own arms-sales ceiling. Nevertheless, some U.S. citizens were unhappy at not getting the full benefit of the deal. For example, Representative Paul Findley (Rep., Ill.) was primarily concerned that the ploy caused "an enormous loss in shipbuilding for the United States."[29]

The United States' business-as-usual attitude was particularly surprising since U.S. corporations had been targets of violent attacks for several months. The United States had about 300 firms involved in Iran. Their employees and their business headquarters were ubiquitous and highly visible. The militant elements of the opposition had little difficulty identifying and attacking them. The larger companies were particularly vulnerable. These included Bechtel Corporation, Westinghouse Electric Company, American Telephone and Telegraph Company, Pepsico Inc., General Telephone Electronics, and General

Tire and Rubber Company. Pepsico Inc. as well as U.S. banks and hotels were attacked.

Major U.S. arms contractors, however, were in an even worse position. Grumman Corporation and Bell Operations Corporation, a subsidiary of Textron Inc. in Iran, were the main targets. Both the buildings and the employees of arms contractors had been targets of attack over the years, but in 1978–79 the assaults substantially increased. During the first massive demonstration in Isfahan, shortly before *Tasu'a* and *Ashura* (December 10–11, 1978), the headquarters of Grumman Corporation was gutted by arson, and their buildings in Tehran were firebombed. Bell Helicopter employees and buildings were also attacked. Besides their ubiquity, the "boisterous lifestyle" of the employees of these companies offended public sentiment in Iran.

The arms purchase cutbacks finally came. The Shah's government wanted to save billions of dollars, nine months after the start of the revolution and about three months before his departure, in order to meet long-neglected social services and agricultural development! At the time there was $12 billion worth of arms on order from the United States alone. General Dynamics, McDonnell Douglas Corporation, Tex Instruments, and Boeing Company were the big losers. They were to sell, respectively, 140 F-16s worth $2.5 billion, 31 F-4E fighter planes worth $350 million, 1,000 strike missiles worth $105 million, and 7 AWACS aircraft worth $1.5 billion. The administration's easing of its own arms sales restrictions in Iran had helped the United States' otherwise unfavorable balance of trade in billions of dollars, and this seemed to be what most concerned many officials in Washington. After all, the Shah was the United States' single largest arms customer in the world, and President Carter had discussed further sales to the Shah in November 1977, even while the demonstrations of Iranian dissidents were disturbing the Shah's visit at the White House.

The single most important strategic loss, however, was the shutdown of the two U.S. listening posts near the Soviet borders. It had been expected that they would be among the first U.S. installations to be dismantled, and shortly after the seizure of power by the revolutionary forces, two of these top-secret posts were occupied. The day after the Shah's departure, Sadegh Ghotbzadeh, an aide of the Ayatollah Khomeini during his exile in France, said in an important news conference, "We're not going to be an intelligence base for anyone."[30] At that time Drew Middleton said, "Removal of the equipment would have direct effect on the debate over a new, second-stage treaty with the Soviet Union to limit strategic arms. But without the CIA's tracking and eavesdropping equipment, now situated in central and northeastern Iran, the United States will find it more difficult to effectively verify Soviet compliance with some provisions of an arms agreement."[31]

Thus the revolutionary process in 1978–79 undermined all the bases of U.S. influence in Iran that had been cultivated over a quarter of a century and had served to protect the Shah's regime against both domestic and external threats, and to protect U.S. strategic and economic interests in Iran. The tangible bases of the quarter-century influence relationship had included oil, security, economic, and political interests. The tangible bases of U.S. influence in Iran were undermined even before the actual seizure of power by the revolutionary forces due to: (1) the termination of security cooperation in the Persian Gulf; (2) the loss of about $12 billion worth of arms on order for the next four to five years; (3) the threat to billions of dollars of nonoil trade and economic cooperation; (4) the exodus of the overwhelming majority of 45,000 U.S. citizens residing in Iran, and (5) the departure of the Shah. After the revolutionary forces seized power, these tangible bases were virtually destroyed.

THE U.S. INFLUENCE BALANCE SHEET

The balance sheet of the U.S. role in Iran during the revolution is inseparable from that of the Shah discussed in the previous chapter, just as the entire process of United States-Iran influence relationship is inseparable from the problems of continuity and change in the Iranian society. This means that an assessment of the U.S. role in 1978–79 must be made largely in terms of the basic Iranian revolutionary situation. Since that situation consisted of two essential sets of actors—the Shah and the opposition—the U.S. role should be assessed with respect to each.

First, however, we must address two questions: When did the United States enter the revolutionary scene in Iran? What was the basic thrust of U.S. policy? Let us take up each one of these questions in turn.

Given the strategic significance that the United States had always attached to its influence in Iran, it seems incomprehensible that

Washington entered the revolutionary scene as late as it did, almost nine to ten months after the outbreak of riots in Qom and Tabriz. Whatever the explanation—such as the top policymakers' preoccupation with the peacemaking process in the Arab-Israeli conflict—there is no escaping this serious question. The attitude of business as usual in spite of widespread demonstrations and ever-escalating strikes was evident with respect to every major issue in the United States-Iran relationship, including continued arms sales.

With respect to the second question, the role of the United States is equally incomprehensible. As previously discussed, the main thrust of the Carter Administration's purported policy toward Iran was two-pronged: supporting the Shah and promoting his political liberalization. Either the administration believed in the feasibility of this approach, or it pretended that it did. I believe that it did, as evidenced by its actual conduct during the revolutionary process. Although bureaucratic differences over this approach existed and created policy incoherence, the main thrust of that approach prevailed in the U.S. policy toward Iran. The question that must be faced, therefore, is why the contradictory premises of that policy were not questioned, or if in fact they were, then why the administration continued to press for its implementation.

Let us now turn to the actual U.S. behavior in the Iranian revolutionary situation. First, how did the United States behave toward the opposition? The record supports the proposition that Washington did not really understand the attitudes of the opposition forces in the first place, and to the extent that it might have, it bet on the wrong faction among the main political forces. Its flawed understanding of the opposition was not merely a reflection of the intelligence community's underestimation of the strength of the opponents of the Shah. Too much talk about this point has overshadowed a more basic failure. The administration optimistically overestimated the commitment to such norms as give-and-take, compromise, dialogue, and the like in the Iranian culture and society. What is most surprising is that even after the National Front and the Iranian Freedom Movement accepted the overall leadership of the Ayatollah Khomeini, Washington continued to believe that the opposition could somehow compromise with the Shah. It was absolutely clear by then that Bazargan and Sanjabi had given up on the Shah.

Between the two main elements of the opposition—the National Frontists and the Muslim fundamentalists—the United States opted for the former. That miscalculation was not merely a matter of over-estimating the strength of the National Front, but of projecting U.S. cultural and political preferences into the assessment of the front. The notion that the National Front was democratically inclined tipped the balance of appraisal of the Iranian situation in its favor. At least by implication, it also seemed to disfavor Khomeini's faction. In principle, there was nothing wrong with favoring the National Front, but to the extent that it distracted U.S. attention from establishing much earlier contacts with Khomeini's group, it made it even more difficult to try to work with Khomeini's leadership later on, both before and after the revolutionary seizure of power.

How did the United States behave toward the Shah's regime? Two basic propositions are in order. First, before the appointment of the military government, the United States complacently relied on the Shah's government to appraise the revolutionary situation. Influence flowed more from Tehran to Washington than the other way around. This deference to the Shah had little to do with his ability; it was a reflection of the U.S. misappraisal of the Shah's capacity to accurately estimate the situation and to set it right. The administration seemed to assume that the Shah was both willing and able to compromise. To have misread the attitudes of the forces of opposition is one thing, but to have misread the Shah's attitudes is quite another. The United States had been involved with the Shah for nearly 37 years. Did it really believe that the Shah would share power with anyone?

Second, the belated U.S. realization that the Shah must leave Iran could not help U.S. interests. The government that the Shah had left behind had no real prospects for survival; U.S. support did not help it either. It lacked widespread popular support and was immediately denounced by the opposition, including Bakhtiar's own colleagues in the National Front. To believe that the military could have kept the Bakhtiar government in power after the departure of the Shah was naive for two reasons. One, by the time of the Shah's departure, the military was already divided. That was enough to have made the Huyser mission impossible. But the more serious misappraisal, I believe, once again reflected inattention to the patterns of Iranian culture, history, and society. The idea of transferring the military's allegiance from the Shah to Bakhtiar was unrealistic. The loyalty of the military to the Shah was personal in nature and, hence, could not be simply shifted to Bakhtiar.

This balance sheet, however, as all the ones before it, is incomplete. It will have to be integrated with all the others in the conclusion for us to see its tentative propositions in the light of the entire study.

NOTES

1. For the text see *Ettela'at*, January 3, 1978. See also *Washington Post*, December 31, 1977.
2. UPI, *Daily Progress*, January 1, 1978.
3. See Mohammad Reza Pahlavi, *Answer to History* (New York: Stein and Day, 1980), p. 153.
4. See Ashraf Pahlavi, *Faces in a Mirror: Memoirs from Exile* (Englewood Cliffs, N.J.: Prentice-Hall, 1980), pp. 198–99.
5. U.S., Congress, House, *Iran: Evaluation of U.S. Intelligence Performance Prior to November 1978*, staff report, Subcommittee on Evaluation, Permanent Select Committee on Intelligence, (Washington, D.C.: U.S. Government Printing Office, January 1979), p. 6.
6. Ibid., p. 7.
7. Ibid., p. 6.
8. Ibid.
9. *Washington Post*, September 11, 1978.
10. See Pahlavi, *Answer to History*, p. 161.
11. *Washington Post*, November 1, 1978.
12. Ibid., November 7, 1978.
13. *New York Times*, November 13, 1978.
14. *Washington Post*, November 20, 1978.
15. Ibid., November 25, 1978.
16. Ibid., November 28, 1978. See also *Washington Post*, December 17, 1978.
17. *New York Times*, December 21, 1978.
18. Ibid.
19. *Washington Post*, December 7, 1978.
20. Ibid., December 13, 1978.
21. Ibid., December 15, 1978.
22. *New York Times*, January 9, 1979.
23. Ibid.
24. See William H. Sullivan, "Dateline Iran: The Road Not Taken," *Foreign Policy* no. 4 (Fall 1980), pp. 175–87, esp. 180.
25. Ibid., p. 181.
26. Ibid., p. 184.
27. *New York Times*, January 17, 1979.
28. *Washington Post*, March 13, 1978.
29. Ibid., August 19, 1978.
30. Ibid., January 18, 1979.
31. *New York Times*, January 18, 1979.

$$8$$

OBSERVATIONS ON AN
INFLUENCE RELATIONSHIP

What does this study as a whole suggest about the overall United States-Iran influence relationship during the Shah's regime, from his accession to the throne in 1941 to his downfall in 1979?

First, this study suggests that the complexities of the United States-Iran relationship and the rudimentary nature of the state of the art in assessing influence defy any simplistic characterization such as the U.S. domination of Iran. The Shah's involvement with the United States in fact spanned nearly 37 years, and included complicated and multifaceted ties on a whole variety of issues in which the play of influence was too dynamic to suggest any static pattern of influence. But on the whole, it is clear that the flow of influence between the two states was more reciprocal than unilateral, although not necessarily equal. With respect to some specific issues, the United States and Iran each exercised a greater degree of influence on the other at a given point in time, depending on the circumstances. To clarify this point further, let us now try to integrate the influence balance sheets at the end of each chapter with respect to the exercise of influence first by Iran and then the United States.

Empirically, the process of influence must be dated back to 1941, when the Shah ascended the throne, rather than 1953 when the United States intervened covertly to return him to power. The Shah decided to become an "ally" of the United States in order to withstand the potential threat of the Muslim fundamentalist, the nationalist, and the communist forces of opposition that burst into the open in Iran immediately after the fall of Reza Shah—and to resist the

142

pressures of the British and particularly Soviet occupation forces. To realize that objective, he singlemindedly—but not singlehandedly—courted U.S. friendship for an entire decade by a variety of methods and tactics. His supporters within the government, the Majlis and the civilian and military bureaucracy helped him loyally. He consistently took the initiative to encourage U.S. support for his regime by inviting U.S. involvement, first and foremost, in rebuilding his father's paralyzed and demoralized armed forces, in aiding the modernization of the Iranian medieval economic structure, in granting oil concessions—an attempt that was aborted by Soviet interference with the aid of their loyal instrument, the Tudeh Party—and in obtaining diplomatic support for Iran's "territorial integrity and political independence."

All these efforts redounded to the advantage of the Shah's nascent regime and his country in two major wartime crises. The United States supported his regime unequivocally in the oil crisis in 1944, and again in 1945–46 during the crisis over the evacuation of Soviet Red Army troops, and over the Soviet interference in Azerbaijan and Kurdistan, where Moscow had established two communist puppet regimes through Soviet material and moral support. The United States also intervened covertly in Iran in a domestic power struggle between the nationalist forces led by Dr. Muhammad Musaddeq against the Shah and returned the Shah to power in 1953.

The U.S. intervention in the Shah's favor did not, however, automatically result in close ties between his regime and the United States. The Shah continued to press for intimate ties with the United States for the next quarter of a century. He nursed the pre-1953 embryonic ties without effective domestic opposition, which he increasingly suppressed and coopted after his return to power. He did sign the oil Consortium agreement of 1954, even though reluctantly—his reservations were played up to get a better deal and greater income. He believed that the advantages of the new oil agreement were threefold: it earned increased revenues, involved the U.S. interests in Iranian oil, and simultaneously terminated the many years of British monopolistic control of the Iranian oil industry for the first time in history. Having relentlessly and successfully pressed the Consortium over nearly two decades for increasingly greater offtake of Iranian oil, he led the Persian Gulf oil-producing states in getting the most beneficial terms in a landmark collective agreement signed in Tehran in 1971. By exploiting the change of the world oil market from a buyer's to a seller's market, he nationalized the Iranian oil industry in 1973, which gave him greater control over it, as contrasted with all other Persian Gulf states, except Iraq. Without joining the Arab oil embargo in the same year, he led the spectacular oil price increases that marked a turning point in the rise of power and influence of the OPEC states in international economics and politics. From then on, he hawkishly pressed for ever-increasing oil revenues enabling him to tighten his control over the political system, increase economic growth, and project Iranian power within ever-larger circles of states in the Middle East and Southwestern Asia.

He used increasing oil revenues to enhance internal and external security. Internally, he created the SAVAK, which developed, over time, functions, methods, and techniques far exceeding the intentions of the CIA and the Mossad—which aided in its creation—yet was compatible with the political and value structures of the Iranian culture. Modern tools were used to inflict ancient cruelties on the forces of political opposition, including torture, harrassment, intimidation, and execution, without any real regard for law. Externally, he joined the United States-sponsored Baghdad Pact alliance, embraced the Eisenhower Doctrine, and signed a bilateral executive agreement for defense with the United States during the Cold War. In the wake of the departure of British forces from the Persian Gulf region, he enthusiastically accepted for his country the role of a U.S. surrogate under the Nixon Doctrine for the protection of the region's stability and security, and then expanded the Iranian security perimeter into the Gulf of Oman and the northwest quadrant of the Indian Ocean. He purchased billions of dollars of U.S. military equipment and training for his armed forces, and dreamed of transforming his country into one of the five conventional military powers of the world. Within and outside the region, he pursued political and diplomatic policies to enhance his international legitimacy, while aiding parallel United States' and Iranian interests.

In the economic field, he used the oil revenues to finance successive economic development plans for rapid industrialization. Iran's spectacular rate of economic growth compared favorably with that of most developing, and even some developed, countries during the mid-1960s, and was paralleled by visible improvement in the material standards of life and per capita income. But the maldistribution of wealth, the accompanying corruption, the increasing rate of inflation, the neglect of agricultural development, and many other socioeconomic dislocations surfaced graphically with the massive infusion of petrodollars into the economy after the explosion of oil revenues. Grandiose plans for industrial development without adequate infrastructure in communication and transportation created all kinds of bottlenecks, but the Shah continued to dream of transforming the Iranian economy to the equivalent of those of West Germany and France. Obsession with the rate of economic growth without equitable distribution of wealth fueled the overheating of the economy.

In the agricultural sector, the Shah heeded President Kennedy's pressure for economic and social change by launching his land and other reforms with the initial aid of his able minister of agriculture, Dr. Arsanjani. The historic destruction of the ancient land-owning system, emancipation of women, increasing rate of literacy, and other reforms were not matched, however, by efforts that would make the peasantry more productive. Nor did the efforts to improve the quality of education succeed in making the newly literate population more educated. The monstrosities of agricultural corporations neither prevented the massive migration of agricultural laborers to the growing urban population centers, nor did they remedy the fragmentation of landholdings. The uprooted peasantry swelled the ranks of the urban poor in cities and towns. The urban and rural poor populations found the common bond of ever-increasing alienation from the regime.

The Shah made the United States one of Iran's major trade partners, but he deeply resented the imbalance of trade against Iran. Among other factors, the rise of unprecedented nonarms imports was due to: massive food imports, as a result of the decline of agricultural productivity; growing imports of consumer goods, including luxury items; the sudden growth of imports of capital goods as a result of vast industrial projects; and a rapidly increasing population. The overall economic dependency of Iran on the United States continued to grow in spite of the rhetoric of diversification and self-sufficiency.

Politically, however, the Shah's regime enjoyed a rare longevity partly because of sustained U.S. support. His courtship of U.S. power and influence in Iran paid off handsomely for decades. With U.S. support, he returned to power after having almost lost his throne. He maintained the regime's internal and external security against its perceived foes, and he projected abroad the Iranian military-political, diplomatic, and economic influence far beyond what was needed to defend Iran's own territorial integrity and political independence. In building and projecting influence for his regime and his country, he managed, in effect, to retain U.S. support for his regime, in spite of his suspicion of a U.S. conspiracy against him toward the end of his rule.

How did the United States fare in this prolonged influence game? Based on what I have already said about the Iranian perspective, the limits of U.S. influence over the Shah's regime should be evident without detailed discussion. But a few points need further elaboration.

First, the United States was not very reluctant when the Shah insistently courted Washington during the first decade of their relationship. The United States had some interests in the region and in Iran before 1941. Apart from the often-mentioned interest in the protection of U.S. missionaries, the United States had demonstrated as early as 1882—when the bill for establishing diplomatic relations was before the House of Representatives for approval—a serious interest in the expansion of its trade with Iran, and believed, interestingly, that diplomatic relations with "the oldest government in the world" would be of "strategic importance" to the United States. Because of isolationism, in general, and the U.S. perception of Iran as a British preserve, in particular, no significant and durable relationship with Iran developed until World War II when U.S. interests in Saudi Arabian oil supplies in the 1930s increased Washington's interest in the developments in nearby Iran across from the Persian Gulf. Even within Iran itself—apart from the quasiprivate missions of Shuster and Millspaugh—U.S. oil companies had been interested in Iranian oil as early as the 1920s.

Second, empirical evidence does not support the twofold mythology that the exercise of U.S. influence over Iran began because of the covert U.S. intervention in 1953, and that because of that single event the U.S. influence over Iran in all issues automatically followed during the next quarter century. Although the United States entered the Iranian political scene in earnest with the arrival of about 40,000 U.S. troops in Iran in 1942 for the main purpose of prosecution of the war against Germany, as early as 1943 Washington publicly endorsed the objective of maintaining Iran's "territorial integrity and political independence" in the Tehran Declaration signed by Roosevelt, Churchill, and Stalin. The U.S. commitment to that objective was no simple diplomatic platitude, as evidenced by the U.S. public support of Iran against the Soviet blandishments for oil concessions in 1944, the U.S. championship of the Iranian demand for the withdrawal of Soviet troops from Iran, and cessation of Soviet inter-ference in Iranian affairs in the 1945–46 crisis. Furthermore, the United States responded favorably to every major move by the Shah's government to expand the United States-Iran relationship in military modernization, financial reorganization, economic planning, and financial aid.

Third, on balance, the United States exerted considerable influence over Iran in spite of serious limits. For the first time in history, U.S. companies acquired a significant foothold in the Iranian oilfields across from those in Saudi Arabia, and after the nationalization of the oil industry, they enjoyed preferential treatment in oil purchases. The overriding U.S. interest in Iran, however, was consistently strategic, dating back, as already seen, to World War II. With the advent of the Cold War, U.S. strategic interests in Iran increased unprecedentedly. The Tehran-Moscow cold war coincided with the East-West cold war. John Foster Dulles's northern tier concept was realized by the formation of the Baghdad Pact organization and the inclusion of Iran as a member after the downfall of the Musaddeq government. The Shah's bête noire corresponded with that of the United States. The Shah, however, was always unhappy with the U.S. reluctance to become a member of the alliance. Washington also acquired the Shah's full support for the Eisenhower Doctrine, and repelled the Soviet pressures on Iran after the breakdown of Soviet-Iranian negotiations for a nonaggression pact; it signed an executive agreement with the Shah's regime—and also separate and similar agreements with Turkey and Pakistan after the Iraqi Revolution and the defection of Iraq from the Baghdad Pact.

More crucial, from the perspective of Washington, the Shah's regime served to protect parallel United States' and Iranian interests in the Persian Gulf region for nearly a decade before its downfall. The U.S. client of the Cold War era turned into a U.S. surrogate in the wake of the departure of British forces from the Persian Gulf region. The United States succeeded in avoiding direct involvement in the region at the height of the war in Vietnam. Under the Nixon Doctrine, the United States not only avoided the commitment of U.S. troops in the region, but also acquired in Iran the world's single largest customer for U.S. arms and military training. The U.S. balance-of-payments difficulties were eased not only by massive arms sales, but also by the growing U.S. export of capital and consumer goods to Iran; the balance of trade consistently favored the United States.

At the same time, hundreds of U.S. private corporations found an investment haven in Iran under the United States-Iran treaty of 1955, and thousands of U.S. nationals engaged in lucrative activities when the job market in the United States was shrinking.

In addition to the above strategic interests, the United States used Iranian territory to monitor Soviet compliance with the terms of the strategic arms limitation treaty. In this respect the advantages to the United States vastly exceeded both its own need for Middle East oil, and the need to protect Western access to the uninterrupted flow of Persian Gulf oil supplies. They helped maintain the global strategic balance between the United States and the Soviet Union.

The second major proposition of this study flows significantly from the first one. It suggests that no single U.S. policy failure can be objectively raised to the level of the primary cause of the collapse of the U.S. influence in Iran in 1978–79. Ever since the Iranian Revolution, the literature on the United States-Iran relationship during the Shah's regime has been replete with all kinds of theories about "who lost Iran." A few of the major arguments need to be mentioned. The U.S. intervention thesis contends that the primary cause of the ultimate collapse of the U.S. influence in Iran was the anti-U.S. sentiments aroused within the Iranian society as a result of the U.S. intervention in favor of the Shah and against the popular leader Dr. Muhammad Musaddeq in 1953. Another theory contends that "U.S. imperialism" was the primary cause of the collapse of Washington's influence in Iran. It insists that because of a "symbiotic relationship" between the U.S. "corporate interests" and the interests of the U.S. government, Washington's dominance in Iran, as elsewhere in the Third World, reflected U.S. capitalistic interests rather than strategic interests. The latter were allegedly used to cloak the former in establishing "the international system of dominance" through United States "guns and dollars in the aftermath of World War II." A third theory posits that President Nixon's 1972 mistaken decision to make the Shah the protector of the Persian Gulf region's stability and security, and to sell him whatever conventional weapons he wanted, was largely responsible for the eruption of the Iranian Revolution. And finally, a fourth, and opposite thesis, blames the collapse of the U.S. influence in Iran on the Carter Administration's human rights policy.

Whether these contentions reflect a liberal-democratic, a leftist or Marxist, or a conservative predisposition of the analyst, the fact remains that all of them seem to share the same basic assumption. That is, the United States controlled the Shah's regime so completely that the main fault for the collapse of U.S. influence must be sought more in the U.S. foreign policy process than in anything else. Even those lesser theories that blame the collapse of U.S. influence in Iran on the failure of Washington's intelligence community, or on U.S. bureaucratic politics and infighting would seem to make the same basic assumption. There are, of course, also what might be termed "sink theories." In order to avoid responsibility for any real critical judgment about the causes of the U.S. failure, such studies simply throw in indiscriminately a catalogue of factors presumably as an objective attempt at explication. But on the whole, the major existing perspectives all seem to make the same basic assumption, that is, an unlimited U.S. control over the Shah's policy decisions.

Ironically, the major Iranian perspectives seem to share the same basic bias. The Muslim fundamentalists, the nationalists, the *Mujaheddin-e Khalq* Islamic Marxists, the *Fada'eyin-e Khalq* Marxist-Leninists, the Tudeh communists, and one might say most Iranians, believe that the United States fully controlled the Shah's regime until the Iranian Revolution. Even the Shah seems to have believed this during his fits of depression at the end of his rule. He blamed his downfall from power on liberals in the State Department and elsewhere in the Carter Administration.

Yet this study has suggested that the flow of influence between the Shah's regime and Washington was reciprocal, multifaceted, and too complicated to lend itself to such simplistic suggestions. As a matter of fact, if analysts are more interested in making a case to suit their own predispositions than in ascertaining empirically the patterns of influence relationship between the two countries, why not argue "Who lost the United States"? After all, it was the Shah who courted U.S. influence in Iran first throughout the decade after his accession to the throne in an effort to consolidate his own power against perceived domestic opponents and foreign foes. It was the Shah who cooperated surreptitiously with CIA agents to bring down the Musaddeq government; it was the Shah who cultivated U.S. influence in Iran by economic, military, political, and diplomatic instruments over a quarter of a century after the 1953 coup. And it was ultimately the Shah's own resistance to sharing power with any major sociopolitical group in the opposition that precipitated the downfall of his regime.

The other major shortcoming of the existing attempts at explication stems from the fact that they often take the symptoms for the causes of the U.S. failure in Iran. The more basic questions are seldom, if at all, asked. For example, why did the United States covertly intervene in Iran in 1953? Why did President Nixon make the cavalier promise of selling the Shah whatever conventional weapons he wanted? And why did President Carter support the Shah to the very end of his rule, in spite of his human rights policy?

To recite from some of my own tentative criticism of United States' and Iranian policies in the text, why did the Eisenhower Administration assure the Shah that he had no obligation toward the United States when Washington helped save his throne and when its leverage on the Shah was the strongest and might have been used to extract a promise to respect the Iranian Constitution—as the British had done so successfully in 1941? Why did the Carter Administration seem to insist on the application of a basically contradictory two-pronged policy of supporting the Shah's regime, and simultaneously pressing it for political liberalization? Or why did the Carter Administration undertake the impossible task of trying to shift the allegiance of the Iranian armed forces from the Shah to the Bakhtiar government?

These questions bring me to the third and the last major proposition of this study. The failure of U.S. policy in Iran fundamentally reflected more the problem of a flawed approach to Iranian society than any single mistaken decision or the simple sum total of many erroneous decisions by U.S. policymakers over the decades. To the extent that the Shah's regime subscribed to that approach, Iran also shared the responsibility for the eventual collapse of the close United States-Iran relationship. The Shah and many members of the political elite subscribed, in fact, to that approach; they did so, of course, for their own reasons.

Despite all the vicissitudes of the United States-Iran relationship over the decades, the U.S. approach to Iran was marked by three major features that, more or less, remained amazingly constant throughout the decades. These three characteristics were intimately interconnected, but I suggest them separately for purposes of analytical clarity. Furthermore, since most of the empirical evidence in support of these characteristics is already included throughout the text of this study, I shall offer only examples for illustration.

1. The U.S. approach to Iran from its inception to the end was guided primarily by strategic considerations. The covert U.S. inter-

vention in Iran in 1953 was launched for fear of a "communist coup d'état," staged by the Tudeh Party and supported by the Soviet Union at the height of the Cold War. President Nixon's cavalier decision to sell the Shah all the conventional arms he wanted was also guided primarily by strategic considerations. Even the critical Senate report, mentioned in the text, conceded that basic point, but unfortunately confined its critique to secondary matters of policy implementation. Finally, as an example, the Carter Administration's inability to adopt a coherent policy toward Iran stemmed largely from the contradictory premises of its approach. The administration supported the Shah, as all previous administrations had, primarily for strategic reasons, although it also wishfully hoped to make a democratic leader out of a despotic ruler in keeping with the precepts of its human rights policy. In practice, however, the strategic consideration still prevailed; the administration, in fact, continued to support the Shah despite considerable disunity within the government.

For his own reasons, the Shah fully subscribed to Washington's emphasis on strategic considerations throughout his rule. But he also used this emphasis as a leverage on Washington. The Shah's main complaint about the U.S. security policy was Washington's refusal to enter into a NATO-type alliance with Iran; to the end he maintained his youthful ambition (1941) of becoming the "ally" of the United States. The Shah, like Washington, believed that the Soviets posed the main threat to his regime and Iran. As a military man, he considered the strength of the Iranian armed forces the sine qua non of the success of all his other policies. Without military strength, he believed, effective social, economic, and political development would be impossible; he meant, of course, that consolidation of power must be based mainly on military strength. He also believed that without a strong military capability Iran would not be able to project power beyond its own boundaries either as a military deterrent to the threats of perceived foreign enemies or as a way to realize his dream of a "great civilization" akin to Cyrus the Great's.

The billions of Iranian dollars that the Shah spent on U.S. arms generally received the support and encouragement of Washington, in spite of occasional lonely voices raised against the massive arms transfers. The arms sales helped the U.S. balance of payments; they presumably helped maintain Western access to the uninterrupted flow of Persian Gulf oil supplies; and, of course, they made it possible for greedy arms manufacturers to profit. Even President Kennedy's disapproval of the Shah's heavy expenditures on arms did not last long; President Johnson resumed arms sales with a zest; and President Carter managed to sell arms even during the first year of the Iranian Revolution, despite his purported arms-sale ceiling.

A great deal of criticism has been directed against both the amounts of U.S. arms sales to Iran and the inappropriateness of the sophisticated weapon systems involved. While the latter criticism concerned the problems of Iran's absorptive capacity and the involvement of too many U.S. military personnel, etc., the former related to the adverse impact of the excessive Iranian military expenditures on social, economic, and political developments in Iran. Without doubt the diversion of badly needed funds from socioeconomic development projects contributed to the deterioration of human conditions in Iran. But the problem of emphasis on strategic considerations that lay at the base of the United States' softening of its criticism of the Shah's arms purchase policy—and even its downplaying of criticism of the Shah's overpricing of Iranian oil—was compounded by other flawed features of the U.S. approach to Iran.

2. This brings us to the second major feature of the U.S. approach to Iran. Policymakers and analysts in Washington—and their Iranian counterparts—revealed a rather simplistic attachment to the processes of "modernization." It was widely assumed that modernization in the form of increasing industrialization, spreading education, improving communication and transportation, growing urbanization, etc. would transform a traditional, parochial, and heterogeneous society such as Iran's into an integrated national community; would transform subjects into citizens, and communalism and tribalism into nationalism; would change primordial loyalties, values, attitudes, ethnic and linguistic particularities, and other "anachronistic" features of the old societies of the Third World into all the ingredients that are necessary for the creation of a civic polity.

Indiscriminate commitment to modernization in the course of the development of the United States-Iran relationship produced three major tendencies that impeded both U.S. and Iranian accurate estimates of the situation in Iran. Before delving into these points, I should caution that the United States and Iranian tendencies were not always necessarily identical. In fact, the record reveals persistent divergency of attitudes between the U.S. and Iranian policymakers toward the problems of modernization. For example, policymakers in Washington were aware, all along, of the primacy of political considerations in the Shah's socioeconomic reform programs. They were also aware of the persistent flaws of all Iranian development plans, starting with the first development plan after World War II and including the last one under the government of Amuzegar.

Nevertheless, the fact remains that U.S. policymakers continued to believe that genuine and successful modernization under the Shah's regime was possible, although they were reluctant to press the Shah too hard for basic socioeconomic change. Largely because of emphasis on strategic considerations, the United States did not, most of the time, wish to be too demanding. The only major instance in which the United States was willing to apply real pressure on the Shah's regime for socioeconomic change was in the early 1960s, under the Kennedy Administration. But even then the president prematurely expressed satisfaction with the Shah's land reform for the fear, perhaps, that too much pressure might risk a fate for the Shah's regime similar to that of Diem's in Vietnam. Let us now return to the three major tendencies that stemmed from an indiscriminate emphasis on modernization in the U.S. approach to Iran.

First, regardless of whatever reservations U.S. policymakers might have had about the Shah's approach to economic development, Washington went along for years with the prevalent thinking in the 1950s and 1960s that the main road to economic development was economic growth. The Johnson Administration's jubilation over the Iranian rate of economic growth prompted the decision to terminate U.S. economic aid to Iran. Many U.S. observers believed that Iran had nearly reached the stage of economic "takeoff." After the explosion of Iranian oil revenues in the early 1970s, U.S. policymakers expressed serious concern about the "overheating" of the Iranian economy, but in practice the Nixon, Ford, and Carter Administrations not only continued to sell arms, but also massively increased the export of U.S. capital goods for Iranian industrialization. They also continued to increase the sale of U.S. consumer goods to Iran despite its continuously unfavorable balance of trade. The obsession of the Shah's government with the GNP as the engine of economic development continued for decades before the Iranian Revolution. Later, his cutbacks of extravagant projects were too little and too late. The rhetoric of self-sufficiency had little to do with the practice of deepening dependency on the U.S. economy.

Second, another flawed tendency in the U.S. attachment to indiscriminate modernization was relative insensitivity to traditional sociopolitical forces. This problem partly reflected Washington's overreliance on the judgment of the Iranian political elite. In dealing with the Iranian government, it was often assumed that Iranian policymakers were better judges of the Iranian society, an assumption that had proved wrong on many occasions. For example, the insensitivity of the Pentagon to the Iranian religious opposition to the privileges of the U.S. military personnel in the early 1960s partially reflected Washington's notion that all would be well if the Shah could get the necessary bill through the Majlis. A better example is the U.S. underestimation of the importance of the religious forces during the Iranian Revolution, although it must be said in all fairness that the Iranian policymakers were even less sensitive. Some even counseled U.S. embassy officials in Tehran not to pay too much attention to such old forces as the Bazaaris and religious leaders. These policymakers represented largely what I call "alien Iranians," or what in *Farsi* is known as those who are "neither here nor there" (*az inja roondeh az unja moondeh*). They represent those Western-educated Iranians who neither really know their own society, nor are truly familiar with Western values in any appreciable depth; the Shah himself was one of them.

Third, the last adverse tendency was a corollary of the second one; that is, U.S. oversensitivity to modern forces of "moderation." As the two previous tendencies, this tendency reflects at base the same optimistic assumptions that policymakers and social scientists alike made for years about the miracles that economic modernization can perform. Even Henry Kissinger admitted after the downfall of the Shah's regime that the Shah had failed to match socioeconomic change with political modernization. But he failed to mention that some students of Iranian affairs had been saying that for years, that the Shah's persistent neglect of building viable political institutions was partially encouraged by the knowledge of Washington's emphasis on strategic rather than on economic, social, and political considerations, and that he himself had been a supreme example of that tendency.

In any event, the tendency to overrate the strength of the middle-class-based political forces, particularly the National Front, took its own toll. For example, those who always remembered the U.S. intervention in Iran shortly after the Eisenhower Administration came into office in 1953 tended to forget that previously the Truman Administration had tried hard to work out an Anglo-Iranian settlement of the oil nationalization dispute. But the Musaddeq government badly miscalculated its own strength, made a farce of democratic government, and refused to consider seriously a compromise settlement with the help of the United States or any other intermediary.

The strength of the National Front was overrated even more during the Iranian Revolution. Little note was taken of the fact that the Iranian political scene had drastically changed since the mid-1960s. The society itself had grown from a population of merely 16 million during the crisis of 1951–53 to nearly twice as many by the mid-1960s, and was marked by the process of "rejuvenation," to borrow a United Nations term, in the sense that about half of the population was between the ages of 16 and 30. The youthful population had been disappointed in the performance of the Bazargan Freedom Movement and the National Front; their opposition to the Shah's regime was considered ineffective. Three of the members of the movement had defected and formed the *Mujaheddin* organization. That organization and the *Fada'eyin* group had, for over a decade, posed a very severe challenge to the Shah's regime through armed struggle before the revolution. Furthermore, during the same period the process of radicalization of Iranian politics had also taken place among the leading clergy, most notably the Ayatollah Khomeini. For all practical purposes the political moderates had shrunk in terms of the followers of the National Front and the Bazargan Freedom Movement amidst the polarization of the Iranian political scene between the extremes on the right and the left.

Nevertheless, many U.S. scholars and statesmen continued to believe in the strength of forces led by the aged Bazargan and Sanjabi more because of their perceived modernistic and liberal political predisposition than because of an accurate assessment of the Iranian situation. The Carter Administration's pressure for political liberalization, therefore, largely meant that the Shah should try to share power somehow with moderate political and religious elements. And, in all fairness, it initially seemed to be a viable approach. Bazargan, Sanjabi, and Shariatmadari were right there in Iran, and their demands were more reformist than revolutionary at first. The tragic fire at the Rex Cinema in Abadan and the massacre at Jaleh Square, however, changed all that, but the optimistic U.S. assessment of the strength of the moderate elements continued. Even the November 5, 1978 surrender of Bazargan and Sanjabi—euphemistically called an "alliance"—to the overwhelming leadership of the Ayatollah Khomeini does not seem to have made any significant change in that optimistic assessment of the Iranian revolutionary situation. Perhaps the fact that the National Front leadership helped organize the massive and impressive demonstrations on the occasion of *Ashura* in December was taken as a sign of support for the aged leadership of the National Front, although in fact that was more a clear demonstration of the response of the crowds to the call of Khomeini. Regardless of the explanation, the fact remains that U.S. policymakers were more optimistic about the chances of success of the moderate elements than the actual situation seemed to warrant.

3. Besides the emphasis on strategic considerations and an indiscriminate attachment to modernization—with all the attendant emphasis on economic growth, relative insensitivity to traditional sociopolitical forces, and overrating of the popular support for perceived moderate forces—the U.S. approach to Iran also suffered significantly from a limited ability to comprehend the less tangible elements of the Iranian political culture. As in the cases of the other two impediments to a better appraisal of the Iranian situation, this problem was longstanding; it only surfaced more graphically during the Iranian Revolution. The Shah certainly did not comprehend the U.S. culture any better. His arrogant rhetoric about lax morality in Western culture, about the failure of U.S. democracy at the time of the creation of the Rastakhiz Party, about the lack of discipline and the decline of the work ethic in Western society, etc. betrayed a superficial understanding of Western values and society.

But that did not excuse the limited U.S. ability to adequately take into account the deeper, more mysterious, more contradictory, more intangible, and more paradoxical psychological and spiritual factors underlying the Iranian political behavior. These factors were not as easy to comprehend as the rate of economic growth or the problems of urbanization, industrialization, and communication. Nor were they so easy to classify and categorize as various sociopolitical forces. And yet the limited ability to comprehend these unquantifiable and intangible forces significantly impeded the U.S. estimate of the Iranian situation over the decades. For example, although the U.S. insistence on the routine nature of the "status of forces agreement" for the exclusion of U.S. military personnel from Iranian criminal jurisdiction in the early 1960s was factually correct, it was culturally insensitive. Within the Iranian political culture, such an agreement was perceived to be the reincarnation of the "capitulations" first imposed on Iran at the end of a disastrous defeat at the hands of czarist Russia in 1828.

Let me cite two examples of underrating the less tangible factors from the revolutionary period. First, the U.S. notions of compromise, give-and-take, and the like underpinned the Carter Administration's insistence on political liberalization. But the underlying value involved was basically alien to the Iranian authoritarian tradition, quite apart from the shortcomings of the personality of the Shah. In Iran most political actors, whether monarchist, nationalist, or religious fundamentalist, tended to view "compromise" as surrender to the enemy. In this respect, the attitude of Musaddeq was not terribly different from Khomeini's, nor theirs from the Shah's.

Second, the dispatch of General Huyser to Tehran with the aim of bringing about a shift of allegiance in the military from the Shah to Bakhtiar seemed unwarranted. At base the loyalty of the military was personal rather than institutional, although the Shah used the symbol of the ancient "Immortals" (*Javidan*) to legitimize the loyalty of the military to the monarchy. All the attempts at military modernization had created little change in the personal nature of that loyalty. The feeble attempts of Ahmad Qavam and Musaddeq to place the military under civilian control had failed; the military continued to behave primarily as the arm of the Shah. The fact that the army split into pro- and anti-Shah factions during the 1951–53 crisis, that the Tudeh was able to infiltrate the army by 1954, that the young air force technicians (*homafars*) joined the revolutionary forces, and even the military commanders broke up into two camps shortly before the seizure of power by the revolutionary forces only partially reflected the rise of the new middle classes in the military. Beneath these apparent changes lay still another ancient tendency in the Iranian political culture—incessant factionalism.

Limited ability to perceive adequately the tenacious hold of tradition in Iranian domestic political and foreign policy behavior might reflect ahistorical impulses in the U.S. culture, or might stem from undue emphasis on the doctrine of social change, or might reflect unfamiliarity with non-Western cultures. Whatever the explanation, it limited appreciation of the challenge of continuity. Such a limitation can prejudice a more accurate appraisal of the situation especially in Third World societies, such as Iran, that are burdened by ancient contradictions. Although a Third World state, Iran is, in Arnold Toynbee's words, "the world's sole superpower of ancient times." With this in mind, the Iranian rulers have seldom been able to escape the aspiration toward grandeur. The Shah was certainly no exception, nor was he an exception in his disregard for the limits of Iran's power and influence. The discrepancy between the ends and means in Iranian domestic and foreign policy processes, I have submitted elsewhere, marked the behavior of Iranian rulers for nearly half a millenium since the rise of Iran in modern times at the turn of the sixteenth century. That gap between the Shah's aspirations and the means at his disposal was evident with respect to every issue area in the United States-Iran relationship examined in this study, whether it concerned the Shah's goal of transforming Iran into one of the world's five nonnuclear military powers, or the objective of raising Iran to the level of West Germany and France in economic power. Yet, most U.S. observers simplistically attributed this and similar problems to the Shah's "megalomania." What they failed to understand was the convergence between the Shah's narcissism and the historical Iranian tendency toward aggrandizement.

Another intangible factor that underpinned the Iranian political behavior during the Shah's regime, and yet was not fully appreciated in the U.S. policymaking community should be added here briefly. That is the time-honored tendency that stems largely from a millennial contradiction between a vague Iranian ethical and emotional commitment to an ideal of a good society, and the actual experience of Iran in history. It manifests itself in both domestic and foreign policy processes. On the domestic level, that ideal reveals itself in individual, interpersonal, and intergroup relations. The ancient motto of "good thoughts, good words, and good deeds" (*pendar-e nik, goftar-e nik, va kerdar-e nik*) is not a class-bound ideal; it applies presumably to all relationships regardless of class origin, status, or ideology. On the level of political leadership, for example, it has always been expressed in the expectation of the society at large to have "truthful" and "just" rulers. "By Ahuramazda's will," said King Darius, "I am of such nature that I am a friend to the just: I am no friend to the unjust. What is right, that is my desire. I am not a friend to the man that followeth falsehood."

Yet in practice, the Iranians throughout the ages have witnessed injustice and falsehood in their society at every level of individual, interpersonal, and intergroup relationships. On the political level, they have seen these deviations from the perceived normative imperatives in a persistent pattern of authoritarian rule. The Shah emphasized this ethical-psychological dimension of the Iranian ideal by invoking pre-Islamic and Islamic precepts, partially to legitimize his regime, but also in a mystical belief that it is one of the most important aspects of Iranian culture and civilization. Khomeini found that ideal in his view of Islamic religion and history. In mobilizing the masses against the Shah's "illegal regime" during the Iranian Revolution, he invoked no single symbol as frequently as the "government of God," which alone was legitimate and legal. His model of a true Islamic government was that of the historical example of 'Ali ibn Abu Talib, the first Shi'i Imam and the fourth Islamic Caliph. The Shah's model was Cyrus the Great, the founder of the Achamenid dynasty. Yet in the behavior of both the Shah and Khomeini, the gap between their ideal of just and good government and their practice of authoritarian control is too evident to need elaboration.

On the international level, the same tension between the ideal and historical reality persists and influences the world outlook and behavior of Iranian policymakers. Ideally Iran has always aspired to the norms of universalism. Adda B. Bozeman dates that ideal back to the sixth century B.C. when the Iranians, she says, "for the first time in historical known terms" were concerned about moral principles and national interests in their foreign policy, and that concern manifested itself even in the practice of its leaders for 200 years when the tyranny of empires plagued the fabric of community everywhere else in the ancient world. Arnold Toynbee was so enamored of Iran's tolerant tradition of universalism that he saw in it a model for unifying mankind in the present world community. The Shah never tired of emphasizing this tradition to bolster diplomatic legitimacy of his regime, but he also believed in it mystically.

Yet the ideal of utopian universalism is contradicted in practice by the intolerant aspects of Iranian nationalism, which often overshadow its positive side, that is, a fierce sense of independence. Waves of foreign invasion, domination, occupation, intervention, penetration, and exploitation over millennia may partly account for spurts of Iranian xenophobia. That, however, is also a manifestation of a deeper tendency in the Iranian society. Iranian rulers in power and sociopolitical groups vying for power have habitually invited foreign patrons to protect them against perceived domestic and foreign foes. If successful, they have taken the credit for it, and if not, they have blamed it on foreigners. The Shah's relationship with the United States in this study is the most outstanding example of this tendency. He courted U.S. influence in Iran for nearly 37 years, and yet blamed his downfall on the United States.

All in all, the complexities of the United States-Iran influence relationship over the decades during the Shah's regime seem to defy any simplistic characterization. The United States did not simply dominate Iran. The flow of influence between the United States and Iran depended on the issue at hand at a given point in time. Most often, it was reciprocal, although not necessarily equal. Second, the collapse of the U.S. influence in Iran in 1978–79 cannot be easily attributed to any single mistaken decision at the time, or the sum total of a series of erroneous decisions over the previous decades. The exercise of U.S. influence in Iran was largely limited by the character and complications of the Iranian political culture. And third, to the extent that the United States policy in Iran can be faulted, the shortcoming stemmed from the overall U.S. approach to Iran. That approach suffered largely from an inordinate emphasis on strategic considerations, an indiscriminate concern with socioeconomic modernization, and a limited ability to take into account the less tangible factors underlying the Iranian political behavior.

_____ *9*

EPILOGUE

The main purpose of this epilogue is to suggest that the principal propositions of this study about the United States' relations with Iran during the Shah's regime are generally applicable to the postrevolutionary period of the past three years. Hence, this chapter is not intended to be a detailed discussion of the United States relations with Iran since the fall of the Shah. A variety of works on aspects of these relations have already been published by scholars and government officials. Only months after the revolutionary seizure of power, I prepared a detailed analysis on the perspectives and projections of Iran's foreign policy for the Joint Economic Committee of Congress.[1] Nor is this epilogue intended to discuss the Iranian revolutionary politics; a number of Iranian and U.S. observers, including myself, have done so elsewhere.[2] And finally, this epilogue is not intended to discuss my own experience as an analyst and occasional consultant to the U.S. government, especially after the outbreak of the hostage crisis. The U.S. hostages were not the only captives in this traumatic crisis. For example, I was besieged for commentary by the media and the public during the entire length of the crisis, and hence welcomed the release of the hostages for more reasons than those that pleased most of the U.S. public.

What is striking is the persistence of the major tendencies of the prerevolutionary decades in the postrevolutionary years. The same simplistic assumptions that were made about the nature of the U.S. relations with Iran during the Shah's regime have been made by and large about Washington's relations with the revolutionary regime,

161

especially the fundamental assumption that whatever has gone wrong in the U.S. relations with Iran must have been mainly the fault of the United States. Just as the Shah's downfall was perceived simply to have been the result of the failure of U.S. foreign policy in one way or another, so has been the seizure of the U.S. Embassy for example. It would seem that the Iranian Revolution did not make any serious dent in the underlying assumption that the U.S. influence over Iran was unlimited. After all, since it is assumed that a super-power always enjoys superior power and influence over a small power, the United States was "humiliated" by a "second-rate" power such as revolutionary Iran. Just as self-flagellation was the result of the "loss" of the Shah's Iran, it has been the outcome of the perception of "America held captive" during "the worst 444 days in American history."

More important, few people in the United States seem to understand that just as the Shah wooed and won U.S. support for decades in order to protect *his* regime against perceived domestic and foreign foes, the revolutionary leadership has rejected the previous U.S. protection of Iran partly as a means of consolidating domestic control and legitimacy. In the context of this basic tendency in the Iranian political culture, seizing the hostages had a more profound meaning than simply reflecting anti-Shah and anti-U.S. sentiments. Once the hostages were taken, for whatever reasons initially—a subject that still requires objective investigation—the hard-line revolutionary elements used the ensuing crisis to establish their control over the emerging political system in terms of the so-called ideology characterized as the "Khomeini line." The "Great Satan" in effect was used as the "Great Savior" of the Iranian Revolution in favor of the militant revolutionary factions. The extremist elements used the crisis effectively to destroy the Bazargan government. Both the provisional prime minister and his Foreign Minister Yazdi were suspected of trying to normalize the relations of revolutionary Iran with the United States, which to the militants meant a return to the Iranian foreign policy of the Shah's days. It was also used to discredit Ghotbzadeh, who worked for an early settlement of the hostage dispute. And Bani-Sadr's last-minute attempt to exploit the settlement of the hostage dispute in favor of his struggle with the Beheshti-Rajai-Rafsanjani triumvirate failed, because he had already lost the fight against the hard-line clerics partly because of his own initial attempt to settle the hostage crisis to his credit.

All this does not mean that President Carter's decision to admit the Shah to the United States for medical treatment was not flawed. Nor does it mean that in making that decision he simply succumbed to Rockefeller-Kissinger pressures. The president did care about the Shah's grave illness; I watched his saddened face in a meeting when he rejected impatiently the idea that the United States should return him to Iran. He believed that such a course of action would clearly mean the Shah's certain execution by the revolutionaries. The real point is that the president both miscalculated the reactions of the Iranian militants, and overestimated the ability of the Bazargan government to effect the reluctant "assurances" it made to U.S. officials about the safety of the U.S. Embassy personnel. The fact that Foreign Minister Yazdi—who joined Prime Minister Bazargan in making such assurances—had negotiated successfully with Ambassador Sullivan for the evacuation of militants from the embassy premises in February 1979 should not have been taken as an indication that it could be done again. By November the weakness of the Bazargan government had been repeatedly demonstrated; Khomeini himself had characterized his prime minister as "weak," and Bazargan had repeatedly offered his resignation because he lacked the needed authority in a country that, he said, had a "thousand chiefs."

More important, the reasons for the failure of U.S. policy toward the revolutionary regime were deeper than this particular flawed decision, or any other ill-fated decision such as the disastrous rescue mission in April 1980. The failure of U.S. policy toward the revolutionary regime was not simply the result of any single decision, or of a combination of several mistaken decisions, just as the downfall of the Shah's regime was not, as seen, merely the reflection of President Nixon's decision in 1972 to sell the Shah whatever sophisticated conventional arms he wanted, or of President Carter's human rights policy in 1977–79, or of the covert U.S. intervention in Iran as early as 1953. Rather it was rooted in a basically flawed approach to revolutionary Iran, just as it had been, as seen, the product of an essentially flawed approach to the Shah's regime. Let me apply quickly a few features of the prerevolutionary flawed approach to the events of the period since the fall of the Shah in order to illustrate the failure of U.S. policy largely because of the persistence of the old approach to revolutionary Iran.

First, one central feature of the U.S. approach to Iran over the decades had been a persistent overemphasis on strategic considerations in the formulation and execution of U.S. policy toward the Shah's Iran. Without repeating the empirical evidence in support of this theme, it may be recalled, Iran had always been regarded as a "strategic prize" in East-West competition, and Washington had emphasized the importance of military instruments of its policy toward Iran. Although shortly after the Iranian Revolution the United States sought to normalize relations with Iran more by nonmilitary means, such as diplomatic, the basic military thrust of U.S. policy toward the entire region revealed to independent observers that the United States had hardly learned the lessons of its past relations with Iran. The following events were seen by the militant elements in Iran as an attempt by the United States to prevent the consolidation of power by the revolutionary forces, and to aid not only the cause of the "counterrevolutionaries" such as those who supported the Shah, but also the more moderate elements of the revolution such as Bazargan who sought to forge a new and "equal" relation with the United States: (1) the visit of the secretary of defense to the Middle East (February 9–19, 1979) amidst the revolutionary seizure of power in Iran; (2) his offer of an unprecedented amount of military and economic aid to "pro-Western" countries; (3) the U.S. "consultative framework" envisaging military cooperation between Egypt, North Yemen, Jordan, the Sudan, Israel, and if possible Saudi Arabia, with the United States; and (4) the secretary's unequivocal and unprecedented statement that the United States would itself defend its vital interests in the Persian Gulf region's oil supplies by military force "if appropriate." The fact that U.S. military efforts, such as negotiations with Oman, Somalia, and Kenya for access to their seaport and airfield facilities, the dispatch of the 80,000-ton carrier Constellation and several escorting warships to the Indian Ocean-Arabian Sea area, and the strengthening of the small naval force in the Persian Gulf itself, as well as the U.S. policy statements mentioned, *preceded* the Soviet invasion of Afghanistan left little doubt in the minds of the Iranian revolutionary extremists that the United States in effect now regarded Iran as a "strategic peril" in the region.[3]

Elsewhere I have discussed the continuing failure of the United States to learn the lessons of its overemphasis on strategic considerations in developing a new Persian Gulf policy in the wake of the Iranian Revolution and the collapse of the Shah's regime.[4] I need not delve into that all-important subject here despite the unprecedented U.S. military buildup in the region, especially first under the so-called Carter Doctrine and then in keeping with Secretary Haig's search for a "strategic consensus" in the Middle East. The point here is that the negative effects of the U.S. emphasis on strategic consider-ations in terms of East-West conflict and of the concomitant feverish military buildup on the early U.S. efforts to normalize relations with revolutionary Iran before the hostage crisis has been so far universally overlooked.

To say this does not mean that the United States should have done nothing to restore the global and regional balance of power, especially after the Soviet invasion of Afghanistan. It only means that the pursuit of a swift normalization of relations with the Iranian revolutionary regime—against the background of the failure of Wash-ington to establish contact with the Khomeini-led forces of opposi-tion before the Shah's downfall—was incompatible with the central military thrust of the emerging U.S. regional policy. This was partly why the militant revolutionary factions disbelieved the claim of the Bazargan government to placing Iran's relations with the United States on the basis of "equality," and pressured Foreign Minister Yazdi to back off from his earlier consent to receive Walter Cutler as the U.S. ambassador to Tehran. The foreign minister had all along been vulnerable to the charges by the militants that he was every-thing from a CIA agent to a U.S. government plant. This was also why the student militants subsequently could deride the meeting between Bazargan, Yazdi, and the U.S. National Security Advisor Brzezinski in Algeria as an act of treason in order to bring down the Bazargan government two days after the seizure of the U.S. Embassy.

Second, another central feature of the U.S. prerevolutionary approach to Iran that continued to plague the U.S. policy toward Iran after the fall of the Shah's regime was the tendency to over-estimate the influence of modern-educated secular sociopolitical personalities in the conduct of U.S. relations with Iran. For all practical purposes, the U.S. officials were cut off from the more traditional, and yet more influential, religious figures, despite the small amount of contact with Beheshti and Shariatmadari. Before the hostage crisis, this limited contact was not that helpful in estab-lishing effective access to the Ayatollah Khomeini, and after the crisis no major political personality, including Shariatmadari, felt able to speak out against the seizure of the U.S. Embassy. In fact, almost every major sociopolitical group and personality agreed with the underlying theme that the behavior of the militant students was basically a reflection of the popular resentment against the past U.S. support of the Shah's regime. The United States' grant of asylum to a "bloodthirsty tyrant" was the final blow to the Iranian revolutionaries. Bani-Sadr's criticism of the militant students on humanitarian and international legal grounds was certainly gratifying to the United States in the context of the bitter and angry denunciation of the United States by most other Iranians, but his attempt to excuse the taking of hostages on the ground of incorrigible U.S. behavior in the past went almost unnoticed in the United States.

The problem was not, as has been so often alleged, that Bani-Sadr and Ghotbzadeh—with whom the United States tried to deal during part of the crisis—did not have the power and authority to release the hostages, but that the U.S. access to the all-powerful Khomeini and his close circles was almost nil. Conscious of this serious predicament, I personally suggested to President Carter about a month after the seizure of the U.S. Embassy that the United States should seek the aid of the United Nations "to find some religious scholars, let's say, solicited anywhere between Mauritania and Malaysia, who would be of outstanding piety and learning and would be able to sit down on the floor with Ayatollah Khomeini and talk his language." Shortly afterward I made the same suggestion in a nationwide interview on *Meet the Press*. I explained that "we have intermediaries, but they have been mainly intermediaries in terms of political or diplomatic figures, but I am talking about religious scholars, who have no necessarily political connections. . . . "[5] The president's response to my suggestion was positive. The U.S. made a "world-wide search" for several people fitting my description. They discussed the hostage crisis with Khomeini, but had "no more success than anyone else."

In any event, the point is that the legacy of the lack of effective access to traditional sociopolitical forces and figures of the Shah's days was becoming apparent. In one of the most severe diplomatic and political crises of our times, the United States found itself helpless to establish even a meaningful dialogue with the angry revolutionary regime. For decades the U.S. officials in Iran had felt at home in dealing with Western-educated Iranians, including those who opposed the Shah's regime. Apparently the situation could not be reversed overnight. It has not been reversed, however, even three years after the fall of the Shah in other societies of the region. In various visits to the Persian Gulf region, I have sensed that U.S.

contacts with indigenous people are still largely confined to modern- and Western-educated elements; we keep talking to the converted, so to speak, while powerful traditional personalities and groups are still largely incognito.

A third tendency that had marked the U.S. approach to the Shah's regime and continued after the revolution was the difficulty in understanding and responding to intangible, and yet important, factors in a non-Western society such as Iran. Just as during the Shah's regime, after its fall we tended to assume that such Western values as give-and-take, compromise, etc. were understood and shared by Iranians as they are by us. Before the Shah fell from power, we believed that the leaders of the opposition and the Shah were capable of compromising, whereas neither the secular nor the religious leaders of the opposition, nor the Shah had the slightest intention of a compromise. The giving comes only after one is already defeated, and not before, because otherwise it is considered to be an act of surrender. The Shah did not, in effect, give the slightest amount of real power to the opposition and was forced to leave the country. The revolutionary regime did not compromise on the hostage crisis; in effect it gave in not simply because it was no longer politically beneficial to hold onto the hostages, but significantly because the revolutionary militants felt that they had no alternative, despite having gained control of the Majlis and the government. The Iranian economy was in shambles and their "pure soil" (*khak-e pak*) was invaded and partly occupied by Iraqi forces in a war that they had provoked but had not started.

Another example of our inability to understand the intangible factors in the Iranian political behavior is not too far to seek. We have spoken and behaved as if the Iranian state is a Western by-product of the post-Westphalia state system. For example, while we invoked—as we should have—the rules of international law to denounce the taking of hostages, we tended to forget that the revolutionary government in Iran did not share the values that underpinned that law.[6] As early as 1944, Ayatollah Khomeini had declared that the Western-type territorial state was "the creation of limited minds," and after the Iranian Revolution he wanted to establish a "government of God" in Iran, rather than following the Shah's policy of trying to transform Iran into a Western-type nation-state under international law. In his classic treatise on *The Law of Nations*, J. L. Brierly says, "... independence does not mean freedom from law but merely freedom from control by other states." The problem with respect to most small states is that they *do not believe* that they are yet "truly free" from the control of great and superpowers. In the case of Iran, however, it has not been a matter of simply believing that Iran is not really free from foreign domination. This brings us to the last illustration of limited U.S. ability to deal with intangible factors in our Iran policy.

As mentioned previously, the gap between ideal and reality in Iranian political behavior has been one of the most prominent features of the Iranian political culture. The fact that Iran had been "the sole superpower" of ancient times or the persistent perception that it has been a "unique" cultural and political leader in history might be related to the tendency of Iranian political rulers and leaders to set goals and objectives far beyond the reach of their means, at least since the birth of "modern Iran" at the turn of the sixteenth century. That tendency, as I have tried to show elsewhere,[7] continued for nearly half a millenium before the Iranian Revolution, and as we have seen in this study it persisted during the Shah's regime, particularly after the fourfold rise of oil prices when he began to dream about quickly transforming Iran into one of the five conventional military powers of the world, and into the equal of France and West Germany in economic power as part of his quest for the "Great Civilization."

The contribution of such unrealizable goals to the Iranian Revolution has already been seen. But the revolution has not changed the underlying tendency: only the dreams have changed; the underlying unrealism persists. The prerevolutionary dream of an Iranian monarchical universalism akin to Cyrus the Great's has now been replaced by a utopian Islamic universalism drawn from 'Ali ibn Abu Talib, the first Shi'i Imam. The Ayatollah Khomeini believes that Iran must become a powerful state in order to "vouchsafe Islam to the entire world," through the export of the Iranian Revolution, which is a moral imperative in the Islamic revolutionary order. The influence of the United States, the Soviet Union, and other "dominant states" (*mustakbarin*) must be eliminated in favor of the "oppressed states" (*mustaz'afin*). Since it was primarily the United States, however, that dominated Iran during the Shah's reign, the cleansing of the Iranian society from U.S. influence through "Islamization" is given top priority in the "Islamic cultural revolution" (*enqelab-e farhangi-e Islam*).[8] Just as the Shah's ambitions were simplistically viewed in the United States as a manifestation of his personal "megalomania" without taking note of this deeper and durable tendency within the Iranian political culture, so is the Ayatollah's world outlook perceived simplistically as a reflection of "irrationality."

The Shah's alignment with Washington and Khomeini's hostility toward the United States have both presumably aimed partly at attaining "justice" in the Iranian society, but the utopianism of neither has been tempered by the realities of the Iranian situation. According to Reinhold Niebuhr:

> The finest task of achieving justice will be done neither by the Utopians who dream dreams of perfect brotherhood nor yet by the cynics who believe that the self-interest of nations cannot be overcome. It must be done by the realists who understand that nations are selfish and will be so till the end of history, but that none of us, no matter how selfish we may be, can be only selfish.
>
> The whole art of politics consists in directing rationally the irrationalities of men.[9]

Will Iran ever learn that art? That is a question for the Iranians. But will the United States ever learn that without understanding the nature of the challenge posed by other societies we cannot bring our power and influence to bear on the pursuit of our foreign policy, no matter how worthy our goals may be?

NOTES

1. See R. K. Ramazani, "Iran's Foreign Policy: Perspectives and Projections," U.S., Congress, Joint Economic Committee, *Economic Consequences of the Revolution in Iran*, Joint Committee Print (Washington, D.C.: U.S. Government Printing Office, 1980), pp. 65–97.

2. As early as March 1979, I characterized the Iranian Revolution as the "revolution of rising alienation," and have elaborated this concept in other writings. See, for example, R. K. Ramazani, "Iran's Revolution in Perspective," Z. Michael Szaz (project director), *The Impact of the Iranian Events upon Persian Gulf & United States Security* (Washington, D.C.: American Foreign Policy Institute, 1979), pp. 19–37; and my "Iran's Revolution: Patterns, Problems and Prospects," *International Affairs* 56, no. 3 (Summer 1980): 443–57.

3. For details see, R. K. Ramazani, "The Genesis of the Carter Doctrine," in George S. Wise and Charles Issawi, eds., *Middle East Perspectives: The Next Twenty Years* (Princeton, N.J.: Darwin Press, 1981), pp. 165–80.

4. See R. K. Ramazani, "Security in the Persian Gulf," *Foreign Affairs* 57, no. 4 (Spring 1979): 821–35; "Weapons Can't Replace Words," *Newsweek*

(international edition), September 22, 1980; and the "America and the Gulf: Beyond Peace and Security," *Middle East Insight*, January/February 1982, pp. 2-9.

5. For the text of my interview, see NBC's *Meet the Press*, Guest: Professor R. K. Ramazani, Washington, D.C.: Kelly Press, December 16, 1979, pp. 1-8.

6. See my foreword, Robert D. Steele, ed., *Iran Crisis and International Law*, Proceedings of the John Bassett Moore Society of International Law (Charlottesville: John Bassett Moore Society of International Law, 1981). For a somewhat similar theme, see Adda B. Bozeman, "Iran: U.S. Foreign Policy and the Tradition of Persian Statecraft," *Orbis* 23, no. 2 (Summer 1979): 387-402.

7. For details, see Rouhollah K. Ramazani, *The Foreign Policy of Iran, 1500-1941: A Developing Nation in World Affairs* (Charlottesville: University Press of Virginia, 1966).

8. See R. K. Ramazani, "Iran: The 'Islamic Cultural Revolution,'" in Philip H. Stoddard, David C. Cuthell, and Margaret W. Sullivan, eds., *Change and the Muslim World* (Syracuse, N.Y.: Syracuse University Press, 1981).

9. Quoted in Marshall R. Singer, *Weak States in a World of Powers: The Dynamics of International Relationships* (New York: The Free Press, 1971), p. 62.

SELECTED BOOKS
IN ENGLISH

Akhavi, Shahrough. *Religion and Politics in Contemporary Iran: Clergy-State Relations in the Pahlavi Period.* Albany: State University of New York Press, 1980.

Alexander, Yonah, and Nanes, Allan, eds. *The United States and Iran: A Documentary History.* Frederick, Md.: University Publications of America, 1980.

Algar, Hamid. *Religion and State in Iran, 1785-1906.* Berkeley and Los Angeles: University of California Press, 1969.

Amirie, Abbas, and Twitchell, Hamilton A., eds. *Iran in the 1980's.* Tehran: Institute for International Political and Economic Studies and Stanford Research Institute, 1978.

Bakhash, Shaul. *Iran: Monarchy, Bureaucracy, and Reform under the Qajars, 1858-1896.* London: Ithaca Press for the Middle East Centre, St. Antony's College, 1978.

Banisadr, Abolhassan. *The Fundamental Principles and Precepts of Islamic Government.* Translated by Ghanoonparvar, Mohammad R. Lexington, Kentucky: Mazda, 1981.

Bayne, Edward A. *Persian Kingship in Transition: Conversations with a Monarch Whose Office Is Traditional and Whose Goal Is Modernization.* New York: American Universities Field Staff, 1968.

Bharier, Julian. *Economic Development in Iran, 1900-1970.* London and New York: Oxford University Press, 1971.

Bill, James Alban. *The Politics of Iran: Groups, Classes and Modernization.* Columbus, Ohio: Charles E. Merrill, 1972.

Binder, Leonard. *Iran: Political Development in a Changing Society.* Berkeley and Los Angeles: University of California Press, 1962.

Bonine, Michael E., and Keddie, Nikki, eds. *Continuity and Change in Modern Iran.* Albany: State University of New York Press, 1981.

Chubin, Shahram, and Zabih, Sepehr. *The Foreign Relations of Iran: A Developing State in a Zone of Great-Power Conflict.* Berkeley and Los Angeles: University of California Press, 1974.

Cottam, Richard W. *Nationalism in Iran: Updated through 1978.* 2nd ed. Pittsburgh: University of Pittsburgh Press, 1979.

De Villiers, Gerard, with Bernard, Touchias, and de Villiers, Annick. *The Imperial Shah: An Informal Biography.* Boston: Little Brown, 1976.

Eagleton, William, Jr. *The Kurdish Republic of 1946.* London and New York: Oxford University Press, 1963.

Elwell-Sutton, L. P. *Persian Oil: A Study in Power Politics.* London: Lawrence and Wishart, 1955.

Fesharaki, Fereidun. *Development of the Iranian Oil Industry: International and Domestic Aspects.* New York: Praeger, 1976.

Fischer, Michael M. J. *Iran: From Religious Dispute to Revolution.* Cambridge, Mass. and London: Harvard University Press, 1980.

Forbis, William H. *Fall of the Peacock Throne.* New York: Harper & Row, 1980.

Graham, Robert. *Iran: The Illusion of Power.* Rev. ed. London: Croom Helm, 1979.

Halliday, Fred. *Iran: Dictatorship and Development.* New York: Penguin, 1979.

Helms, Cynthia. *An Ambassador's Wife in Iran.* New York: Dodd, Mead, 1981.

Heravi, Mehdi. *Iranian-American Diplomacy.* New York: Theo. Gaus' Sons, 1969.

Hoveyda, Fereydoun. *The Fall of the Shah.* New York: Simon and Schuster, 1980.

Keddie, Nikki R. *Religion and Rebellion in Iran: The Tobacco Protest of 1891-1892.* London: Frank Cass, 1966.

——. *Roots of Revolution: An Interpretive History of Modern Iran.* New Haven and London: Yale University Press, 1981.

Kuniholm, Bruce R. *The Origins of the Cold War in the Middle East: Great Power Conflict and Diplomacy in Iran, Turkey, and Greece.* Princeton: Princeton University Press, 1980.

Lambton, Ann K. S. *Landlord and Peasant in Persia: A Study of Land Tenure and Land Revenue Administration.* London and New York: Oxford University Press, 1953, reprinted 1969.

Ledeen, Michael, and Lewis, William. *Debacle: The American Failure in Iran.* New York: Knopf, 1981.

Lenczowski, George. *Russia and the West in Iran, 1918-1948: A Study in Big-Power Rivalry.* Ithaca, N.Y.: Cornell University Press, 1949.

——. ed. *Iran under the Pahlavis.* Stanford: Hoover Institution Press, 1978.

McDaniel, Robert A. *The Shuster Mission and the Persian Constitutional Revolution.* Minneapolis and Chicago: Bibliotheca Islamica, 1974.

Millspaugh, Arthur Chester. *Americans in Persia.* Reprinted. New York: Da Capo Press, 1976; Washington: Brookings Institution, 1946.

Nobari, Ali-Reza, ed. *Iran Erupts.* Stanford: Iran-America Documentation Group, 1978.

Pahlavi, Ashraf. *Faces in a Mirror.* Englewood Cliffs, N.J.: Prentice-Hall, 1980.

Pahlavi, Mohammad Reza. *Mission for My Country.* New York: McGraw-Hill, 1961.

——. *Answer to History.* Briarcliff Manor, N.Y.: Stein and Day, 1980.

Ramazani, Rouhollah K. *The Foreign Policy of Iran: A Developing Nation in World Affairs, 1500-1941.* Charlottesville: University Press of Virginia, 1966.

——. *The Persian Gulf: Iran's Role.* Charlottesville: University Press of Virginia, 1972.

——. *Iran's Foreign Policy 1941-1973: A Study of Foreign Policy in Modernizing Nations.* Charlottesville: University Press of Virginia, 1975.

——. *The Persian Gulf and the Strait of Hormuz.* The Netherlands: Sijthoff & Noordhoff, 1979.

Roosevelt, Kermit. *Countercoup: The Struggle for the Control of Iran.* New York: McGraw-Hill, 1979, 1980.

Rubin, Barry. *Paved with Good Intentions: The American Experience and Iran.* New York and Oxford: Oxford University Press, 1980.

Sachedina, Abdulaziz Abdulhussein. *Islamic Messianism: The Idea of the Mahdi in Twelver Shi'ism.* Albany: State University of New York Press, 1981.

Saikhal, Amin. *The Rise and Fall of the Shah.* Princeton, N.J.: Princeton University Press, 1980.

Salinger, Pierre. *America Held Hostage: The Secret Negotiations.* New York: Doubleday, 1981.

Shuster, William Morgan. *The Strangling of Persia.* New York and London: The Century Company, 1912.

Stemple, John D. *Inside the Iranian Revolution.* Bloomington: Indiana University Press, 1981.

Sullivan, William H. *Mission to Iran.* New York: W. W. Norton, 1981.

U.S., Congress. Joint Economic Committee. *Economic Consequences of the Revolution in Iran.* Washington, D.C.: U.S. Government Printing Office, 1980.

Wilber, Donald N. *Contemporary Iran.* New York: Praeger, 1963.

Yar-Shater, Ehsan, ed. *Iran Faces the Seventies.* New York: Praeger, 1971.

Zabih, Sepehr. *The Communist Movement in Iran.* Berkeley and Los Angeles: University of California Press, 1966.

Zonis, Marvin. *The Political Elite of Iran.* Princeton, N.J.: Princeton University Press, 1971.

INDEX

Abbas Mirza, Prince, 5
'Adl, Parviz, 96
Aid (*see* U.S.)
Airborne Warning and Control System
    (AWACS), 49 (*see also* U.S.)
Allen, Ambassador George, 11
    (*see also* U.S.)
Amini, Dr. Ali, 55, 75, 132 (*see also*
    Kennedy, Khomeini, Meyer)
Amuzegar, Jamshid, 68–69, 103–08
    (*see also* Qom uprising, Tabriz
    uprising, U.S.)
Anglo-Iranian Oil Company (AIOC),
    12, 16, 21–35 (*see also* Musaddeq,
    oil, Razmara)
Anglo-Russian invasion, 2, 4
Ansari, Hushang, 61, 113 (*see also*
    human rights, Kissinger,
    Rastakhiz, U.S.)
Arab-Israeli War of 1973, 27–28
Army Mission Headquarters
    (ARMISH), 47 (*see also* U.S.)
Azerbaijan, 6, 9, 9–12
Azhari, Gen. Gholam Reza, 50, 108–
    16 (*see also* U.S.)
Azmudeh, Gen. Eskandar, 105 (*see
    also* Tabriz uprising)

Badri, Gen. Abdul Ali, 122 (*see also*
    Bakhtiar, Huyser)
Baghdad Pact Organization (CENTO),
    37–39 (*see also* U.S.)
Bakhtiar, Shahpour, 116–22 (*see also*
    Bazargan, National Front,
    Khomeini, Sanjabi, Sullivan)
Bakhtiar, Taymour, 117–18 (*see also*
    SAVAK)
Ball, George W., 131 (*see also* U.S.)

Bani-Sadr, Abol-Hassan, 162, 166
    (*see also* Khomeini: U.S.)
Baqa'i, Dr. Muzaffar, 14 (*see also*
    Grady)
Bazaar merchants, 3, 5, 14 (*see also*
    Bazargan; Khomeini)
Bazargan, Mehdi, 82–83 (*see also*
    Bani-Sadr, Khomeini, Sullivan,
    U.S.)
Behbehani, Ayatollah, 74 (*see also*
    ulama)
Benjamin, Minister, 6 (*see also* U.S.)
Boeing Company, 33 (*see also* U.S.)
Britain, 2, 3, 4 (*see also* oil, U.S.)
Brzezinski, Zbigniew, 111, 129, 134,
    165 (*see also* Azhari, Khomeini,
    Sullivan, U.S.)
Burujerdi, Ayatollah, 74, 79 (*see also*
    ulama)
Byrnes, Secretary James, 10

Carter, Jimmy, 49, 90–98 (*see also*
    Khomeini, U.S.)
Central Intelligence Agency, 73 (*see
    also*, Musaddeq, Roosevelt, K.,
    U.S.)
Church, Frank, 50 (*see also* U.S.)
Churchill, Winston, 4 (*see also* Britain)
Conference on International Economic
    Cooperation (CIEC), 31 (*see also*
    oil)
Congress, U.S., 6 (*see also* U.S.)
Consortium, oil, 21–55 (*see also* U.S.)
Constitution, 3, 4, 18, 87
Cranston, Alan, 50
Culver, John C., 50

Doshan Tappeh, 121 (*see also Fada'*

Turner, Admiral Stanfield, 130 (*see also* Carter, CIA, U.S.)

ulama, 3, 5, 7, 74 (*see also* Behbehani, Burujerdi, Kashani, Khomeini)
U.N. Security Council, 16
U.S.: aid to Iran, 54–57; alliance with Iran, 38–40, 138; arms sales to Iran, 47–52, 136; companies in Iran, 50–52, 136–37; and economic development of Iran, 161–68; hostages in Iran, 161–69; intervention in Iran, 12–18, especially 16–18; oil interest in Iran, 21–35, 135–36; "special relationship" with Iran, 40–47; trade with Iran, 57–60 (*see also*, Carter, Eisenhower, Kennedy, Kissinger, Nixon, Roosevelt, F. D., Truman, Vance)

Vance, Cyrus, 49, 129 (*see also* Brzezinski, Carter, U.S.)
Von Marbod, F., 50 (*see also* U.S.)

Yamani, Sheikh Zaki, 28 (*see also* oil, OPEC)

Zahedi, Ardeshir, 120 (*see also* Carter)
Zahedi, Fazlollah, 17, 22 (*see also* Eisenhower, Musaddeq, Roosevelt, Kermit, U.S.)

ABOUT THE AUTHOR

R. K. Ramazani is Edward R. Stettinius Professor of Government and Foreign Affairs at the University of Virginia where he has taught since 1954. He is a native of Tehran and a U.S. citizen.

Besides this volume, he has authored 7 other books, including the prize-winning *The Foreign Policy of Iran, 1500–1941*, and recently *The Persian Gulf and the Strait of Hormuz*. He has contributed to 20 other books and published numerous articles.

Dr. Ramazani is a former vice-president of the American Institute of Iranian Studies. He has been a consultant to the U.S. government, the Rockefeller Foundation, and the United Nations.

STUDIES OF INFLUENCE IN INTERNATIONAL RELATIONS
Alvin Z. Rubinstein, General Editor

SOUTH AFRICA AND THE UNITED STATES:
The Erosion of an Influence Relationship
Richard E. Bissell

SOVIET-INDIAN RELATIONS: Issues and Influence
Robert C. Horn

SOVIET INFLUENCE IN EASTERN EUROPE: Political Autonomy
and the Warsaw Pact
Christopher D. Jones

U.S. POLICY TOWARD JAPAN AND KOREA: A Changing Influence
Chae-Jin Lee and Hideo Sato

SOVIET AND AMERICAN INFLUENCE IN THE HORN OF AFRICA
Marina S. Ottaway

THE UNITED STATES AND IRAN: The Patterns of Influence
R. K. Ramazani

SOVIET POLICY TOWARD, TURKEY, IRAN AND AFGHANISTAN:
The Dynamics of Influence
Alvin Z. Rubinstein

THE UNITED STATES AND PAKISTAN: The Evolution of an
Influence Relationship
Shirin Tahir-Kheli

THE UNITED STATES AND BRAZIL: Limits of Influence
Robert Wesson